Theory for Classics

Theory for Classics: A student's guide, is a clear and concise handbook to the key connections between Classical Studies and critical theory in the twentieth century. Louise A. Hitchcock looks at the way classics has been engaged across a number of disciplines.

Beginning with four foundational figures—Freud, Marx, Nietzsche, and Saussure—Hitchcock goes on to provide guided introductions of the major theoretical thinkers of the past century, from Adorno to Williams. Each entry offers biographical, theoretical, and bibliographical information along with a discussion of each figure's relevance to Classical Studies and suggestions for future research.

Brisk, thoughtful, provocative, and engaging, this will be an essential first volume for anyone interested in the intersection between theory and Classical Studies today.

Louise A. Hitchcock is a Senior Lecturer in the Centre for Classics and Archaeology at the University of Melbourne. She is a former Fellow of the American School of Classical Studies in Athens, senior Fulbright Fellow in Cyprus, and ECA Fellow and Visiting Annual Professor at the Albright Institute in Jerusalem. She has published extensively on theoretical approaches to Bronze Age architecture and archaeology.

Theory for Classics
A student's guide

Louise A. Hitchcock

Based on the original book in the series
by William E. Deal and Timothy K. Beal

NEW YORK AND LONDON

First published 2008
by Routledge
2 Park Square, Milton Park, Abingdon, Oxon OX14 4RN

Simultaneously published in the USA and Canada
by Routledge
270 Madison Ave, New York, NY 10016

Transferred to Digital Printing 2008

*Routledge is an imprint of the Taylor & Francis Group,
an informa business*

© 2008 Louise A. Hitchcock

Typeset in Sabon by Keyword Group Ltd, UK
Printed and bound in Great Britain by Antony Rowe Ltd,
Chippenham, Wiltshire.

British Library Cataloguing in Publication Data
A catalogue record for this book is available from the
British Library

Library of Congress Cataloging in Publication Data

Hitchcock, Louise.
Theory for classics: a student's guide/Louise A. Hitchcock
p. cm.
Includes bibliographical references (p.).
1. Critical theory. I. Title.
B809.3.H58 2008
001.3—dc22
2007027954

ISBN 10: 0-415-45497-2 (hbk)
ISBN 10: 0-415-45498-0 (pbk)
ISBN 10: 0-203-93291-9 (ebk)

ISBN 13: 978-0-415-45497-1 (hbk)
ISBN 13: 978-0-415-45498-8 (pbk)
ISBN 13: 978-0-203-93291-9 (ebk)

For Brian Thomas O'Neill

Contents

Acknowledgements

I am grateful to many colleagues, friends, and students for their help and support with this project. First, I would like to thank Donald Preziosi for his mentoring and steadfast confidence in me throughout the years. Second, I am thankful to William Germano, Richard Stoneman, and Amy Laurens at Routledge for giving me the opportunity to revise the core text in the series for classics, and for their direction and encouragement. There are many friends, colleagues, and students on four continents who have not only helped me, but who have actively supported my interest in theory and its relationship to the past: K. O. Chong-Gossard, Barbara Creed, Joy Damousi, Jeanette Hoorn, and Tony Sagona at the University of Melbourne; within the discipline of classics: James I. Porter, Nancy Sorkin Rabinowitz, Paul Rehak, Alan Shapiro, and John Younger.

This book was written during my sabbatical year as the visiting Annual Professor at the Albright Institute of Archaeological Research in Jerusalem. I am grateful to the staff, board of trustees, fellows, and fellowship committee at the Albright for providing an opportunity to work in a quiet, supportive, and collegial atmosphere. I am especially grateful to the Director, Sy Gitin and to Joan Branham, the Vice-President and Chair of the Fellowship Committee. I wish to thank Ed Silver of the University of Chicago for his enthusiasm, insightful feedback, which shaped the final direction of this work, and his many positive comments and suggestions. I am also grateful to my student, Erin McGowan, for her proofreading of the text. I, alone, am responsible for any errors of fact or interpretation. This book is dedicated to my husband, Brian O'Neill, for taking over where my mother, Anne Morris Hitchcock, left off, in giving unswerving support of everything I've done and will do.

Introduction

Classics and theory—who needs it?

What is theory and why is it important for classics and classical studies?

Like so many words in the English language, theory comes from the Greek *theoria*, which means "a viewing" or "spectacle" and offers a way of seeing. In this way, theory serves like a pair of conceptual spectacles that you use to frame and focus on what you're looking at. It can serve as a tool for discerning, deciphering, and making sense. Alternatively, theory can provide a position from which to engage in a critique of the status quo.

One central question that is debated by some in the academic study of classics is "What is classics?" Responses to such a question are diverse. For some, it is the study of classical languages, primarily Greek and Latin texts. Conquests by Alexander the Great, followed by the Roman Empire, extended the geographic boundaries of the classical world. In recent times, Michael Ventris' now-famous radio announcement in 1952 that Mycenaean tablets written in the Linear B script were an early form of Greek, and the discovery earlier in the twentieth century that Hittite was an Indo-European language extended the study of classical languages and Indo-European dialect into the Bronze Age. Interest both in the context of classical inscriptions and in the Minoan predecessors of the Mycenaean Greeks has extended the boundaries of classics further into archaeology, pre-history, and art history, with art history itself owing much of its development as a discipline to classical archaeology. In addition, classics maintains disciplinary linkages with philosophy, comparative literature, history, art history, and anthropology. These linkages are particularly evident in the United States, which is academically represented in Greece by the American School of Classical Studies. This stands in contrast to European countries, as well as Canada and Australia, which maintain research institutes or schools of archaeology in Athens. Thus, in some universities, there is a strict division between classics, art history, and archaeology, and in others this boundary is blurred. In his 1869 lecture on "Homer and Classical Philology," Nietzsche commented extensively on the multi-disciplinary nature of philology in the study of the past, while James Porter (2005) (In "What is 'Classical' About Classical Antiquity?," p. 27 and *passim*) has more recently observed, "'Classical Antiquity' is not consistently classical."

It is safe to say that classics is an evolving discipline and that its practices have always been theoretical in terms of the conceptual tools used to study the classical world.

Increasingly, it is clear that over the past two centuries the academic study of classics has no grand unifying theory that brings into sharp focus all things classical. And, there never will be such a theory. Classics is an increasingly diverse subject, where every theory frames and focuses our attention on some things while leaving other things outside the frame or out of focus. Different research questions and types of texts or bodies of data lend themselves to different theories and different approaches.

As scholars of the classical world continue to extend or push beyond the boundaries of the discipline, there is a growing movement to explore new or different theoretical perspectives by which to interpret the ancient world. Theories of culture, history, language, and gender and other forms of identity that were unfamiliar to many in the past are today reframing and refocusing how we study the classics. As a result, the canon of theories and methods available to the academic study of the ancient world has been both dramatically transformed and expanded. While this makes the discipline of classical studies an increasingly exciting and vibrant field, it also presents teachers and students of the classics with significant challenges. New as well as older theoretical approaches, which make it possible to ask innovative questions and reveal novel possibilities for studying and interpreting the past, are frequently difficult to understand. The starting point is not a clear one. *Theory for Classics* provides concise introductions to the theories of many of the most prominent scholars both inside and outside the classics whose work has either proven to be or has the potential to be important within the field.

This book, derived from books in the original series, is written with three audiences in mind. First, it is for undergraduate students in courses on theory and methodology for the academic study of classics and classical civilizations. Although there are many theoretical approaches to classical texts published in the journal *Arethusa*, numerous volumes by renowned classicists that focus on the relevance of specific theorists with strong academic backgrounds in the classics (such as Nietzsche, Bakhtin, and Lacan), and many excellent introductions to the study of theory, there is not an introductory book on theory which is specifically aimed at the study of the classical world.

Second, this book is for graduate students. Not only will it serve master's or doctoral students seeking theoretical frameworks for thesis or dissertation research, it will also prove useful as they prepare for a career in teaching.

Finally, *Theory for Classics* is intended for teachers and scholars of classical antiquity, who need a resource to help them introduce students to contemporary theoretical perspectives and who are themselves interested in how these perspectives might speak more directly to classical studies.

Genesis

To paraphrase a famous, oft-used quote (by Bernard of Chartres, Isaac Newton, and Nietzsche among many others) from the Medieval and Renaissance through contemporary periods, this book stands on the shoulders of books originally published in the *Theory 4* series, revising and drawing heavily from them in all instances, and hopefully adding something to them. The impetus for the book was the core text, *Theory for Religious Studies* by William E. Deal and Timothy K. Beal, had its origins in the classroom. My own contribution in the revision of this text also draws heavily from *Theory for Art History*, by Jae Emerling. Thus, it represents an interaction with classics, its related disciplines and discourses, and my own theoretical interests. Students dedicated to the discipline of classics find they are immersed in what have become the traditional practices in classics, which is mastery of the languages, study of dialect, and documentation of archaeological remains. Although the time required to master the primary material through empirical study leaves little time to question disciplinary practices or extra-disciplinary research, some students are also familiar with the basic tenets of structuralism expressed through binary oppositions operative in much of Western thought, e.g. order–chaos, public–private, sacred–profane, self–other, male–female, culture–nature, and so on.

Introducing less normative or commonsensical theories and perspectives, frequently associated with the epithets "post-modern," "post-structuralist," or "deconstruction" is another matter. The conceptual time and effort required to understand these difficult texts, theories, and viewpoints can be great, particularly when balanced against an already heavy burden of primary data to master, when the utility is not readily evident and may remain elusive for a period of years or even decades. Many of the ideas offered by contemporary theory seem to fly in the face of conventional logic of contemporary society and even worse, do not directly address issues linked to the understanding of classical languages and civilizations. Many new and difficult terms and concepts are employed—such as discourse, representation, gender, ideology, embodiment, subjectivity, deconstruction, and originary—which are unfamiliar to many students and do not at first glance seem to have much to do with the classics. A frequent complaint is that many of these terms are not found in a standard dictionary hence, they are not "real" words.

Other than being part of current academic fads and fashions (one can often date a modern text through terms and paradigms invoked), what do the theories introduced in this book offer to students of classics?

The theories summarized in this book offer the reader a variety of perspectives that move him/her beyond the traditional approaches to the classics. They raise questions and address issues related to what it means to study individuals and institutions, political and religious power, assign meaning to the past, and study marginalized categories of evidence.

Furthermore, they require us to see the past not simply as isolated texts, events, or categories of objects and monuments, but as interconnected aspects of culture that both impact and are impacted by social life in the past and the present.

Although once a contender for being the "queen of disciplines," classics today struggles alongside other humanities disciplines in many institutions to legitimize itself and to justify its continued existence. The multicultural composition of many large countries has resulted in a host of new humanistic disciplines deemed more relevant, including Africana, Chicano, Islamic, indigenous, cultural, and modern language studies, which are competing with classics and edging it out of its once privileged position in the curriculum. The greatest threat to the humanities as a whole, however, is their continued devaluation by the increasing short-sightedness and bureaucratization in the running of many universities, which demand an immediate financial return on their investment and devote more money to marketing than to the real purpose of the university, learning for its own sake and the intangible, but very real long-term benefits, which result. Knowing how to think, write, read, and envision the future, are the most marketable skills of all. The greatest irony in this situation is the key role that the study of classics has played in structuring contemporary society from statesmen such as Thomas Jefferson to many of the theorists surveyed in this book (i.e., Nietzsche was a professor of philology and Freud used archaeological ruins and classical texts such as the Homeric poems as a means to model human consciousness), over one-half of whom were either trained in ancient languages (classical and/or biblical) or have engaged with ancient texts (sometimes with varying success) or both. Although many in the classics have ignored theory, theorists have not ignored the classics as detailed in Leonard's (in *Athens in Paris*) recent study of the interest in classics by many French theorists. If it is a truism that theory is good to think with, another is that classics is good to do theory with. Thus, it's impossible to conceive of where a vision of the future will come from if we break with or attempt to engage with our classical past from a point of historical amnesia, rather than a place of informed choice.

Conversations

This book is not only a guide about how theory since the 1960s has transformed the landscape of academic classical studies, but also an invitation to join in the conversation—regardless of the theoretical stance one adopts.

The contemporary perspectives introduced in this book did not miraculously emerge in isolation from the minds of their authors fully formed like Athena from the head of Zeus. Many were heavily influenced by their engagement with classical and biblical antiquity, as noted above, and all were developed in conversation with those who preceded them. In this regard, four theoretical predecessors are particularly important: Sigmund

Freud, Karl Marx, Friedrich Nietzsche, and Ferdinand de Saussure. Together, these four constitute a common context for theoretical discourse since the mid-twentieth century. Indeed, their concepts and questions continue to set the agenda for contemporary theory. Whether one embraces them or not, one should have a basic understanding of their contributions. Therefore, this book begins with a section on these four predecessors to contemporary theory.

Just as theorists introduced in this book were engaged in dialogue with their own theoretical predecessors, today's students of the classics are invited to enter into conversation with the theories and theorists described here. Whether one ultimately declares oneself a deconstructionist, a structuralist, or a feminist, or a Foucauldian, a Nietzschean, a Bakhtinian, a Derridean, or rejects theory altogether, it is important to attend to the questions these thinkers raise and to approach them with an open mind. What happens to our understanding of ancient texts, monuments, or ancient religion, for example, when we question the nature of language? Does language represent a natural correspondence between word and external referent (i.e., a red-figure pot or oral poetry), or as structuralists would argue, is language a semiotic (sign) system in which the linguistic sign is both arbitrary and based on difference? The point is that these critical modes of inquiry allow us to see classics in ways not considered in traditional practice.

How to use this book

This book is designed to be a useful resource. Most readers, it is assumed, will not read it from cover to cover, but will go to it for help with particular theorists and theories. The four predecessors introduced in the opening section are presented in alphabetical order by last name, as are the 26 entries in the main section. Every entry in the book has three main parts: a list of Key concepts, the main body of the text, and a section for Further reading.

At the beginning of each entry is a short bulleted list of Key concepts that have been identified as particularly important for readers to understand. These concepts are listed in the order of their appearance in the main text.

The main body of each entry begins with a brief biographical sketch. In the discussion that follows, the names of other thinkers included in the volume are highlighted. Key concepts are highlighted in bold where they are most thoroughly explained; thus, a reader interested in one particular key concept can quickly scan the entry for the discussion of it. Each entry also offers a discussion of some possible implications for classics and/or classical archaeology. A conscious choice was made to leave the engagement with ancient philosophy aside, as this could easily be the focus of a separate text and it is assumed that students of philosophy gain exposure to contemporary theory as part of the normal curriculum. It is impossible to indicate here all of the possible implications of theory for classics, but a suggestion of the ways in which a certain thinker's work has been used as well as how it may be used in the future is given. Examples are drawn primarily from myth and literature, ancient history, historiography, and archaeology. It is hoped that readers of this text will go on to explore and discover new ways of applying the ideas presented here.

Finally, each entry has a Further reading section which includes two subsections: first, a "By" subsection listing those primary texts essential for a more complete understanding of a thinker; second, an "About" subsection listing texts about the theorist as well as texts on classics and/or classical archaeology that include a significant discussion of the theorist or an application of the theorist's ideas. Texts deemed particularly useful are marked with an asterisk (*). In some instances, these applications are implicit, rather than explicit. In the body of each entry, when a particular text by a theorist is mentioned the date given in parenthesis indicates the year that work was originally published. The bibliography is neither exhaustive nor exhaustively cited, it is simply intended as an introduction.

Theory for Classics suggests multiple ways that we might come to understand classical studies. What follows will require some effort on the part of the reader, not so much in reading the entries as in following up on what is presented here and becoming more well versed in theory. The goal is to provide initial access to the works surveyed here, to explain their key concepts, and to give direction for further study. As readers move beyond the introductions to the primary texts, it is my hope that they will develop a more complex and subtle understanding of the necessity of theory for the study of classics.

Further reading

Branham, R. Bracht, Glenn W. Most, Ralph Hexter, Giulia Sissa, Daniel Selden, Page duBois, and W. R. Johnson. "Panel Discussion: Classics and Comparative Literature: Agenda for the, 90s." *Classical Philology*. 92.2 (1997) 153–88.

Gold, Barbara K. "Teaching Classics: The Jesuit Way versus the Big Business Approach." *The Classical Journal* 84.3 (1989) 253–9.

Leonard, Miriam. *Athens in Paris: Ancient Greece and the Political in Post-War French Thought. Classical Presences*. Oxford and New York: Oxford University Press, 2005.

Newman, J. K. "Text vs. Author." *The Classical Journal* 84.3 (1989) 232–8.

Payne, M. (ed.) *A Dictionary of Cultural and Critical Theory*. Oxford: Blackwell Publishers Ltd, 1996.

Porter, James I. "What is 'Classical' About Classical Antiquity? Eight Propositions." *Arion* 13.1 (2005) 27–61.

Schnapp, Alain. *The Discovery of the Past*. Translated by Ian Kinnes and Gillian Varndell. New York: Harry N. Abrams, 1997.

Part I

Predecessors

1 Sigmund Freud

Key concepts:

- unconscious
- repression
- Oedipus Complex
- psychoanalysis
- sublimation
- illusion
- pathography

Sigmund Freud (1856–1939), the founder of psychoanalysis as an academic discipline, was born into an assimilated, secular Jewish family in the Moravian town of Freiburg, Germany. However, the most formative place in Freud's development was in *fin de siecle* Vienna where he took a medical degree at the University of Vienna in 1881. After winning a modest medical scholarship, he proceeded to work with Jean-Martin Charcot (1825–1893) at the Salpêtrière hospital in Paris from 1885 to 1886. Freud was influenced by Charcot's work on hysteria, which he diagnosed as a disease and treated with hypnotism. When Freud began his practice as a physician in Vienna in 1886, he focused on nervous disorders. Freud distinguished his method from Charcot's by abandoning hypnotism in favor of encouraging patients to freely narrate their experiences. It was in Vienna that he initially proposed and refined his psychoanalytic discourse, presented in the landmark publication of *The Interpretation of Dreams* in 1900. Freud fled to London in 1938 to escape the advancing Nazis and died there in 1939.

The intellectual and theoretical legacy of Freud's work in the humanities, especially literature, art history, and philosophy, is arguably one of the most important in the tradition of modernity. In addition to his assertion of the unconscious, his thesis that dreams possess an underlying logic, one that is discernible through a method of psychoanalytic interpretation, remains a centerpiece of Western cultural discourse. In a 1922 essay for a general audience Freud provides three definitions of psychoanalysis: (1) a discipline focused on investigating the unconscious; (2) a therapeutic method for treating nervous disorders; and (3) a growing body of data, providing an empirical component to his research. Together, these three definitions provide a helpful introduction to Freud's approach.

The aim of Freud's psychoanalysis was to investigate inaccessible mental processes through an analysis of the **unconscious**. Freudian terms such as the unconscious and repression have become commonplace, but in contemporary usage their precise meanings within Freud's system are often lost. These two terms form a dynamic system that defines the very structure of Freudian psychoanalysis. The unconscious is, most simply put, the nonconscious part of the mind. As such, it affects conscious thought and behavior but is not directly accessible for interpretation. "We have learnt from psycho-analysis," Freud argues, "that the essence of the process of **repression** lies, not in putting it to an end, in annihilating, the idea which represents an instinct, but in preventing it from becoming conscious ... the repressed is a part of the unconscious .... How are we to arrive at a knowledge of the unconscious? It is of course only as something conscious that we know it, after it has undergone transformation or translation into something conscious" ("The Unconscious," p. 573).

What the analyst must decipher is the various compromise formations— the distortions caused by the opposing forces of unconscious desire and those of repression—that become evident through an analysand's retelling. Freud carried out his examinations through analysis of slips of the tongue, jokes, and above all dreams, which he called the "royal road" to the unconscious mind. Dreams, Freud believed, represent fulfillments of unconscious wishes and desires that the conscious mind censors because they are socially taboo or a threat to the integrity of the self. For Freud, the content of the unconscious is essentially those drives that are inadmissible to the conscious self and are therefore forced out consciousness through mechanisms of repression. These include drives and memories related to the "primal scene" (childhood recollection of seeing her/his parents having sex) as well as taboo desires related to the Oedipus Complex. Although repressed, they inevitably resurface in dreams, "Freudian slips," and other forms of expression.

For Freud, the unconscious (*id*—primal instincts) is not static. It is bound in a series of complex mechanisms with the super-ego ("a special agency ... self-criticism"), i.e., rational thought, reason, or one's conscience ("The Uncanny," p. 211). The site of conflict, tension, and negotiation is the ego (*das Ich*). It is the dynamic tension or play between these forces that distorts or disguises unconscious desire. The task of the analyst is to locate these compromise formations and decipher them. Freud writes that:

> almost everywhere there can be found striking omissions, disturbing repetitions, palpable contradictions, signs of things the communication

of which was never intended .... One could wish to give the word "distortion" the double meaning to which it has a right, although it is no longer used in this sense. It should mean not only "to change the appearance of," but also "to wrench apart," "to put in another place."
(Moses and Monotheism, p. 52)

What makes Freud's work extraordinary, then, is his attempt to develop a systematic means to access and interpret the unconscious. In the passage quoted here he explicitly elides the actions of psychical processes with those of textual interpretation (one influenced by the Jewish interpretive strategies of *Midrash* (commentary)) in a gesture that renders one's conscious life, the life history of the ego, a text littered with "suppressed and abnegated material," i.e., the traces of another origin (ibid.).

The **Oedipus Complex** is particularly important to Freud's understanding of human consciousness and the origin nervous disorders. Although the tragedy of Oedipus lies in the shame of his unwitting murder of his father and marriage to his mother, the broader Freudian meaning of the Oedipus Complex concerns the young child's attraction to the parent of the opposite sex and jealousy of the parent of the same sex. Although girls and boys experience this attraction and negotiate this complex differently, resolution is achieved by making a transition from jealousy of, to identification with, the same sex parent. Freud believes that the Oedipus Complex is a universal event, and the failure to negotiate it successfully is the primary cause of nervous disorders. The larger significance in this and other myths lies in absorbing the universal meaning in it by every new generation, whether it means resolving the parental tension in Oedipus or restoring order from the chaos in the story of Electra.

Freud's second definition of **psychoanalysis** as a therapeutic method for treating nervous disorders involves an act of interpretation "concerned with laying bare these hidden forces"; one that from its inception, Freud desired to raise to the status of a science, what he called "an impartial instrument" ("The Uncanny," p. 220). By investigating his patients' life history, Freud sought to objectively demonstrate his contention that "in mental life nothing which has once been formed can perish—that everything is somehow preserved and that in suitable circumstances .... It can once more be brought to light" (*Civilization and its Discontents*, p. 16). The presence of these "hidden forces" is made evident through everyday occurrences such as forgetting proper names, incidental mannerisms, slips of the tongue (i.e. Freudian slips or parapraxes), bungled actions, and, most importantly, dreams. Collectively all of these elements comprise the psychopathology that Freud is keen on identifying and interpreting. It is the analyst's task, he argues, to pinpoint these slips, these inabilities, the unsaid within discourse, so as to help the patient attain knowledge of the repressed experiences that cause neuroses.

Of course, it was primarily with his identification of the constitutive elements of dreams, the dream work as Freud terms it, that psychoanalysis stakes its claim to our attention. Dreams, Freud believed, represent the fulfillment of unconscious wishes that the conscious mind censors because they are socially taboo, unpleasurable, or a threat to the integrity of the self (the ego). What has been repressed is represented in dream imagery. This representation occurs only after the repressed material has undergone distortion [*Entstehung*] brought about by condensation, displacement, pictorial arrangement, and secondary revision. Condensation is the process whereby a number of people, events, or meanings are combined and reduced to a single image in a dream. Displacement, on the other hand, is the process by which one person or event is dispersed into many linked associations, whether it is a similar sounding work or a symbolic substitution. The remaining element of pictorial arrangement and secondary revision are the means by which the dream is finalized; together they arrange the dream contents in such a way that the manifest content (the dream as the dreamer experiences it, i.e. the literal text of the dream) does not completely hide the latent content (the repressed unconscious material). It is this opening in the otherwise seamless construction of the dream work that allows Freud to intervene.

Freud's intervention, his "talking cure" as one of his early patients phrased it, a therapeutic method for treating nervous disorders, requires the analysand to narrate his or her life history. Lying on a couch, the analysand recounts his or her life history with little interruption from the analyst, who sits behind the patient listening for subtle manifestations of unconscious processes that indicate neurosis. Freud's urging (in *On Beginning the Treatment*) that "the patient must be free to choose at what point he shall begin" has been seen as influenced by Homer's invocation of the Muse to "start from where you will" at the beginning of *The Odyssey* (Nobus, In "*Polymetis* Freud," p. 262). In this more or less uninterrupted, free association by the patient, language is not taken at face value. Rather Freud's self-imposed task is to sift through the language of the conscious mind for traces of the unconscious, i.e., traces that index the presence of latent or repressed content. In the act of recounting one's life history certain elements pique the analyst's curiosity: an odd turn of phrase, a mishandled image, the repetition of a certain word, a nervous tic, and so on. These elements hint at the faulty areas of the construction of the self, which indicates the absent-presence of what has been repressed: the little thread, which if pulled unravels the entire fiction. This is why the ego, one's conscious sense of self—what you presume to be self-evident and non-contradictory—is, in fact, a fiction.

In psychoanalysis, the speaking human subject is approached as a divided subject, a site of conflict between conscious and unconscious drives that do not form a single, integrated, whole self. Therefore, the enunciations of the "I" of language are not to be accepted without hesitation because more often than not they represent only the alibis of the ego. What Freud is after is the trace of the origin: the alibi (literally, what is *in another place*).

Freud's third definition of psychoanalysis is a growing body of scientific research, including case studies, research data on the mind and brain, and interpretations of other aspects and works of culture. Indeed, Freud did not restrict himself to analyzing individual human subjects, nor did he ignore other fields of academic research in the natural sciences and humanities. Rather, he was a prolific interpreter of culture, approaching it through archaeology, anthropology, linguistics, literature, and religion.

The model of psychic preservation, the presence of the past in the present, is one Freud borrows from archaeology, drawing inspiration from a variety of sources, from Schliemann's discovery of Troy to ancient Rome. In *Civilization and Its Discontents* (1930), Freud posits an analogy between the psychic preservation and an archaeological model, specifically Rome, the Eternal City. He explains how the topography of Rome is shot through with ruins and remnants of the past; they are found "dovetailed into the jumble of the great metropolis which has grown up in the last few centuries since the Renaissance" (p. 17). Freud takes the model of an archaeological site with its subsequent layers of ruins and maps it onto human consciousness because this is how the past is preserved in the present; it is a model of immanence. He argues that we should compare the past of a city with that of the mind. He asks us to "suppose that Rome is not a human habitation but a psychical entity with a similarly long and copious past" (ibid.). In both models, what Freud posits is a spectral palimpsest that recalls his famous explanation of the *Wunderblock*, wherein all that has been written on the *tabula rasa* is preserved in the wax on which it rests. This model of immanence is important because it provides a spatial metaphor that enables one to read the traces or residual effects of the past in the present. Moreover, it helps us to understand Freud's insistence when it comes to the constant action required to repress an unconscious desire. He is adamant when he asserts that the "process of repression is not to be regarded as an event which takes place *once*, the results of which are permanent, as when some living thing has been killed and from that time onward is dead; repression demands a persistent expenditure of force .... The maintenance of a repression involves an uninterrupted expenditure of force" ("Repression," p. 572).

From Freud's first major text *The Interpretation of Dreams* (1900) through works dealing with religion, such as *Totem and Taboo* (1913), and even in later work such as *Civilization and Its Discontents*, a conception of the human being is given. It posits that humans are driven by two primal instincts: self-preservation and libidinal satisfaction. These instincts abide no normative social laws besides satisfaction. This drive towards satisfaction is a destructive force. Unchecked, only violence and death would result from our march toward unabashedly selfish fulfillment. Thus, Freud argues that there is a need for civilization and social order to repress these instincts; to make civilization as such possible these instincts must be addressed. One of the primary means for dealing with these instincts that Freud identifies is **sublimation**.

In sublimation, he argues, repressed material is "promoted" into something grander or is disguised as something "noble". For example, sexual urges may be given sublimated expression in the form of intense religious experiences or longings, or the production of art and literature, so that essentially, it performs a cathartic function (see also **Kristeva**). "Sublimation," Freud writes, "of instinct is an especially conspicuous feature of cultural development; it is what makes it possible for higher psychical activities, scientific, artistic or ideological, to play such an important role in civilized life" (*Civilization and Its Discontents*, p. 44). Substitutive satisfactions are **illusions** in contrast with reality because what we desire is satisfaction and yet "there is no possibility at all of its being carried through; all the regulations of the universe run counter to it" (ibid., p. 23). Thus, we are made to derive enjoyment in illusory, second-tier forms. However, sublimation provides Freud with a means to further investigate how repressed material continues to exert a determining influence over conscious life, how and why primal instincts are perpetually present, always threatening to take over. This potential for desublimation occurs not only on the individual level, but on the collective level as well because sublimatory ventures like religion and art are social illusion. Sublimation has important implications for interpreting myth and for understanding the history of classics as a discipline, through investigating and analyzing the motivations of some of its major figures, such as Winckelmann's homosexuality or Schliemann's psychopathic tendencies.

Freud's interest in (de-)sublimation—the uncensored articulation of psychic fantasy—along with the "aesthetic yield of pleasure" this offer can help introduce Freud's engagement with literature, religion, and art. Throughout his career Freud consistently turned his attention to these to aid his development of psychoanalytic methodology. These areas of study greatly impacted how he thought of interpretation and its ends. Inversely, the importance of Freudian thought to the study of literature and art history cannot be underestimated. It fundamentally changed the way in which we relate to, read, and interpret cultural production. Often overlooked here is the politics implicit in Freud's model. He argues that socio-political life can be improved only if the mass of repressed material (in both the individual and collective spheres) is addressed in a systematic fashion. Importantly, it is myth, literature, and art that provide the opportunity to diagnose "the wishful phantasies of whole nations," their "*secular dreams*" ("Creative Writers and Day-Dreaming," p. 442), thus providing classicists with a tool for exploring cultural norms through analyzing the role of myth and literature in the formation of civic and ethnic identities in the past and in the present.

Another way of examining the significance of satisfaction and desire is through prohibitions, which was explored by Freud in *Totem and Taboo* (first published in German in 1913). There, Freud develops a theory of religion based on a reconstruction of the psychological origins of primitive society. Following other religionists of his time, Freud notes two prohibitions, or taboos, common among most tribal cultures: incest and eating the tribe's totem animal. Unlike others, however, Freud insists that these actions would not have been prohibited unless there had been the desire to do them. While Freud linked these prohibitions to the Oedipus Complex, hypothesizing a tribal scene where the sons murdered the chief in order to have his wives/their mothers, then making the murdered father a totem figure, there are larger implications in terms of identifying social norms through an analysis of what is prohibited. For example, the prohibitions on worshipping idols in the Old Testament, suggest that those pagan practices were still going on, while the practice of ostracism in ancient Athens indicates a certain level of anxiety about status combined with political motivation.

Freud's study of art has important implications for the study of classical archaeology. It is well known that Freud was an avid collector of antiquities. His interest in them arose upon the death of his father, an event that also spurred his desire to complete *The Interpretation of Dreams*. Freud's collection of artworks served as an index of the passing of his father and as the material presence of the Western cultural past that played a role in the construction of psychoanalysis: a method of unearthing an individual's forgotten past, the very one that dictates the shape of the future. In his essay "'Mille e tre': Freud and Collecting" (1994), John Forrester writes that "Freud's collection of antiquities, and the very idea of psychoanalysis itself … was a compendium of his version of civilization, as opposed to its diffusion and fragmentation in the world of everyday life—a world that nonetheless could be measured and weighed in the scales of the analytic method" (p. 242). Freud's collection was, no doubt, also a symbol of his achievement, just as in the estrangement he felt when visiting the Acropolis, for Freud, these were symbols of a place that had seemed unattainable in the poverty of his youth. For many, the study of classics continues to be a symbol of status and achievement. With Freud's antiquities collection, the difficulty of separating manifest and latent content, the autobiographical as opposed to the impersonal construction of a work for others to enjoy, becomes evident. But it is precisely with this difficulty that the future import of Freud's work for art historical and classical discourse rests. Thus, writing about or studying the past is never a neutral or objective practice, but is bound up and co-constructed in the formation of one's identity.

The literature of classical antiquity also plays a key role in Freud's theorizing or modeling of the unconscious. Homer is placed at the top of his list of the ten most magnificent works of literature. In "*Polymetis* Freud," Dany Nobus has discussed Freud's familiarity with Homer from his adolescence onward, his referencing of Homer in many contexts, sometimes using the original Greek and quoting entire passages, and the particular influence of *The Odyssey* on Freud's work. In a notable example from *The Interpretation of Dreams*, Freud draws an analogy between the persistent character of unconscious dream-wishes and the ghosts in the Kingdom of the Dead in Book 11 of *The Odyssey* (p. 255). Armstrong's new study of Freud

(*A Compulsion for Antiquity*, 2005) explores his engagement with many other texts in the classical canon.

In his famous essay "Leonardo Da Vinci and a Memory of His Childhood" (1910), Freud deploys the term "**pathography**." In the broadest sense it refers to a method of interpretation that relies upon the biography of an artist. But Freud is more precise in his phrasing. He refers to the manner in which the pathology, the unconscious repetitions, and preoccupations of an artist are written [*graphia*] in the produced work. It is a translation of selected aspects of a life history more often than not those concerned with traumatic experiences, repressed desires, and other symptoms. Is it possible to utilize Freud's call for interpretative attention to "the significance of minor details" so as to make present the death of an artist's intention (which is represented over and over again in the yet again of reception), which simultaneously marks the beginning of its *Nachleben* (after-life)? The *Nachleben* of works is the terrain of both classical archaeologists and art historians. But it is one that must work through discourse (whether it is historicist, formalist, theoretical) in order to return the viewer to the artwork or artifact, the thing itself, and is hence, anti-biographical.

Similarly classical archaeologists look for patterns in the depictions of tiny details in sculpture and vase painting to assign works to a particular artist, school, or workshop; and more broadly they look at patterns in the distributions of artifacts to interpret or assign social meaning. In "Clues and Scientific Method," Carlo Ginzburg has suggested that Sigmund Freud was taken with Giovanni Morelli's essays on the attributions of art works based on the depiction of insignificant details. Both were doctors, trained in looking for minor symptoms as a key to interpreting illnesses. It has been further suggested that Freud was influenced by Morelli in developing his techniques of psychoanalysis, revealing mental disorders through the close observation of unnoticed features or minor mannerisms as revealing clues of mental disorder, whereby the details are a key to deeper realities. In classics, this approach was adopted and developed by Sir John Beazley to assign classical Greek vases to particular artists or workshops. Although Beazley never explicitly articulated his method, James Whitley (in "Beazley as Theorist") has shown how the methods of Freud and Morelli were subsequently used by Beazley. Mary Beard (in "Mrs. Arthur Strong, Morelli, and the Troopers of Cortés") has subsequently argued that Eugénie Sellers Strong introduced the Morellian approach to the study of classical art even earlier. The important point, however, is that this positivist method has been influential in shaping the discipline of classics and that it is neither natural nor neutral, but the product of particular historical circumstances.

Freud's best-known and most imaginative work on religion is *Moses and Monotheism* (written between 1934 and 1938), in which he reconstructs the origins of ancient Israelite religion through his analysis of the exodus story in the Hebrew Bible. He argues that Moses was an Egyptian Prince who followed the monotheistic teachings of Akhenaten, and fled to the wilderness, taking the Hebrew slaves as his followers. Although few historians of Israelite religion are convinced by Freud's reconstruction, it has implications for trying to tease out the idea of what Jan Assmann (*Moses the Egyptian*) calls *mnemohistory* or remembered history—the significance of past as it was remembered, rather than the past as it really happened. Thus, in Assmann's study, cultural memory as well as its effects and motivations are privileged, rather than focusing on a positivist account of the past. Assmann's study of Moses the Egyptian as inspired by Freud and the idea of remembered history has important implications for the study of literature, myths, and ruins such as the Homeric poems and Hesiod's *Theogony*. Studying them as well as sanctified ruins of earlier periods from the perspective of cultural memory permits us to examine how the Greeks viewed their past and constructed their present in terms of the remembered past. The aspects of history, which we choose to privilege in academia, also say something about our relationship with the past.

Although many classicists prefer to focus on the conscious meanings of authors, historical figures, texts, art works and monuments, and prominent figures in the discipline, psychoanalysis can inform the very contours of historical practice, regardless of whether or not one is for or against its premises. This relation is a reciprocal one as illustrated by the influence that both ancient remains and classical texts have had on the development of many aspects Freud's work.

Further reading

By Freud

Moses and Monotheism. Translated by Katherine Jones. New York: Vintage Books, 1939.

The Interpretation of Dreams. In *The Standard Edition of the Complete Psychological Works of Sigmund Freud*, edited by James Strachey. IV. London: Hogarth Press, 1953–74.

On Beginning the Treatment (Further Recommendations on the Technique of Psycho-Analysis I). In *The Standard Edition of the Complete Psychological Works of Sigmund Freud*, edited by James Strachey. XII. London: Hogarth Press, 1953–74.

Introductory Lectures on Psycho-Analysis. In *The Standard Edition of the Complete Psychological Works of Sigmund Freud*, edited by James Strachey. XV–XVI. London: Hogarth Press, 1953–74.

Totem and Taboo: Some Points of Agreement between the Mental Lives of Savages and Neurotics. In *The Standard Edition of the Complete Psychological Works of Sigmund Freud*, edited by James Strachey. XIII. London: Hogarth Press, 1953–74.

Civilization and Its Discontents. Translated by James Strachey. New York: W. W. Norton and Company, 1962.

* "Two Encyclopedia Articles." In *Standard Edition of the Complete Works of Sigmund Freud*, edited by James Strachey. XVIII. London: Hogarth Press, 1953–74.

"The Future of an Illusion." In *Standard Edition of the Complete Works of Sigmund Freud*, edited by James Strachey. XXI. London: Hogarth Press, 1953–74.

* "A Disturbance of Memory on the Acropolis." In *Standard Edition of the Complete Works of Sigmund Freud*, edited by James Strachey. XXII. London: Hogarth Press, 1953–74.

"The Unconscious," "Repression," "Creative Writers and Day-Dreaming," and "Leonardo Da Vinci and a Memory of His Childhood." In *The Freud Reader*, edited by Peter Gay. New York: W. W. Norton and Company, 1989.

"The 'Uncanny'" and "The Moses of Michelangelo." In *Writings on Art and Literature*. Stanford: Stanford University Press, 1997.

About Freud

Armstrong, Richard H. *A Compulsion for Antiquity: Freud and the Ancient World*. Cornell: Cornell University Press, 2005.

Assmann, Jan. *Moses the Egyptian: The Memory of Egypt in Western Monotheism*. Harvard: Harvard University Press, 1997.

Beard, Mary. "Mrs. Arthur Strong, Morelli, and the Troopers of Cortés." In *Ancient Art and Its Historiography*, edited by A. A. Donohue and Mark A. Fullerton. Cambridge: Cambridge University Press, 2003.

Bowie, Malcolm. "Freud and Art, or What Will Michelangelo's *Moses* Do Next?" In *Psychoanalysis and the Future of Theory*. Oxford: Blackwell, 1993.

Forrester, John. "'Mille e tre': Freud and Collecting." In *The Cultures of Collecting*, edited by John Elsner and Roger Cardinal. Cambridge, MA: Harvard University Press, 1994.

* Gay, Peter. *Freud: A Life for Our Times*. New York: W. W. Norton, 1988.

Ginzburg, Carlo. "Morelli, Freud, and Sherlock Holmes: Clues and Scientific Method," In *The Sign of Three: Dupin, Holmes, Peirce*, edited by Umberto Eco and Thomas A. Sebeok. Bloomington: Indiana University Press, 1983.

Hertz, Neil. "Foreword." In *Writings on Art and Literature* by Sigmund Freud. Stanford: Stanford University Press, 1997.

Lloyd Jones, Hugh. "Psychoanalysis and the Study of the Ancient World," In *Greek Comedy, Hellenistic Literature, Greek: Religion and Miscellanea*. Oxford: Oxford University Press, 1990.

Meisel, Perry (ed.). *Freud: A Collection of Critical Essays*. Englewood Cliffs, NJ: Prentice-Hall, 1981.

* Nobus, Dany. "*Polymetis* Freud: Some Reflections on the Psychoanalytic Significance of Homer's Odyssey." Comparative Literature Studies 43.6 (2006) 252–68.

Ricoeur, Paul. *Freud and Philosophy: An Essay on Interpretation*. Translated by Denis Savage. New Haven: Yale University Press, 1970.

Spitz, Ellen Handler. *Image and Insight: Essays in Psychoanalysis and the Arts*. New York: Columbia University Press, 1991.

Whitley, James. "Beazley as Theorist." *Antiquity*. 71.271 (1997) 40–7.

Wollheim, Richard. *Sigmund Freud*. New York: Viking Press, 1971.

Wollheim, Richard. "Freud and the Understanding of Art." In *Sigmund Freud*, edited by Harold Bloom. New York: Chelsea House, 1985.

2 Karl Marx

Key concepts:

- historical materialism
- dialectic
- modes of production (relations and forces)
- proletariat, capitalists, bourgeoisie
- base/superstructure
- ideology
- alienation
- commodity fetishism

Karl Marx (1818–83) was a German political philosopher. He was born in Trier, Germany, to liberal Jewish parents who had converted to Protestantism in order to advance the law career of his father. In 1836, after a year at the University of Bonn, Marx entered the University of Berlin, where he concentrated on philosophy. Deeply influenced by Hegelian thought, he was a member of a student group known as the Young Hegelians, who espoused a radical, atheistic version of Hegel's *The Phenomenology of the Spirit* (1807).

Marx's doctoral thesis on Greek philosophy was accepted in 1841. Unable to find a university position, he became a journalist for the liberal newspaper the *Rhenish Gazette*. He wrote articles on a wide range of topics, touching especially on political and social concerns, and served briefly as the paper's editor before it was censored by the Prussian government for, among other things, articles about workers' conditions.

In 1843 Marx, newly married, moved to Paris to take a position as co-editor of a new publication, the *German-French Annals*. This journal expressed communist ideas, but failed to draw the interest of French readers. Deemed subversive by the Prussian government, the publication was confiscated and its editors sought for arrest. Once again unemployed and now unable to return to Germany, Marx devoted his energy to writing a work of political philosophy that would express his socialist views. At this same time (1844), Marx befriended Friedrich Engels (1820–95), son of a German industrialist, who became Marx's lifelong collaborator and benefactor.

At the insistence of the Prussian government, the French expelled Marx and other German communists from Paris. Marx moved to Brussels, supported financially by Engels. They both attended the Congress of the Communist League in London in 1847. It was here that Marx asserted his views about how to bring about a communist revolution. As a result, he and Engels were commissioned to articulate the League's working doctrines, which resulted in the publication of *The Communist Manifesto* (published in German) in 1848.

After the 1848 French Revolution, Marx moved first to Paris, then to Cologne, then back to Paris as conservative factions regained control of Germany, and then, late in the summer of 1849, to London where he remained throughout the rest of his life. Marx lived in poverty for a time, but with Engels' support and his own family inheritances, he eventually enjoyed a comfortable lifestyle in London with his family. He continued to organize social movements and to write. In 1852, and continuing for a decade, he became a regular contributor to the *New York Tribune*. Marx published the first volume of *Das Kapital* (*Capital*), a critique of capitalist economics, in German in 1867. *Das Kapital* brought attention once again to Marx's ideas and a second edition was published in 1871. Translations into other languages soon followed, though an English translation did not appear until after Marx's death. Two subsequent volumes of *Das Kapital* remained unfinished at the time of his death but were later completed by Engels.

Marxism, or Marxist theory, is based on the ideas formulated by Marx and Engels as a critique of industrial capitalism. It focuses attention on social history in relation to political economy, particularly with regard to class struggle. From a Marxist perspective, history is not driven by ideas, values, or some overarching spirit. Rather, it is a record of struggle, rooted in material existence, for food, shelter, products of labor, and control over the means of production. Marx's ideas—disseminated in part through various interpretations of and elaborations on Marxism—exerted a tremendous impact on twentieth-century politics as well as on social theory, literary theory, cultural studies, philosophy, sociology, archaeology, anthropology, and the arts.

We can conceive of Marxist theory in at least two ways. First, Marxist theory is a revolutionary critique of capitalist society. Marx was personally concerned with the need for social change in light of what he saw as the injustice and oppression caused by nineteenth-century industrial capitalism and the economic relations it engendered. His analyses of how industrial capitalism operated and how it caused oppression were directed at changing this system and thereby ending the human suffering that it produced. Second, and more important for our purposes, Marxist theory is a way to analyze not only economic relations (the base in Marx's terms), but also those values and viewpoints created by industrial capitalism that impact ostensibly non-political endeavors such as religion, literature, and other cultural products (the superstructure). These types of analyses can and have been extended to preindustrialized, but stratified societies. Furthermore, Marxist theory emphasizes the ideological nature of all human enterprises, thus providing a dynamic means to interpret administrative and economic documents, political and religious texts, literature, public art, and household production.

Central to Marxist thought is a philosophy of history known as **historical materialism,** which views historical change as a result of the actions of human beings within the material world, and not of the hand of God or some other extra-human force. Ludwig Feuerbach, who criticized the idealism of Hegelian thinking, which stressed ideas, the spiritual nature of the universe, and historical teleology, influenced Marx's materialist view of history. For Marx, what propels history is a **dialectic** relationship between social classes, expressed in economic and other conflicts. Hegel, too, had understood history as dialectical, with change taking place through a series of successive movements from thesis to antithesis to synthesis. But whereas Hegel saw this as a history of a divinely inspired human spirit, Marx saw it as a history of human struggle over material goods, their production, and the means of production. This is why Marx is said to have stood Hegel on his head: Material circumstances shape ideas, not vice versa.

Marxism describes the historical development of different **modes of production,** a concept referring to the ways in which societies organize economic relations in order to allow for the production of goods. The Marxist characterization of capitalism as an oppressive, exploitative, and unjust system for organizing labor and production focuses on analyzing social relations and the tools used in the production of goods. Labor is not performed in isolation, but within larger human networks. Human patterns of economic organization, or **relations of production,** interact with human labor and organization, or **forces of production.** Therefore, the separation of a worker from the products of his or her labor by specialization and division of labor defines the means by which humanity has been divested of its very being—its social being, which results in **alienation.** From its earliest articulation, Marxism is presented as a discourse that is always already political *and* ontological.

Although modes of production differ across historical periods, Marxist cultural analysis is especially focused on industrial capitalism, viewing it as an economic system that depends on and promotes social and economic inequality, and therefore it is an unjust mode of production. Marx's discussion of class struggle in capitalist society presupposes that economic development progresses from primitive to feudal to capitalist and that class struggle corresponds to the dominant mode of production in each society. Inevitably, Marx argues, contradictions exist between those in control and those controlled, thereby resulting in class conflict. It is this dialectic of class confrontations and struggle that creates a new society. Historical change is possible only within the context of dialectical conflicts between classes. It is only with the evolution of a socialist mode of production that class distinctions and conflicts end in a classless, socialist state.

In a capitalist mode of production, the relations of production are such that the labor of workers is used to turn raw materials into finished goods (commodities) whereas the owners who control the sale and distribution of these products, collect their surplus value. Such a system, Marx argues, inevitably results in the creation of class inequality in which the **proletariat**— workers who sell their labor power for a wage in order to make a living— enables the **capitalists** who own and control the means of production (i.e., natural resources, factories, machines, and other material resources) to recover a profit at the expense of the workers. A third class, the **bourgeoisie**, are neither owners nor workers, but service providers such as doctors and teachers. Although they provide services to both other classes, they are usually identified as having the same class interests as capitalists.

For Marx, economic organization of the means of production shapes other aspects of society. The concepts of **base** and **superstructure** explain this relationship. Base refers to a society's economic mode of production (e.g., industry), which determines its superstructure, that is, its political, social, religious, moral, scientific, and other cultural institutions. From this perspective, art, religion, and literature are not an independent or autonomous mode of human activity but are structured and determined by a society's mode of production and the relations (economic and social) it constructs. Marxism is a materialist theory that views artistic production and belief systems as a part of society's superstructure, which includes universities and museums.

The economic base is supported by a superstructure, which justifies it. This superstructure seeks to naturalize class differences as an overarching reality that people have no possibility of, or desire to change. Naturalizing these cultural differences through art and belief systems (religious and political) is known as **ideology**. Such a system is understood by Marxist thinkers as fundamentally exploitative and only changeable through dialectical struggle between classes. Struggle occurs because the inequities and contradictions of an unequal system become evident over time as exploited classes attain class consciousness. Marxist philosophy forecasts that the dialectical struggle will eventually destroy capitalism and establish a class-free, socialist society in its place. This event will mark the end of history in the sense that further economic change will no longer occur because unequal class relations that fueled dialectical struggle have ceased to exist.

Marxism draws our attention to the processes of **alienation**, especially that caused by the stratification of society into different classes, where upper classes have privileged access to the goods produced by the lower classes. Alienation occurs in two ways. First, a capitalist mode of production is a system in which workers produce goods from which only capitalist owners profit. This is a labor divided, and thus, alienated from the fruits of its own efforts. Second, workers are alienated from themselves in a capitalist system. According to Marx, this occurs because workers become commodities when they must sell their alienated labor in the marketplace, just as other goods are sold. Thus, the workers become alienated from their own humanity and that of others. It is for this reason that Marx describes his goal of a class-less, communistic society as "the *positive* supersession [*Aufhebung*] of *private property* as *human self-estrangement*, and hence the true *appropriation* of the *human* essence through and for man; it is the complete restoration of man to himself as a *social*, i.e. human, being, a restoration which has become conscious and which takes place within the entire wealth of previous periods of development" ("Private Property and Communism" (1844), p. 212). Marx's thought forward a progressive, dialectical overcoming of capitalist mode of production that is informed by the struggles and inequalities of the past. It is only through the dialectical struggle that humanity can free itself from alienation and its attendant ideology.

Ideology, Marx contends, is a false consciousness that distorts social and material reality, thereby functioning to keep people in their place within the capitalist system. This distortion prevents people from viewing the relations of production as they really are. Therefore ideology is an aspect of super-structure: It is produced by the economic base and functions to legitimate that base. Ideologies promote beliefs about politics, religion, and social relations. But ideologies are not autonomous; they depend, Marx explains, on the prevailing economic mode of production and serve as a justification for its continued existence.

In this Marxist light, the teaching of classics and related practices of classical archaeology and museology—elements of the superstructure—are not innocent endeavors, but rather are ideologically implicated in larger political and economic processes. For example, it is well known that the study of Greek and Latin has been associated in the past with the education of the upper classes in Britain. Today, this is no longer the case, and classicists looking for other reasons to justify the discipline are reinvigorating it through shifting emphasis to other approaches such as gender studies, settlement archaeology, ethnicity, colonialism, as well as phenomenology and embodiment.

Within ancient history and archaeology, there is a fairly recent tradition of Marxist thinkers who have sought to foreground the ideology inherent in the manipulation of text, imagery, and a prestige goods economy as tools of legitimation in ancient societies. The study of ancient economy in the classical world and much of the inspiration for the study of premonetary and household economy has developed out of the work of Moses Finley, a social historian, blacklisted as a communist, who went on to found his own school of ancient history at Cambridge. Finley was concerned with the study of social and institutional structures, particularly the ancient economy, focusing on questions that could not be answered by a literal reading of historical sources. Treating texts and archaeological remains as two kinds of historical evidence, he also promoted the use of quantitative analysis in the practice of ancient history and viewed the writing of history as a form of ideology.

Other applications of Marxist thought to the past have foregrounded the social and human origins and significance of cultural production. Marxist approaches have also focused on the study of institutionalized inequality such as slavery, as pioneered in the work of Keith Hopkins. On a less successful and cruder level, Marxists have tried to project modern concepts of capitalist exploitation of the masses into the prehistoric past as in Chourmouziadis' (*Neolithic Dimini* (In Greek) (1979)) interpretation of the Neolithic settlement at Dimini. Peter Rose (*Sons of the Gods, Children of the Earth*) has applied Marx to literary works from Homer to Pindar in order to analyze their role in serving particular class interests. Rose also provides a useful survey of various attempts to apply Marxist and Althusserian concepts of archaeology to classics in "Divorcing Ideology from Marxism and Marxism from Ideology."

Contemporary values in capitalist society have fostered a situation in modern times whereby ancient art and artifacts have attained a curious position. Under the reign of capitalism, there are no longer relations between human beings. The social sphere is defined by **commodity fetishism** in which there is only "a social relation between the products" (*Capital*, p. 43). Products become commodities because they are endowed with qualities symbolizing exchange value and the remnants of social interaction. A commodity is an intriguing "social hieroglyphic" that must be deciphered in order to reveal the presence of another economy: the absent exchange of social relations between persons as opposed to things (ibid., p. 45). Rather than treating ancient objects solely as important documents of the past with a social function, they are have attained the inescapable status as commodities. The result has led to looting and destruction of ancient sites, forgeries, and illegal tax-write-offs when collections of sometimes-dubious authenticity are donated to art museums.

From a Marxist view, then, religious, economic, and political structures (which were sometimes one and the same) in the ancient world can be adequately understood only when we take into account how texts, rituals, art, trade, organization and division of labor, and social relations are implicated in a culture's material conditions, especially the dominant economic modes of production.

Further reading

By Marx

The Grundrisse. Edited and translated by David McLellan. New York: Harper and Row, 1972.

Marx and Engels on Literature and Art: A Selection of Writings. Edited by Lee Baxandall and Stefan Morawski. New York: International General, 1973.

The Marx-Engels Reader. Edited by Robert C. Tucker. 2nd edn. New York: W. W. Norton and Company, 1978.

Karl Marx: A Reader. Edited by John Elster. Cambridge: Cambridge University Press, 1986.
Early Writings. Translated by Rodney Livingstone and Gregor Benton. London: Penguin, 1992.
The Communist Manifesto: A Modern Edition. New York: Verso, 1998.
Capital: An Abridged Edition. Edited by David McLellan. Oxford: Oxford University Press, 1999.
"Private Property and Communism." In *The Continental Aesthetics Reader*, edited by Clive Cazeaux. London and New York: Routledge, 2000.

About Marx

Althusser, Louis. *For Marx*, translated by Ben Brewster. New York: Pantheon, 1969.
Baxandall, Lee. *Marxism and Aesthetics: A Selected Annotated Bibliography*. New York: Humanities Press, 1968.
Carver, Terrell (ed). *The Cambridge Companion to Marx*. Cambridge: Cambridge University Press, 1992.
Chourmouziadis, George H. *To Neolithiko Dimini*. Volos: Etairia Thessalikon Erevnon, 1979.
Derrida, Jacques. *Specters of Marx: The State of Debt, the Work of Mourning, and the New International*. Translated by Peggy Kamuf. London and New York: Routledge, 1994.
Elster, Jon. *Making Sense of Marx*. Cambridge: Cambridge University Press, 1985.
*Finley, Moses I. *The Ancient Economy*. Berkeley: University of California Press, 1973.
Finley, Moses I. *Ancient Slavery and Modern Ideology*. London: Chatto and Windus, 1980.
Finley, Moses I. *Economy and Society in Ancient Greece*. London: Chatto and Windus, 1981.
Hopkins, Keith. *Conquerors and Slaves*. Cambridge and New York: Cambridge University Press, 1978.
Lukács, Georg. *Studies in European Realism*. Translated by Edith Bone. New York: Grosset and Dunlap, 1964.
McGuire, Randall H. *A Marxist Archaeology*. New York: Academic Press, 1992.
Macherey, Pierre. *A Theory of Literary Production*. Translated by Geoffrey Wall. London and New York: Routledge, 1978.
*McLellan, David. *Karl Marx: His Life and Thought*. New York: Harper and Row, 1973.
*Miller, Daniel and Tilley, Christopher "Ideology, power, and prehistory: an introduction." In *Ideology, Power, and Prehistory*. Edited by Daniel Miller and Christopher Tilley. Cambridge: Cambridge University Press, 1984.
Negri, Antonio. *Marx Beyond Marx*. Translated by Harry Cleaver, Michael Ryan, and Maurizio Viano. South Hadley, MA: Bergin and Garvey, 1984.
Rose, Peter W. "Divorcing Ideology from Marxism and Marxism from Ideology: Some Problems." *Arethusa* 39.1 (2006) 101–36.
Rose, Peter W. *Sons of the Gods, Children of the Earth: Ideology and Literary Form in Ancient Greece*, Ithaca, NY. Cornell University Press, 1992.
Singer, Peter. *Marx: A Very Short Introduction*. Oxford: Oxford University Press, 2000.
Wolff, Jonathan. *Why Read Marx Today?* Oxford: Oxford University Press, 2002.

3   Friedrich Nietzsche

Key concepts:

- Dionysian and Apollonian
- aesthetics
- death of God
- overman
- (will to) power
- tragic culture
- good, bad, and evil
- slave morality

Friedrich Wilhelm Nietzsche (1844–1900) was born in Röcken, Prussia. He was the eldest of three children. His father and both grandfathers were ordained Lutheran ministers, and early on he seemed destined for the ministry (other children called him the "little pastor"). His father died at the age of 36, when Friedrich was only five. About five months later his baby brother Joseph also died, and was buried wrapped in his father's arms.

Nietzsche received an excellent education, beginning the study of Greek and Latin in 1851. From 14 to 19 he studied classics at Schulpforta, an elite boarding school. Nietzsche entered the University of Bonn in 1864 to study theology and philology, but a year later he moved to the University of Leipzig to focus exclusively on philology, the study of classical languages. In 1867 he took leave of his studies to serve a year in the Prussian military as an artillery officer. By 1869, at the age of 24, he was appointed professor of classical philology at the University of Basel, on the recommendation of his mentor, Professor Friedrich Ritschl. He delivered his inaugural lecture on "Homer and Classical Philology" on May 28, 1869. At the time of his appointment he had yet to complete his exams and dissertation, but the University of Leipzig waived those requirements and awarded him the doctoral degree. In 1870 he took leave from the university to serve as a medic in the Franco-Prussian war, but was discharged within months due to illness.

As a result of failing health, Nietzsche took leave of his professorate in 1876 and then resigned in 1879. Having given up his Prussian citizenship without being granted Swiss citizenship, he remained "stateless" for the rest of his life. For the next decade, he wrote prolifically while traveling and visiting friends throughout Europe and elsewhere.

In January 1889, while in Turin, he suffered a mental breakdown from which he never recovered. The apocryphal story is that he collapsed after wrapping his arms around the neck of a horse that had just been brutally whipped by a coachman. After a year in a sanitarium in Jena, he lived with his mother until her death in 1897 and then spent his last years in the care of his sister, Elizabeth, a devout anti-Semite who published *The Will to Power* (based on his 1880s notebooks) and who later brought his works to the attention of influential fascists, including Hitler and Mussolini. Despite certain passages in his writings that easily support the anti-Jewish ideology of the Nazis, Nietzsche railed against German nationalism and was alienated from his sister on account of her anti-Semitism.

Nietzsche described his work as philosophizing "with a hammer." Although trained in classical philology, he is best known as a critic and philosopher of prevailing western European cultural values. However, classical philology remained his reference point, and it is fruitless to distinguish his philosophy and philology. In particular, Nietzsche's work challenged the Christian foundations of European values. But his philosophy was not simply negative or destructive, which is a common misreading. On the contrary, his critical eye on Western civilization was inspired by a desire to affirm what he understood to be the source of life—a kind of primordial, creative energy beyond rationality and beyond moral categorization as good or evil. He argued that Western civilization was in decline because it had drained that life force, ceding power and authority to those who fear it.

Nietzsche's first book, *The Birth of Tragedy* (published in German in 1872), describes this creative, primordial life force as **Dionysian**, after the ancient gender-bending god of wine, masquerade, violence, and orgy. Contrary to the prevailing view, which privileged ancient Greece as a world of noble harmony and rational order with Dionysian excess transferred to the east, Nietzsche argues that Greek culture existed in the tension between two opposing forces: on the one hand, the Dionysian forces of amoral desire, non-rational and creative exuberance, and intoxicated "blissful ecstasy"; and on the other, the **Apollonian** forces of moral order and sober rationality. The Apollonian force is order; the Dionysian is the chaotic life force that precedes the order of civilization and is its creative source. Nietzsche believes that in the centuries since ancient Greece, Western civilization had gradually repressed the Dionysian, leaving modern society predominantly Apollonian starved of creative energy and in poor health.

In "Homer: The Very Idea" (p. 60), James Porter observes that Nietzsche regarded modernity as viewing the classical world as a buried, ideal world. "Modern man," Nietzsche asserts, "is merely a counterfeit of the sum of cultural illusions that are allegedly nature" (*Birth of Tragedy*, p. 62). To correct this situation Nietzsche explains that pre-Socratic Attic tragedy was, in fact, equally Apollonian *and* Dionysian; thus, his prescription for modern (specifically, nineteenth-century western Europe) society is a resurrection of the Dionysian, through the art and music of German Romanticism.

Two important philosophical positions underlie Nietzsche's redefinition of "the science of **aesthetics**" (*Birth of Tragedy*, p. 33). First, following on the work of Immanuel Kant and Arthur Schopenhauer, Nietzsche argues that there is no simple opposition between appearance and truth. Rather, he insists that the world is constructed through representation. In other words, because self-consciousness constructs reality, there is no representation of a thing-in-itself. Because of humanity's reliance on language we are condemned, Nietzsche argues, to a life of metaphor, an endless contemplation of images. This is characterized as an anthropocentric existence wherein there is no possibility of bridging the gulf "between this real truth of nature [Dionysian] and the lie of culture [Apollonian] that poses as if it were the only reality that is similar to that between the eternal core of things, the thing-in-itself, and the whole world of appearances" (*Birth of Tragedy*, p. 61).

Nietzsche's second philosophical position, which allows us to understand the first more fully, is a call for the inversion of Kantian aesthetics. In *On the Genealogy of Morals* (1887) he offers the following:

> Kant thought he was honoring art when among the predicates of beauty he emphasized and gave prominence to those which established the honor of knowledge: impersonality and universality. This is not the place to inquire whether this was essentially a mistake; all I wish to underline is that Kant, like all philosophers, instead of envisaging the aesthetic problem from the point of view of the artist (the creator), considered art and the beautiful purely from that of the "spectator," and unconsciously introduced the "spectator" into the concept "beautiful" ... "That is beautiful," said Kant, "which gives pleasure *without interest*".
>
> (p. 104–5)

Here it is easy to see that the poles of creator and spectator correspond to those of the Dionysian and the Apollonian. Moreover, this call for an inversion of Kantian aesthetics is an extension of Nietzsche's overarching conception of the immanence of the Apollonian and Dionysian. More than simply calling for the substitution of the latter for the former, his definition of art is contingent upon an ever-changing dynamic relation between the

Apollonian forces of restraint, disinterest, and dissimulation, and the Dionysian forces of intoxication (the dissolution of the individual into the sphere of the collective), intuition, and the delimitation of the human subject. The artist maintains a relation to the "primordial artist of the world" and in this relation the artist is revealed to be both "subject and object, at once poet, actor, and spectator" (*Birth of Tragedy*, p. 52). Because he also considers external "reality" to be valid only as an aesthetic phenomenon, Nietzsche defines aesthetic experience as not what occurs in an isolated, privileged sphere of existence, but as the very founding experience of life. It is in and through art that life can be experienced as such.

The aspect of this system of thought is interesting in that Nietzsche theorizes the interdependence of these opposing poles. The gulf that separates subject and object, appearance and truth, Apollonian and Dionysian is traversed by what he terms "an aesthetic relation" [*ein ästhetisches Verhalten*] ("On Truth and Lie in an Extra-Moral Sense" (1873), p. 58). It is art that moves between the spheres of Apollo and Dionysos; it is art that keeps the possibility of "continual rebirths" in play (*The Birth of Tragedy*, p. 66). This is accomplished by the reticence of the aesthetic, which does not concede to know the external world on its own terms. On the contrary, the aesthetic sphere, for Nietzsche, is determined by the Dionysian motives of the artist as opposed to spectator, i.e., the "true artist" who refuses to deny the intuition that there exists something beyond the world of appearance and self-consciousness. Although the aesthetic cannot represent the thing-in-itself, it is able to construct a relation with "the mysterious X of the thing in itself" ("On Truth and Lie in an Extra-Moral Sense," p. 55). This "mysterious X" must remain inaccessible and unrepresentable but, through art, it makes its presence felt, thereby undermining the concept of experience that Western civilization has inherited from Platonic idealism. It is a nihilistic "playing with seriousness" that allows Nietzsche to present the aesthetic relation between the Apollonian and the Dionysian as that which has the ability to affect "redemption in illusion" ("On Truth," p. 61; *Birth of Tragedy*, p. 61). Just as the world is conceived by an artist, Nietzsche redefines art as a drive, a force or rhythm, that "continually manifests an ardent desire to refashion the world which presents itself to waking man, so that it will be as colorful, irregular, lacking in results and coherence, charming and eternally new as the world of dreams" ("On Truth and Lie in an Extra-Moral Sense," p. 59). Simply put, the metaphysical is the aesthetic in Nietzsche's work only insofar as there is no simple binary opposition of appearance and truth. The truth appears through the rhythm of intuition and language, music and image.

It should be noted that Nietzsche privileges music over the plastic arts. Music, for him, is closest to metaphysics; it is what "allows the symbolic image to emerge in its highest significance" (*Birth of Tragedy*, p. 103). However, as the Dionysian needs the Apollonian, so music needs the plastic arts. It is in the translation between the spheres that the immanence of the two poles of cultural production becomes evident. In fact, the plastic arts as representations of phenomena are crucial to Nietzsche's system because he believes that an organism translates external stimulation into an image. This means that the image is an immediate translation of external stimuli (perceptions as such). This point helps to explain why toward the end of *The Birth of Tragedy* Nietzsche finally articulates his basic points of departure: "What aesthetic effect results when the essentially separate art-forces, the Apollonian and the Dionysian, enter into simultaneous activity? Or more briefly: how is music related to image and concept?" (p. 101). This intimacy between intuition (music) and image (plastic arts) affords him the opportunity to declare that "art is *worth more* than truth" and that "we possess *art* lest we *perish of the truth*" (*The Will to Power*, pp. 453, 435).

Nietzsche's work is invaluable for classical archaeology because he insists that the reception of an artwork is irreducible to formalistic-linguistic concepts or mere appreciation of "beauty." Rather than continuing on the dead-end street of a viewer's sensuous apprehension (*aisthesis*) of an artwork, Nietzsche's work radically departs from Kant. As Giorgio Agamben explains in *The Man Without Content* (1994):

> The problem of art, as such, does not present itself within Nietzsche's thought because all his thought is about art. There is no such thing as Nietzsche's aesthetics because Nietzsche never thought of art starting from ... the spectator's sensuous apprehension—and yet it is in Nietzsche's thought that the aesthetic idea of art ... as a creative-formal principle, attains the furthest point of its metaphysical itinerary.
>
> (p. 85)

Nietzsche calls for a shift in focus from the spectator and the perception of the work of art to the artist and the work of the work of art because he wants to replace Kantian aesthetics (which expresses only a will to decline, a stoic resignation) with "an aesthetic relation" that asserts the will to life that is the nucleus of his philosophy.

For Nietzsche, the study of art is less about categorization or appreciation and more about disclosing the ways in which art is *vital* to individual and collective experience. (The difficulty arises because the criteria by which one would judge or arrive at what constitutes this category of "true art" are yet to be determined.) Art exists, for Nietzsche, within the flux of the Apollonian and the Dionysian, i.e., within the sphere of tragedy.

Despite the importance of Nietzsche's observations on aesthetics, creativity, and representation, the first thing that comes to most minds concerning Nietzsche is, of course, his pronouncement of the **death of God** in *The Gay Science* (1882; section 125) and the Prologue to *Thus Spoke Zarathustra* (1983-85). Nietzsche's meaning is frequently misunderstood, as he is neither calling for nor celebrating the death of God. Instead, he is describing what he sees as a fact of modern Western civilization, namely that it no longer lives by faith in "God" as a monolithic, ultimate author and guarantor of moral law who sees into the hearts of all people and will judge them accordingly. For Nietzsche, the most important thing about the death of God is what must die with him, namely, the Christian conceptions of human sinfulness, fallenness, and indebtedness. Nietzsche's interest in making this pronouncement is to free people from bondage to a slave morality according to which life is lived in hopes of some future, other-worldly reward. We see this most clearly, perhaps, in his Prologue of *Thus Spoke Zarathustra*, a philosophical work of poetry, allegory, and fiction, in which Zarathustra (Zoroaster the founding prophet of Zoroastrianism), the hero of exuberant freedom and affirmation of life on earth, meets a saint in the forest. Whereas Zarathustra loves the earth and human beings, the saint has given up on humans and seeks only to love God. As the saint departs, Zarathustra wonders to himself, "Could it be possible? This old saint in the forest has not yet heard anything of this, that God is dead!" (p. 12). Immediately following this interchange with the old saint, Zarathustra begins preaching the coming of the **overman** (*Übermensch*, often translated as "superman"), that is, the human being who has achieved self-mastery and realization, who has overcome the notion of human nature as fallen and sinful, and the slave morality that goes with it.

In *The Birth of Tragedy* we see Nietzsche's conception of the world as a turbulent sea of non-rational forces that are both destructive and generative. Nietzsche saw the world not as a moral universe, created and managed by a moral God, but as a chaotic "monster of energy" in which humans live, move, and have their being. **Power**, therefore, must be understood not as an object to be held but as a never-ending struggle within this ever-changing sea of forces. Life, therefore, is driven by a will to power that is antecedent to morality. The will to power is not just a will to live but a will to wield and use power and to subsume other wills in the process. He concludes his text with a call for a rebirth of **"tragic culture"** which can "'live resolutely' in wholeness and fullness" because "the tragic man of such a culture" is not afraid "to desire a new art, the art of metaphysical comfort, to desire tragedy as his own proper Helen" (*Birth of Tragedy*, p. 113).

In Nietzsche's *On the Genealogy of Morals* (1887), he explores the origins of the contemporary moral categories of **good, bad,** and **evil.** He argues that these categories are not essential or universal categories but are culturally constructed through operations of social power throughout history. Goodness is simply that which is valued by those in power and badness is its opposite, either as a threat to their power (e.g., enemies) or as the antithesis of it (e.g., the weak). In the earliest stages of human history, Nietzsche argues, the good and the bad were determined by the dominant knightly-aristocratic class. That which furthered their health and happiness in the world was good; that which did not was bad. Then came moralistic religion, the champions of which Nietzsche calls the priestly-aristocratic class.

Whereas the knightly-aristocratic values were based on this-worldly physical pleasure and the furtherance of life, the priestly-aristocratic values were just the opposite, glorifying selflessness and weakness, and calling the knightly aristocratic affirmation of life and health not just bad, but downright "evil." (Like other late nineteenth-century German historians, Nietzsche identifies this priestly-aristocratic class quite explicitly with Roman Catholic and Jewish priesthoods and legal codes.) Against them, this priestly-aristocratic class has established a **slave morality** that glorifies weakness and makes people feel bad for all that comes naturally, that is, for their will to power, pleasure, and the enjoyment of life.

Historians and anthropologists would rightly doubt Nietzshe's provocative, if also simplistic, history of society as he presents it in *Genealogy*. The importance of this work, however, lies not in his account of religion in relation to this historical schema, but in his genealogical approach. Instead of seeing religious ideas and values like "evil" as universal truths or divine revelations, he approaches them as products of history that take form over time through ongoing social struggle. They are, in short, effects of power. The analysis of power as situated, distributed, and negotiated, combined with a genealogical approach, later becomes central in the work of **Foucault**, and has implications for how we study institutions of the past and in the present, which shape our discipline.

Similarly, in another famous essay, "On the Use and Abuse of History for Life," (1873) Nietzsche regards histories as constructed with deep and sometimes unconscious agendas. (This work formed the basis for **Adorno's** project of Enlightenment critique.) The essay notes the transformative power of the past for good and for bad, calling the past the "gravedigger of the present." The importance of Nietzsche's observation lies in confronting the contemporary tendency to forget the importance of the past and to treat it as disconnected from and irrelevant to the present. Yet as James Porter observed (In *Nietzsche and the Philology of the Future* (2000) p. 15) immersion in the past is a modern desire, thus, to study the past is to be modern, the study of antiquity is required for self-definition. Nietzsche used his inaugural lecture on "Homer and Classical Philology" (1869) to initiate his exploration of the relationship between past and present. Nietzsche saw classics and philology as disciplines that were entered from not one, but from multiple perspectives (In *Homer and Classical Philology*):

> We may consider antiquity from a scientific point of view; we may try to look at what has happened with the eye of a historian, or to arrange and compare the linguistic forms of ancient masterpieces, to bring them at all events under a morphological law; but we always lose the wonderful creative force, the real fragrance, of the atmosphere of antiquity; we forget that passionate emotion which instinctively drove our meditation and enjoyment back to the Greeks.

Although the later theorists we will be reading have built upon and departed from Nietzsche's philosophy, his refusal to view the past as ideal and transcendent, rather than historical, situated, and contingent is as relevant for the present as when he was writing in the nineteenth century. Nietzsche noted, in "We Philologists," (translated in 1910) that while the elements of the past were exhaustible, that "if we make it our task to understand our own age better by means of antiquity, then our task will be an everlasting one."

Further reading

By Nietzsche

*"Homer and Classical Philology," In *The Complete Works of Friedrich Nietzsche.* *Vol. 3*, edited by Oscar Levy. Translated by John McFarland Kennedy. T. N. Foulis, 1910. http://www.gutenberg.org/etext/18188

*"We Philologists," In *The Complete Works of Friedrich Nietzsche. Vol. 8*, edited by Oscar Levy. Translated by John McFarland Kennedy. T. N. Foulis, 1910. http://www.gutenberg.org/etext/18267

Beyond Good and Evil. Translated by Walter Kaufmann. New York: Random House, 1966.

The Birth of Tragedy and *the Case of Wagner.* Translated by Walter Kaufmann. New York: Vintage Books, 1967.

On the Genealogy of Morals. Translated by Walter Kaufmann. New York: Vintage Books, 1967.

The Gay Science, with a Prelude of Rhymes and an Appendix of Songs. Translated by Walter Kaufmann. New York: Random House, 1974.

The Will to Power. Translated by Walter Kaufmann. New York: Random House, 1967.

**Thus Spoke Zarathustra.* Translated by Walter Kaufmann. New York: Viking, 1968.

"On Truth and Lie in the Extra-Moral Sense." In *The Continental Aesthetics Reader*, edited by Clive Cazeaux. London and New York: Routledge, 2000.

*"On the Use and Abuse of History for Life." In *Untimely Meditations. Part 2.* 1874. Translated by Ian Johnston, 2007. http://www.mala.bc.ca/~Johnstoi/ Nietzsche/history.htm.

About Nietzsche

Agamben, Giorgio. *The Man without Content.* Translated by Georgia Albert. Stanford: Stanford University Press, 1999.

Bataille, Georges. *On Nietzsche.* Translated by Bruce Boone. New York: Paragon, 1992.

Bishop, Paul (ed.). *Nietzsche and Antiquity: His Reaction and Response to the Classical Tradition. Studies in German Literature, Linguistics, and Culture.* Rochester, NY: Camden House, 2004.

Deleuze, Gilles. *Nietzsche and Philosophy.* Translated by Hugh Tomlinson. New York: Columbia University Press, 1983.

Ferry, Luc. "The Nietzschean Moment: The Shattered Subject and the Onset of Contemporary Aesthetics." In *Homo Aestheticus: The Invention of Taste in the Democratic Age.* Translated by Robert De Loaiza. Chicago: University of Chicago Press, 1993.

Heidegger, Martin. "The Word of Nietzsche: 'God is Dead'." In *The Question Concerning Technology and Other Essays*, edited by William Lovitt. New York: Harper and Row, 1977.

Kaufmann, Walter. *Nietzsche: Philosopher, Psychologist, Antichrist*. Princeton: Princeton University Press, 1950.

Kofman, Sarah. *Nietzsche and Metaphor*. Translated by Duncan Large. Stanford: Stanford University Press, 1993.

Nehamas, Alexander. *Nietzsche: Life as Literature*. Cambridge, MA: Harvard University Press, 1985.

Porter, James I. "The Invention of Dionysus and the Platonic Midwife: Nietzsche's *Birth of Tragedy*," *Journal of the History of Philosophy* 33.3 (1995) 467–97.

*Porter, James I. *Nietzsche and the Philology of the Future*. Stanford: Stanford University Press, 2000.

*Porter, James I. "Homer: The Very Idea." *Arion, 3d series*. 10.2 (2002) 57–86.

Shapiro, Gary. *Archaelogies of Vision: Foucault and Nietzsche on Seeing and Saying*. Chicago: University of Chicago Press, 2003.

Vattimo, Gianni. *Nietzsche: An Introduction*. Translated by Nicholas Martin. Stanford: Stanford University Press, 2002.

4 Ferdinand de Saussure

Key concepts:

- structural linguistics/structuralism
- semiotics
- *langue/parole*
- synchronic/diachronic
- sign (signifier and signified)
- arbitrariness of the sign
- paradigmatic meaning
- binary opposition (meaning as difference)
- syntagmatic meaning

Ferdinand de Saussure (1857–1913) was a Swiss linguist whose posthumously published *Course in General Linguistics* (1916) became a catalyst for the development of structuralism. Saussure was born in Geneva, Switzerland, into a family with a lineage of noted academics going back to the eighteenth century. Saussure himself displayed a gift for languages from an early age. At the University of Geneva, he not only studied linguistics but also theology, law, and chemistry. In 1878, at 21 years old, he published *Memoir on the Original System of Vowels in the Indo-European Languages*, a comparative study of vowel usage in proto-Indo-European languages.

Saussure received his doctorate from the University of Leipzig in 1880. From 1881 to 1891 he taught linguistics at the École des hautes études in Paris. In 1891 he returned to the University of Geneva where he taught courses on Sanskrit and general linguistics for the remainder of his career. Although he published very little himself, his students at the University of Geneva compiled and transcribed their notes from his general linguistics course lectures and had them published in 1916 under the title *Course in General Linguistics*.

Saussure's perspective on language had an impact on many fields of academic inquiry including anthropology, archaeology, architecture, art history, literature, philosophy, psychology, and religion. The decisive element in his work is the assertion that linguistic meaning resides in the relationships between words. These relationships are inscribed in space and time. This philosophy of language is commonly referred to as **structural linguistics** or **structuralism** since its strategy for examining language and meaning centers on investigating structures within a system. Structuralism brought about a major shift in twentieth-century thought by initiating the "linguistic turn," which has become shorthand for the conviction that meaning does not exist outside language as a system of signs.

In the *Course in General Linguistics*, Saussure advocates the scientific study of language, which, for him, concerns "the life of signs within society." This method departs from historical linguistics as practiced by European philologists in the late nineteenth and early twentieth century, who sought to trace Indo-European languages as well as other language families back to a common origin. Saussure called his new linguistic science "semiology," a term derived from the Greek word for "sign" (*semeîon*). Semiology, also called **semiotics**, is the science of signs, that is, the study of the structure of language (as well as other signs) as a system of signification rather than the study of the history of language.

In order to study language as a system of signs, Saussure makes a distinction between *langue* and *parole*. *Langue* ("language") refers to language as a structured system operating at a particular time and place, and to the linguistic rules that determine how a language can be used in practice. In contrast, *parole* ("speech") refers to particular instances of speech within the system. Without *langue*, *parole*—what individuals say, language in use or semantics—would be impossible. For Saussure, the object of inquiry, then, is *langue*, which constitutes the overarching linguistic system that makes specific utterances possible.

As the terms *langue* and *parole* suggest, the study of language as a system requires a **synchronic** ("at the same time") rather than a **diachronic** ("through time") approach. Synchrony refers to the study of language—especially spoken language—as it is used at a particular moment in time. Diachrony refers to the study of language over time. Nineteenth-century philology employed a diachronic methodology that derived from a central assumption that language could only be understood through a study of its historical changes. By tracing a word back to its etymological origin, one would then be able to follow the path back to its present meaning.

Saussure advocates a synchronic approach to language as a system. Instead of etymology as the conveyor of the word's meaning, he asserts that meaning is produced by a word's relationship to other words occurring at a particular time, within a particular system of relationships, which are spatially determined. For instance, the contemporary word "dog" means something not because of its historical derivation from the Middle English *dogge*, which is in turn derived from the Old English *docga*, but rather because of the relationship of "dog" to other words like "puppy" and "cat." In Saussure's analysis, all of these terms are part of a differential system, and their meanings and significance derive synchronically from relationships with other signs within that system.

As illustrated by the previous example, a central claim made by Saussure's semiotics is that words do not have an inherent significance because meaning resides in relationships of difference and similarity within a larger linguistic system. Simply put, words are not units of self-contained meaning. A related concern—whether language is natural or conventional—also plays an important role in Saussure's linguistic analysis. Those advocating a natural view of language propose that there is an intrinsic relationship between a word name and a thing named. On the other hand, if language is conventional, as Saussure maintains, both concrete things and abstract concepts are named on the basis of an arbitrary, cultural decision to use a certain sound to represent a certain idea.

How does Saussure arrive at the conclusion that language is primarily conventional and cultural? He begins with the idea of a linguistic **sign**. A sign may be a word or some other form; he often refers to a sign as an "acoustic image." Regardless of its particular form, however, every sign consists of a **signifier** and a **signified**.

$$Sign = \frac{signifier}{signified}$$

A linguistic sign comprises an acoustic image, such as the phonemes d-o-g spoken or written (the signifier) and the object or concept associated with the acoustic image (the signified). What determines the meaning of a sign is not its acoustic sound, phonemic rendering, or linguistic origin, but its place within the larger network of interrelationships—i.e., within the larger linguistic structure. Thus a structuralist approach focuses on the relationship of individual parts to the larger whole—the structure—within which significance is determined.

One of Saussure's crucial insights, then, is that the meaning of the sign is fundamentally relational. On one level, the relationship between the signifier and the signified is **arbitrary**. That is, there is no *a priori* relationship between a signifier and a signified. The fact that *dog* signifies a four-legged domestic animal in English, while *chien* and *inu* point to this same animal in French and Japanese respectively, is evidence that there is no necessary, predetermined relationship between the letters d-o-g and a common pet. The word *dog* is an arbitrary, culturally agreed-upon designation. We could call dogs by some other term as long as we agree culturally on that usage. There is no particular dog designated by the word, nor is some inherent quality ("dogness") contained in or conveyed by the acoustic image *dog*.

In Saussure's semiotics, the concept of the signifier as an acoustic image is famously illustrated in Belgian Surrealist René Magritte's famous painting *The Betrayal of Images* (1928–9). This seemingly simple representation of a pipe is irremediably complicated by the inclusion of the words: "*Ceci n'est pas une pipe* [This is not a pipe]." The arbitrariness of the sign is made evident here, but there is also another turn of the screw. The visual image— the painting—bears no "natural" relation to either the acoustic image "pipe" or the signified (a wooden instrument one uses to smoke tobacco). But Magritte's work begs a further question; concerning whether or not visual language is something altogether different from either *langue* or *parole*.

Since signs are arbitrary, the meaning of any particular sign is determined in terms of similarity and difference in relation to other signs. Language is both a differential and a relational system of meaning. **Paradigmatic meaning** is founded on **binary oppositions**, such as light-dark, inside-outside, margin-center, male-female, and so on. Within these binary pairs, the meaning of one is basically the opposite of the other. Meaning is predicated on difference. "In language," Saussure argues, "there are only differences. Even more important: a difference generally implies positive terms between which the difference is set up; but in language there are only differences *without positive terms* .... [Moreover] the idea or phonic substance that a sign contains is of less importance than the other signs that surround it" (*Course in General Linguistics*, p. 120). This insight on the differential function of meaning in language has serious implications for the concepts, identities, and cultural articulations that take place in and through language.

The differential manner whereby binary oppositions work to define one another, i.e., how meaning is structurally negotiated through oppositional difference, opened the door for the "linguistic turn" of post-structuralism in the late twentieth century. In post-structuralist thought, binary oppositions like black-white, male-female, straight-queer, colonizer-colonized, night-day, are pressed to reveal a fundamental denotive instability. There is no structure that guarantees the meaning of either term. This insight, in turn, allows for a critique of the inherent paradoxes of larger discourses such as racism. These paradoxes are premised both on a denial of the interdependence of binary terms and on the subtler gradations of meaning within the margins of such oppositional meaning; i.e. twilight is neither night nor day.

A second type of meaning, within structuralism and frequently neglected, thus exacerbating the post-structuralist critique of structuralism and paradigmatic meaning, is syntagmatic meaning. **Syntagmatic meaning** relies upon relationships among words, in a chain. These relationships might be spatial if the chain of signifiers is written or otherwise inscribed in space (i.e. a room full of objects or an iconographic narrative), or temporal if the chain (i.e. a sentence) is spoken. Syntagmatic refers to the spatial and temporal relationships that words, images, monuments, and objects are placed in. Within such a chain, signifiers assume part of their meaning based on their relationship to (as opposed to their difference from) other signifiers. For example, one might say, "I am going to the bank." The statement is somewhat ambiguous as it could imply going to a repository for money or going to the edge of a river. In saying, "I am going to the bank to go fishing," the meaning becomes clearer, but is derived from the relationships among the signifiers, which are spatially determined (if written), or temporally determined (if spoken).

The consequences of Saussure's insights are fundamental to twentieth-century academic research, in part because semiotics, by definition, is an interdisciplinary venture. By asserting the "arbitrariness of the sign," Saussure's work draws attention to the problematic of intent and contingency in any spoken, written, visual, or experiential text. There is no guarantee that an author's intended meaning can be inscribed in the language or other signifying system that he or she uses. The system of language cannot be pinned down to insure the conveyance of a particular meaning (see **Derrida**). In addition, the idea of context, used as a means to devise the parameters which narrow the possibilities of the potential meaning of any given sign, can no longer be taken as a given. A context does not pre-exist as an accumulation of signs or a text, rather the context is constructed anew with each use of language, with each utterance, each text. This fact problematizes the traditional notion of a "natural" relationship between an author/artist/performer/maker and his or her works.

Within classics, Saussure's work has had a somewhat problematic reception, but his work is nonetheless important, particularly in the study of myth, literature, philosophy, and archaeology. The notion that signs derive their identity or comprehensibility by virtue of their difference from other signs; that their properties can only be classified in relation to other signs derives from the Stoic category of relative disposition. Mythical, religious, and historical narratives frequently derive their meanings through binary opposition. Like art historians, classical archaeologists have applied semiotics to the visual realm in order to discern patterns in various categories of iconography, identify architectural vocabularies and spatial syntax as Preziosi has done with Minoan architecture, and interpret the meaning of archaeological assemblages.

Saussure's work instigates a fundamental rethinking of the nature of representation. This includes the representation of the subject—the constitution of all subjects (individual and collective) in and through language—as well as the notion of the representation of "reality." Beyond changing how classicists must read their objects of study and raising questions about the very nature of textual and visual representation, semiotics, by raising the status of the text and discourse, implicates the very activity of the classicist in the production of his or her object of study. This is because there can be no simple binary oppositions or originary meanings in the understanding of things and texts. The centrality of Saussure's work to social theory as a whole rests in large part on his theory of language, but also on working through the consequences of that theory, the most important of which may very well be self-reflexivity, which begins not with how we wield language but in looking at how it constitutes us.

Further reading

By Saussure

Course in General Linguistics. Translated by Wade Baskin. New York: McGraw-Hill, 1959.

About Saussure

Belsey, Catherine. *Poststructuralism: A Very Short Introduction*. Oxford: Oxford University Press, 2002.

Culler, Jonathan. *The Pursuit of Signs: Semiotics, Literature, Deconstruction*. Ithaca: Cornell University Press, 1981.

Culler, Jonathan. *Ferdinand de Saussure*. Rev. edn. Ithaca: Cornell University Press, 1986.

Eco, Umberto and Sebeok, Thomas A. (ed). *The Sign of Three: Dupin, Holmes, Peirce*. Bloomington: Indiana University Press, 1983.

Lévi-Strauss, Claude. "The Structural Study of Myth." In *Structural Anthropology*. New York: Basic Books, 1963.

Mitchell, W. J. T. *Iconology: Image, Text, Ideology*. Chicago: University of Chicago Press, 1986.

Nöth, Winfried. *Handbook of Semiotics*. Bloomington and Indianapolis: Indiana University Press, 1995.

*Preziosi, Donald. *Minoan Architectural Design*. Berlin, Mouton, 1983.

*Tilley, Christopher. "Claude Lévi-Strauss: Structuralism and Beyond." In *Reading Material Culture*, edited by Christopher Tilley. Oxford: Basil Blackwell, 1990.

Part II
The Theorists

5 Theodor W. Adorno

Key concepts:

- culture industry
- mimesis
- autonomy of art
- dialectics of appearance
- authoritarian personality

Theodor Wiesengrund Adorno (1903–1969) was born in Frankfurt am Main, Germany. His academic career is marked by a series of remarkable and influential encounters. While at the University of Frankfurt, in addition to music composition, Adorno studied sociology and psychology with Siegfried Kracauer. Music remained a lifelong interest for Adorno, who even trained as a concert pianist under Alban Berg. His first published essays were on the modernist composer and pioneer of atonalism, Arnold Schönberg.

In 1926, Adorno's first attempt at the *Habilitationsschrift* (a thesis required for promotion to a university position) entitled *The Concept of the Unconscious or The Transcendental Theory of the Mind* was rejected. But his second attempt, which has become a widely influential work, *Kierkegaard: The Construction of the Aesthetic* (1933), was successful. Adorno established the Institut für Sozialforschung in Frankfurt with his longtime friend and collaborator Max Horkheimer in 1931. With the rise of Nazism in Germany, Adorno and other Jewish intellectuals were expelled from their university posts. As a result, he went into exile in Oxford, England, before heading to the United States, where he lived and worked in New York City, Los Angeles, and Berkeley.

Adorno returned to Frankfurt after the war, where he reestablished the Institute of Social Research in 1949. The intellectuals, economists, and sociologists associated with the institute included Horkheimer, Herbert Marcuse, and Jürgen Habermas, among others. It is this group of thinkers that comprise the first generation of what has been termed the "Frankfurt School" of social or critical theorists. Upon Horkheimer's retirement in 1959, Adorno assumed the role of director and held that post until the late 1960s. The student uprisings and social unrest in Paris during May 1968 spilled into West Germany, where students occupied the Institute's buildings. Adorno's comments on the protests were widely ridiculed and he fled to Switzerland, where he died in 1969 while working on his unfinished magnum opus *Aesthetic Theory* (1970).

Adorno's work has been central to discussions of modernity. His work bears the influence of his friendship with Walter **Benjamin**, who encouraged Adorno's interest in the work of Karl **Marx**. The published correspondence between him and Benjamin constitutes one of the most intriguing and important intellectual documents of the twentieth century. Texts such as *The Dialectic of the Enlightenment* (1947), cowritten with Horkheimer, *Negative Dialectics* (1966), and *The Philosophy of Modern Music* (1958) serve as touchstones of postwar critical thought. Adorno's work, however, has been criticized for being elitist, Eurocentric, and too reliant upon a dialectical method associated with modernity. Nonetheless, his interdisciplinary approach to the study of the "culture industry" and his argument for the autonomy of art have played a considerable role in the manifold discourses bearing the prefix "post": postmodernism, post-structuralism, post-Marxism, and even post-colonialism. In this regard it is significant that Adorno's major works were written during his exile in the United States, where the importance of his work to many American scholars and activists is inestimable. Moreover, his aphoristic and performative writing style shares something with the post-structuralist writing practices of Jacques **Derrida**, who shared Adorno's contention that no thought—even critical theory itself—escapes the pull of the market place, nor does it exist as a kind of second-order language that transcends the discourse it critiques. Their paratactical style of writing is meant to undermine the traditional authoritative voice of the scholar as it constructs a space from which to critique the exchange economy of advanced capitalism.

Adorno's discussions of the "**culture industry**" began with his disagreements with Benjamin over the latter's belief in the transformative potential of film and radio to radicalize the masses. In his early essay "On the Fetish-Character in Music and the Regression of Listening" (1938), Adorno insists that technology denies artistic innovation by promoting passive viewers or listeners, thereby stunting political consciousness. (It should be noted that Benjamin's thought underwent a crisis that caused him to abandon this early utopic position.)

Adorno develops his position further in *The Dialectic of the Enlightenment*, which serves an excellent introduction to Adorno's work. Drawing on the work of Friedrich **Nietzsche** and Marxist thinkers such as Georg Lukács, Adorno promotes a critique of Marxism, which analyzes the relationship between enlightenment, myth, and the domination of nature. In responding to what he calls "the darkening of the world" brought about by fascism, Stalinism, and the Holocaust, Adorno argues that the world has retreated into myth and barbarism, which is dialectically present in the "origin" of modern society that begins with the Enlightenment. Here, it is the control and mastery of nature as part of the Enlightenment project that drives history rather than class conflict. Adorno contrasts the **mimetic** aspects of magic in its relationship to nature, which is imitative, to the ordering aspects of myth, which seeks "to report, to name, to say the origin" and to "present, preserve, and explain" (*Dialectic of Enlightenment*, p. 31). It is in this vein that Adorno and Horkheimer carry out their reading of the *Odyssey*. For them, Odysseus comes to stand as a symbol of the bourgeois individual, confronting and ultimately prevailing over natural forces. Adorno's ideas could be used to further explore the role of myth in creating contemporary society as well as examining the historically privileged position of literature as opposed to magic within the discipline of classics.

The concept of the "culture industry," which is also analyzed, refers not only to popular culture, but also to the entire sphere of popular media and culture that produces commodities for mass consumption. In late capitalism, the culture industry even renders art a mere commodity. For Adorno, a commodity is defined in Marxist terms: It is a mass-produced object whose exchange value is its only use value. In this system, the consumer is passive, politically apathetic, and objectified.

Adorno argues that the illusory pleasures offered by the "culture industry" only serve the ends of profit and the further exploitation as well as pacification of the masses. The "standardization" of culture is accomplished in the name of a unified economic and political power. Whether these issues have only become more pressing with the globalization of the attendant entertainment industry or less so with opportunity for individual expression via the Internet remains open to debate. And, this sort of "bread and circuses" approach in creating a consumer culture is not new, but was played out in ancient Rome as indicated by Juvenal's famous saying in *Satire X*. Yet, to counter this rather pessimistic diagnosis of the current state of affairs, Adorno posits "true art" as the diametric opposite of popular media and culture. This concept of the arts that Adorno forwards has been viewed as elitist and essentializing in its claims of universality, but it marks one of the most extended and complex meditations on the role of art in contemporary society.

Adorno's argument is grounded in a complex understanding of the **autonomy of art** that runs throughout his works. With the fusion of economic and political power in late capitalism, art is alienated; it is presented as a mere commodity. And here, however, Adorno differs from Marxist thinkers such as Bertolt Brecht, Jean-Paul Sartre, and the New Left, art maintains an autonomy that gives it a critical distance from which it can observe and critique the socioeconomic sphere. It is not a product of society in any direct manner. Contrary to Sartre's famous calls for a "committed" art, for instance, Adorno demurs: "This is not the time for political works of art" ("Commitment" in *Notes to Literature*, vol. 2, p. 93). There is no doubt that this conception of autonomy is one of Adorno's more contentious arguments, yet it is essential to his masterful rethinking of Kantian and Hegelian aesthetics as well as to his understanding of how the political intersects with the philosophic and the aesthetic. Furthermore, he asserts that the concept of autonomy (a concept perhaps better explained by Pierre **Bourdieu**'s notion of the "field of cultural production" which more easily accounts for art's autonomy and its extenuating circumstances) is critical to grasp the "truth content" available to us. It is this "truth content" of the work of art that Adorno posits as a proleptic necessity to any possible revolutionary transformation of society.

The attempt to synthesize these ideas on commodity fetishism, the culture industry, genre, and the autonomy of art into a general theory of aesthetics is to be found in Adorno's posthumously published *Aesthetic Theory* (1997). It is a wide-ranging and difficult text that references numerous works, in which Adorno attempts a radical examination of classical aesthetics (notions of beauty, nature) and modern aesthetics (he returns to Benjamin's concept of the aura and the notion of the "beautiful semblance"). Adorno's view of genre, which treats it as a retrospective imposition on a dynamic work, thus subordinating it to the intellectual regimes of mass culture, has important implications for how we translate ancient texts and works of art into the present. Only recently has the achievement this work represents begun to be fully appreciated. For many years it was overshadowed by Hans-Georg **Gadamer**'s thoughts on aesthetics in *Truth and Method* (1960), which evinces the centrality of Martin **Heidegger** to continental philosophy.

In what is not so much a continuation as a refinement of his earlier thinking, Adorno posits art as a site of struggle against conformity and passivity. He addresses what he terms the **"dialectics of appearance"** [*Dialektik des Scheins*]. For Adorno, the aesthetic is not a realm of mere appearance or illusion, rather it is the medium of truth. Aesthetic appearance is an index of "truth content." What he is arguing against is clearly stated in an excerpt from *Minima Moralia: Reflections from Damaged Life* (1951):

> Cultivated philistines are in the habit of requiring that a work of art "give" them something. They no longer take umbrage at works that are radical, but fall back on the shamelessly modest assertion that they do not understand. This eliminates even opposition, their last negative relationship to truth, and the offending object is smilingly catalogued among its kind, consumer commodities that can be chosen or refused without even having to take responsibility for doing so.
>
> ("Addressee Unknown")

It is against this neutralization of art that Adorno constructs the constellation of his argument. A primary claim of *Aesthetic Theory* is that the dialectical goal of the autonomy of art is to question appearance, to dissolve the closed, illusory realm of appearance into a "caesura" or "riddle." Thus, the autonomy of art enables it to resist its classification and domestication within the exchange economy. In doing so, however, it denies the existence of any stable, locatable truth as such. What Adorno presents here is an aesthetic theory in which art, literature, and music can index "truth content" through their "enigmatic character."

Although Adorno's privileges abstract art, he does this to avoid the traps of representational or mimetic art as well as to emphasize that art is not an imitation of reality, rather it is the radical other of reality. This idea of "otherness" is congruent with **Benjamin**'s concept of the aura. Adorno asserts that art as autonomous must resist the incursions of mass-produced culture (kitsch). Both of these ideas are relevant to ancient art as well. For example, Christopher Tilley (in "On Modernity and Archaeological Discourse") has urged archaeologists to emphasize the otherness of the past in order to open the field of meanings for art and material culture of the past. However, Adorno's concept of the autonomy of art—as a site of resistance that indexes "truth content" in aesthetic form—retains a more pointed ethical outrage and commitment to the memory of the past and the abuses of state and economic power: "Art, which even in its opposition to society remains a part of it, must close its eyes and ears to it: it cannot escape the shadow of irrationality. But when art itself appeals to this unreason, making it a *raison d'être*, it converts its own malediction into a theodicy .... The content of works of art is never the amount of intellect pumped into them: if anything it is the opposite" ("Commitment," p. 93; translation emended). Adorno's views of art as a commodity have implications for decontextualized study of classical sculpture, vases, monuments, and other items as well as for the ethical issues involved in collecting ancient art and the looting of archaeological sites.

In addition to being influential in the realms of art, music, political theory, and cultural criticism, Adorno's work has been influential in the analysis and study of literature. *The Authoritarian Personality* is another highly influential work overseen by Adorno in collaboration with other colleagues of the Frankfurt school. This work postulates that a particular personality type is receptive to authoritarian systems. Used predominantly in the social sciences, it has been employed by Bernd Seidensticker to analyze the character of Pentheus, in Euripides, *The Bacchae*. Although relying on statistics and empirical data to make its point, *The Authoritarian Personality* has criticized approaches claiming to be scientific and quantitative. Such criticisms serve as reminders that science and statistics are constructs, which require interpretation, while Adorno's engagement with mythology, literature, and art demonstrates the value of humanities in shaping political and social values.

Adorno's *Jargon of Authenticity* represents a critique of **Heidegger**'s existentialism, itself influenced by an early twentieth century German attempt to develop an autonomous intellect with authenticity as its primary value. For Adorno, authenticity implies additional meaning, which he associates with **Benjamin**'s notion of the aura, but as an aura of decay or jargon. Drawing her inspiration from Adorno's concepts of authority and authenticity, Joanne M. Stearns (in "Jargon, Authenticity, and the Nature of Cultural History-Writing: *Not Out of Africa* and the *Black Athena* Debate") examines and critiques the central and normative position of classics in Western civilization.

Further reading

By Adorno

With Else Frenkel-Brunswik, Daniel J. Levinson, and R. Nevitt Stanford. *The Authoritarian Personality*. New York: Harper, 1950.

With Max Horkheimer. *Dialectic of the Enlightenment*. New York: Continuum, 1972.

Negative Dialectics. Translated by E. B. Ashton. London and New York: Routledge, 1973.

The Jargon of Authenticity. Translated by Knut Tarnowski and Frederic Will. London and New York: Routledge, 1973.

The Philosophy of Modern Music. Translated by Anne G. Mitchell and Wesley V. Blomster. New York: Seabury Press, 1973.

Minima Moralia: Reflections from Damaged Life. Translated by E. F. N. Jephcott. London: Verso, 1974.

Prisms. Translated by Samuel and Shierry Weber. Cambridge, MA: MIT Press, 1981.

Kierkegaard: Construction of the Aesthetic. Translated by Robert Hullot-Kentor. Minneapolis: University of Minnesota Press, 1989.

Notes to Literature. 2 vols. Edited by Rolf Tiedemann, translated by Shierry Weber Nicholsen. New York: Columbia University Press, 1991–1992.

Aesthetic Theory. Translated by Robert Hullot-Kentor. Minneapolis: University of Minnesota Press, 1997.

Theodor W. Adorno and Walter Benjamin: The Complete Correspondence 1928–1940. Edited by Henri Lonitz, translated by Nicholas Walker. Cambridge, MA: Harvard University Press, 2001.

About Adorno

Benjamin, Andrew (ed.). *The Problems of Modernity: Adorno and Benjamin*. London and New York: Routledge, 1988.

Buck-Morss, Susan. *The Origin of Negative Dialectics: Theodor W. Adorno, Walter Benjamin, and the Frankfurt Institute*. New York: Free Press, 1977.

Gibson, Nigel, and Andrew Rubin. *Adorno: A Critical Reader*. Oxford: Blackwell, 2002.

Huhn, Tom, and Lambert Zuidervaart (eds). *The Semblance of Subjectivity: Essays in Adorno's Aesthetic Theory*. Cambridge, MA: MIT Press, 1997.

Jameson, Frederic. *Late Marxism: Adorno, or, the Persistence of the Dialectic*. London and New York: Routledge, 1990.

Jay, Martin. *Adorno*. Cambridge, MA: Harvard University Press, 1984.

Jay, Martin. *The Dialectical Imagination: A History of the Frankfurt School and the Institute of Social Research, 1923–1950*. Berkeley: University of California Press, 1996.

Seidensticker, Bernd. Über das Vergnügen an tragischen Gegenständen: Studien zum antiken Drama. Edited by J. Holzhausen. Munich and Leipzig: Saur, 2005.

Rose, Gillian. *The Melancholy Science: An Introduction to the Thought of Theodor W. Adorno*. New York: Columbia University Press, 1978.

Stearns, Joanne Monteagle. "Jargon, Authenticity, and the Nature of Cultural History-Writing: *Not Out of Africa* and the *Black Athena* Debate." In *Ancient Art and Its Historiography*, edited by Alice A. Donohue and Mark D. Fullerton. Cambridge: Cambridge University Press, 2003.

Tilley, Christopher. "On Modernity and Archaeological Discourse." In *Archaeology After Structuralism*, edited by Ian Bapty and Tim Yates. London: Routledge, 1990.

Wellmer, Albrecht. *The Persistence of Modernity: Essays on Aesthetics, Ethics, and Postmodernism*. Translated by David Midgley. Cambridge, MA: MIT Press, 1991.

Wiggerhaus, Rolf. *The Frankfurt School: Its History, Theories, and Political Significance*. Translated by Michael Robertson. Cambridge, MA: MIT Press, 1994.

Wolin, Richard. "Utopia, Mimesis, and Reconciliation: A Redemptive Critique of Adorno's Aesthetic Theory." *Representations* 32 (1990) 33-49.

Zuidervaart, Lambert. *Adorno's Aesthetic Theory: The Redemption of Illusion*. Cambridge, MA: MIT Press, 1991.

6 Louis Althusser

Louis Althusser (1918–90) was a French Marxist political philosopher. He was born in Algeria and educated in Algiers and France. He was admitted to the École normale supérieure in 1939, but World War II disrupted his studies when he was called to military duty. During the German occupation of France, Althusser was captured and placed in a German prison camp where he remained until the end of the war. Freed, he resumed his studies. In 1948 Althusser completed a master's thesis on the German philosopher Hegel and later passed the *agrégation* in philosophy and was given a teaching appointment.

Althusser was a practicing Catholic for the first 30 years of his life, and during that period displayed a strong interest in Catholic monastic life and traditions. In the late 1940s, he joined the Communist Party and remained a member for the remainder of his life. During the May 1968 Paris strikes, he was in a sanitarium recuperating from a bout of depression, an illness he struggled with throughout his life. Unlike some of his intellectual contemporaries, Althusser supported the Communist Party in denying the revolutionary nature of the student movement, though he later reversed this view.

Althusser murdered his wife in 1980. Declared incompetent to stand trial, he was institutionalized but released in 1983. He subsequently lived in near isolation in Paris and died in 1990 of a heart attack. During these last years of his life he wrote two different versions of his autobiography, both of which were published posthumously in 1992 (both are included in the 1995 edition of *The Future Lasts Forever*).

Althusser is especially important for the ways in which he reinterpreted Marx's ideas and made them resonate with the intellectual currents prevalent in Europe in the 1960s, especially structuralism. His work is sometimes referred to as "structuralist Marxism" or "postmodern Marxism." In addition to structuralism, Althusser's work is marked by a positive reconsideration of psychoanalysis, a body of thought simplistically rejected by the Communist Party. Thus Althusser's rereading of **Marx** is informed by the work of Jacques **Lacan**. In important ways, Althusser's "return to Marx" runs parallel to Lacan's famous "return to Freud" (see Jay, "Lacan, Althusser, and the Specular Subject of Ideology," note 147, p. 373). Althusser's return to the founding texts of Marxist discourse was aimed at liberating Marxist ideas from their Soviet interpretation, as well as from humanistic ones. This rereading was meant to revitalize Marxist ideas and to put them back to use for revolutionary purposes.

Of Althusser's many writings, three have been particularly influential: *For Marx* (1965), *Reading Capital* (1968), and the oft-cited long essay "Ideology and Ideological State Apparatuses" (1969; included in *Lenin and Philosophy and Other Essays*). Althusser's influence has been widespread, helping to shape such diverse fields as cultural studies, film studies, literary theory, history, art history, and classics.

Althusser's reassessment of Marxism includes his rejection of some key Marxist assumptions about society. For example, he argues against the deterministic aspects of the orthodox Marxist formation of **base** and **superstructure**. Base refers to the particular economic mode of production operating in a given society. Different societies are organized around different economic systems (modes of production)—for instance, agricultural or industrial. The concept of superstructure refers to political (i.e., socialist or capitalist), social, religious, and other non-economic aspects of a society. Superstructure, then, includes the political and cultural aspects of a society, such as civic, religious, and other institutional structures. The traditional Marxist view is that the base determines the superstructure. In other words, political, social, and religious spheres are not autonomous, but are determined by the economic mode or base. Althusser prefers to talk about the idea of social formations as decentered structures composed of three conflicting, indeterminate practices: the economic, the political, and the ideological. In Althusser's rethinking, the base and the superstructure are in a relationship that affords the superstructure considerable autonomy. Although in the end, he concedes that the economic is determinant even if it is not dominant in a particular historical moment.

The term **practices** has a specific meaning for Althusser, indicating processes of transformation: "By *practice* in general," he writes, "I shall mean any process of *transformation* of determinate given raw material into a determinate *product*, a transformation effected by a determinate human labour, using determinate means (of 'production')" (*For Marx*, p. 166). Economic practices use human labor and other modes of production in order to transform raw materials (nature) into finished (social) products. Political practices deal with the uses of revolution to transform social relations, and ideological practices concern the uses of ideology to transform lived social relations, that is, the ways a subject relates to the lived conditions of existence. Theory is often treated as the opposite of practice, but for Althusser theory is praxis. Thus, Marxism is a practice of class struggle. The separation between theory and practice is a key issue in archaeology, where theory is frequently seen as something distinct and apart from the materiality of the past. Those who realize that the past is textually mediated reject this simplistic binarism (see also **Lacan**).

The term **ideology** is central to Althusser's work. In "Ideology and Ideological State Apparatuses," Althusser melds ideas taken from both Marxist and psychoanalytic thought in order to develop his theory of ideology and its relation to subjectivity. His primary concern in this essay is with the question of how a capitalist society reproduces existing modes of production and their relationship to people: Why do people support this process when, according to Marxist thought, they are in effect acceding to their own domination by the ruling classes? Althusser formulates his answer through the concepts of ideology, ideological state apparatuses, and interpellation.

The creation and subsequent reproduction of capitalist society occurs at two levels, the repressive and the ideological. On the one hand, social control can be coerced by the exertion of repressive force through a variety of institutions including the police, military, judiciary, and prisons—what Althusser calls **Repressive State Apparatuses** (RSAs). These institutions suppress dissent and maintain the social order as envisioned by the ruling power. But application of repressive force is neither the only way nor even the most effective way to guarantee assent to capitalism. In addition to the RSAs, Althusser argues that ideology must also be employed to maintain the dominant social formation. He refers to these ideological modes of control as **Ideological State Apparatuses** (ISAs)—including education, family structure, religion, sports, the arts, and the mass media—which reproduce capitalist values, standards, and assumptions. Ideological discourse produced by ISAs acts on individual subjects in such a way that they see themselves and others as standing within and benefiting from the dominant ideology, subject to it, and willingly supportive—consciously or unconsciously—of the replication of this ruling power. In short, ideologies are presented to us, but at the same time we act, in effect, as willing agents of ideological agendas. In Althusser's thought, the ISAs represent the means by which capitalist ideology operates as a seductive system in which individuals are instantiated as subjects without being conscious of this subjugation as such. What Althusser adds to Marxist *doxa* is his knowledge of **Lacan**'s discussion of subject formation within language and the visual (imaginary) realm.

Departing from the earlier Marxist notion that ideology is false conscious-ness, Althusser understands ideology as an inevitable aspect of all societies —even socialist societies where capitalist exploitation has presumably been eradicated—that serves, in part, to provide human subjects with identities. For Althusser, ideology is a requisite, fundamental structure of subject formation. For this reason, he argues, that "ideology represents the imaginary relationship of individuals to their real conditions of existence" ("Ideology and Ideological State Apparatuses," p. 162). Distinguishing between the imaginary and the real (see **Lacan**'s theory of the mirror stage) allows Althusser to counter the traditional Marxist notion that ideologies are false because they mask an otherwise accessible and transparent world. In contrast to this notion of ideology as misrepresentation, Althusser views ideology as a narrative or story we tell ourselves—i.e. one that we author— in order to understand our relationship to the modes of production. A real, objective world is not accessible to us, only representations of it. A conse-quence of this line of thought is that our very sense of ourselves and our lived experience is a by product of ideology. There is no exit from ideology in Althusser's political philosophy.

Ideologies, then, are discourses that have marked effects on each individ-ual subject. Althusser understands this effect through the concept of **inter-pellation** (from the Latin *interpellare*, to hail or accost someone). This concept describes the way ideology hails and positions ("interpellates") individual subjects—or to state it another way, *subjects us*—within partic-ular discourses. As Althusser puts it, "ideology 'acts' or 'functions' in such a way that it ... 'transforms' the individuals into subjects" ("Ideology and Ideological State Apparatuses," p. 174). We assume our interpellated posi-tion, identify with received social meanings, locate ourselves within these meanings, and enact its goals under the guise of having freedom to make this choice in the first place. Althusser's structuralist notion of ideology is anti humanist because it questions the centrality of the autonomous, freely choosing individual in the process. On the contrary, individuals are subjected to ruling ideologies, misrecognizing ideological interpellation for the actions of a freely choosing individual.

Althusser provides an example of interpellation in action. Suppose, he says, an individual is hailed (interpellated) in the street by a policeman who says "Hey, you there!" This individual turns around to face the police-man. Althusser states; "By this mere one-hundred-and-eighty-degree physical conversion, he becomes a *subject*. Why? Because he has recognized that the hail was 'really' addressed to him, and that 'it was *really him* who was hailed' (and not someone else)" ("Ideology and Ideological State Apparatuses," p. 174). The hailing or interpellation of the individual creates a subject who is, without necessarily knowing it, acceding to the ideology of state authority, its laws, and the systems that support and generate it. Ideology transforms us into subjects that think and behave in socially proscribed ways.

Although ideology is understood to subject individuals to the needs and interest of the ruling classes, it is not, according to Althusser, fixed and unchangeable. Rather, ideologies always contain contradictions and logical inconsistencies, which are discoverable. This means that the interpellated subject has atleast some room to destabilize the ideological process. Change or revolution is possible. Althusser's work has implications for the study of ancient art, monuments, and texts as well as the contemporary discipline of classics, which can be analyzed for the role they play in reproducing, legitimizing, or opposing existing social structures in the past and in the present.

Works of art have a curious and often contradictory position in Althusser's thought because he attempts to construct a threshold between art and ideology—one that would enable what he designates as "real art" to distinguish itself from mere ideology. "The problem of the relations between art and ideology," he writes, "is a very complicated and difficult one. However, I can tell you in what directions our investigations tend. I do not rank real art (as opposed to ancient art, which frequently had an ideological meaning and function—also **Benjamin**) among the ideologies, although art does have a quite particular and specific relationship with ideology" ("A Letter on Art," p. 221).

Marx develops the concept of alienation in his work on commodity fetishism. For this reason, Althusser also argues that the aesthetics of consumption and the aesthetics of creation are identical. This is because they both "depend on ... the category of the *subject*, whether creator or consumer ('producer' of a 'work', producer of an aesthetic judgment), endowed with the attributes of subjectivity (freedom, projects act of creation and judgment; aesthetic need, etc.)" and secondly, "the category of the *object* (the 'objects' represented, depicted in the work, the work as a produced or consumed object)" (pp. 230–1). Although contemporary art can construct a critical distance, ancient art remains immanent to ideology and fetishization, requiring textual mediation to create a critical distance.

Althusser's work is also widely applicable to the study of classical texts. In particular, it draws our attention to the specific ways various types or genres of discourse (myth, ritual, theater, political treatises, historical accounts, art, and monuments) function to interpellate or "recruit" its subjects into a particular ideological framework. Other implications of Althusser's work include the way particular ancient texts, cultures, genders, or time periods are privileged today in order to give legitimacy to contemporary political interests (see also **Lyotard** on metanarratives). Even texts that might seem innocuous such as relations between parents and their children or more specifically, the role of men in Athenian democracy might be seen as naturalizing a patriarchal ideology. For example, Nancy Sorkin Rabinowitz (*Anxiety Veiled: Euripides and the Traffic in Women*) has interpreted women as fetishized commodities in the plays of Euripides, where they are constituted as wives, sacrifices, or destroyers. At the other end of the spectrum, Andrew Riggsby (in *Caesar in Gaul and Rome*) has used Althusser to explore the ideological aspects of Caesar's commentary on his campaigns in Gaul.

Further reading

By Althusser

For Marx. Translated by Ben Brewster. New York: Pantheon, 1969.

(With Étienne Balibar) *Reading "Capital"*. Translated by Ben Brewster. London: New Left Books, 1970.

"Ideology and Ideological State Apparatuses," and "A Letter on Art in Reply to André Daspre." In *Lenin and Philosophy and Other Essays*. Translated by Ben Brewster. New York: Monthly Review Press, 1971.

The Future Lasts Forever: A Memoir. Translated by Olivier Corpet, Yann Moulier Boutang, and Richard Veasey. New York: The New Press, 1995.

About Althusser

Elliott, Gregory. *Althusser: The Detour of Theory*. London and New York: Verso, 1987.

Elliott, Gregory (ed.). *Althusser: A Critical Reader*. Oxford: Blackwell, 1994.

Jay, Martin. "Lacan, Althusser, and the Specular Subject of Ideology." In *Downcast Eyes: The Denigration of Vision in Twentieth-Century French Thought*. Berkeley: University of California Press, 1993.

Kaplan, Ann, and Michael Sprinkler (eds). *The Althusserian Legacy*. London: Verso, 1993.

Miller, Daniel, and Tilley, Christopher. "Ideology, power, and prehistory: an introduction." In *Ideology, Power, and Prehistory*, edited by Daniel Miller and Christopher Tilley. Cambridge: Cambridge University Press, 1984.

Payne, Michael. *Reading Knowledge: An Introduction to Barthes, Foucault, and Althusser*. Oxford: Blackwell, 1997.

Riggsby, Andrew. *Caesar in Gaul and Rome: War in Words*. Austin: University of Texas Press, 2006.

Rose, Peter W. "Divorcing Ideology from Marxism and Marxism from Ideology: Some Problems." *Arethusa* 39.1 (2006) 101–36.

Smith, Steven B. *Reading Althusser: An Essay on Structural Marxism*. Ithaca: Cornell University Press, 1984.

Sorkin Rabinowitz, Nancy. *Anxiety Veiled: Euripides and the Traffic in Women*. Ithaca: Cornell University Press, 1993.

7 Mikhail Bakhtin

Key concepts:

- theoretism
- everyday life
- unfinalizability
- dialogism
- dialogical truth
- heteroglossia
- centrifugal vs. centripetal
- carnival
- carnival laughter
- grotesque realism
- chronotope

Mikhail Mikhailovich Bakhtin (1895–1975) was a radical theorist of literature and language. Influenced by the writings of Karl **Marx**, he was particularly interested in social transformation and revolution within dominant social and intellectual structures. Born in Orel, Russia, he was educated in philology and classics at the University of Petrograd (1914–18) during World War I and the Russian Revolution. He taught in Nevel and then Vitebsk, where he married Elena Aleksandrovna and became part of an intellectual circle that also included Valentin Voloshinov and Pavel Medvedev. He moved to Leningrad in 1924 and five years later he was arrested for alleged participation in the underground Russian Orthodox Church. On account of ill health caused by a bone disease, his initial sentence of ten years in a Siberian labor camp was reduced to six years of internal exile in Kazakhstan, where he worked as bookkeeper on a collective farm. After his exile, he had no long-term stable employment until 1945, when he began teaching Russian and world literature a Mordovia Pedagogical Institute in Saransk, where he remained until his retirement in 1961. Indeed, his academic life was so obscure that when scholars became interested in his work in the 1950s (based mainly on *Problems of Dostoevsky's Poetics*, originally published in Russian in 1929), many were surprised to find that he was still alive. In 1969 he moved to Moscow, where he remained until his death in 1975.

In western Europe, initial interest in Bakhtin's work is owed primarily to Julia **Kristeva**'s famous 1969 essay, "Word, Dialogue, and Novel," in which she engages his theory of dialogism (see below) in order to develop her theory of intertextuality. Kristeva also wrote the introduction to the French translation of *Problems of Dostoevsky's Poetics*, published in 1970.

Bakhtin worked on many topics over half a century of writing, from ethics to aesthetics. In all of his work, however, there is a general concern with the relationship between ethical responsibility and creativity. Put another way, he was interested in the relation between system and change, fixation and flux, law and revolution. How is change, as creative transformation of what is established and taken for granted, possible? What are the tensions within society and within the self, between the desire for normativity and stability on the one hand and innovation and openness on the other? What is one's ethical responsibility to maintain and support established social order on the one hand and to bring about social transformation on the other?

From his earliest writings, he attacked "**theoretism**," that is, the reduction of human creativity to a theoretical system. Theoretism impoverishes the truth of human life by subordinating all the complexity and messiness of human subjectivity and social relations to a static intellectual system.

Resisting theoretism, Bakhtin attended to the particularities of everyday life. Such attention to the minutiae of the everyday undermines the scholarly impulse toward universal theories. By the same token, he was drawn not to the grand or catastrophic events of human history—wars, disasters, revolutions, inaugurations—but **everyday life**, the "prosaic" details of the lives of ordinary people, details that are in many ways most revealing of human society and how social transformation takes place in history.

Throughout his work, Bakhtin emphasized "**unfinalizability**," that is, the impossibility of any final conclusion. Nothing in life has been finalized, and nothing in life can ever be finalized. The literary genre as an unfinalizable means of interpretation is regarded as Bakhtin's most significant contribution. As he writes in *Problems of Dostoevsky's Poetics*, "Nothing conclusive has yet taken place in the world, the ultimate word of the world and about the world has not yet been spoken, the world is open and free, everything is still in the future and will always be in the future" (p. 166). Life is riddled with surpluses, remainders, loopholes, and anomalies that keep things unfinalizable and therefore always hold open the possibility of surprise, change, and revolution. In this respect unfinalizability might be understood as that which undermines theoretism.

Related to unfinalizability is Bakhtin's theory of dialogism and dialogical truth, initially discussed in *Problems of Dostoevsky's Poetics* (see also his essay from the same period on "The Problem of Content," reprinted in his *Art and Answerability*). Whereas his earlier work focuses on the formation of the subject as an unfinalizable complex of identities, desires, and voices, his theory of dialogism focuses on discourse and language. **Dialogism** conceives of all discourse, in literature and in speech, as dialogical, that is, an intersection of multiple voices. When someone speaks and writes, his or her words are not simply streaming forth from within herself as sole author and source. Rather, her discourse, like her identity, is essentially a merger of the many voices and languages that constitute her as a subject. Every subject is made up of multiple voices, past and present, being a space of dialogue. It is this theory of dialogism that **Kristeva** used to develop her theory of intertextuality, which conceives of every text and every discourse as a dialogical space, an "intersection of textual surfaces" ("Word, Dialogue, and Novel," p. 65).

So too with regard to what Bakhtin describes as "**dialogical truth**." He identifies two kinds of discourses about truth: monological and dialogical. As the word implies, monological truth is presented as a single voice. It is one with itself and allows for no contradiction, no countervoice, like a declaration from the Pope or the President. It is presented as though it is the final word—impossible as that may be. Dialogical truth, on the other hand, is the "truth" that emerges in the midst of several unmerged voices. It is an undirected intersection of voices manifesting a "plurality of consciousness" that does not join together in one monologic voice. It is unsystematizable and unfinalizable. The "truth" of dialogical truth is not some particular statement about what is true and what is false, but rather the particularity and uniqueness of the event itself. It is not the unity of a system but the unity of a dynamic event, a dialogue that involves struggle and contradiction. In *The Dialogic Imagination*, Bakhtin also uses the term heteroglossia to refer to multiple types of discourses. **Heteroglossia** refers to the dialectical relationship between centripetal (official) and centrifugal (unofficial) discourses within the use or deployment of a single language. A **centripetal** discourse is associated with homogeneity, centrality, and the use of language to establish hierarchy. **Centrifugal** discourses exert a decentralizing influence, which tend to be associated with the use of language in popular or carnivalesque contexts and literary genres.

In *Problems of Dostoevsky's Poetics*, Bakhtin focuses on dialogism in literature. Most literary presentations of dialogue, Bakhtin readily concedes, are really presenting not dialogism but a series of monologic voices. Nonetheless he insists on the power of novelistic literature to be truly dialogical (as in Dostoevsky), drawing in multiple voices without subordinating them to any one voice, creating a space of interplay in which the reader becomes a participant who must negotiate among these voices.

Another Bakhtinian concept that has gained much attention from scholars in a wide range of disciplines is **carnival**, an idea discussed in *Rabelais* *and His World*. Carnivals are playful subversions of the established social and political order of things, which might otherwise appear fixed. Through common practices of masquerade, the burning of effigies, the desecration of sacred objects and spaces, and excessive indulgences of the body, carnivals loosen the hold of the dominant order, breaking free—though only for a time—from law, tradition, and all that enforces normative codes of social behavior. Another feature of the concept of carnival is **carnival laughter**, the festive, ambivalent and sometimes, dark laughter directed at everyone. In Bakhtin's thinking about carnival time—a time when the conventions of society are suspended or ignored—as throughout his work, we recognize his insistent attention to those aspects of life and language that underscore unfinalizability, keeping people and societies open to creative transformation. Unfinalizability is also evident in Bakhtin's concept of grotesque realism. **Grotesque realism** stands in opposition to the idealized and complete subject of both socialist realism and classical realism. Instead it refers to the cyclical, incomplete, and unfinished transformation of the human body as seen both in physical imperfection and in "its food, drink, defecation, and sexual life," in short, the materiality of human life.

The name that Bakhtin gives to the dialogical space is the **chronotope** (meaning time-space, which is inseparable), a term borrowed from Einstein's Theory of Relativity. For Bakhtin, the chronotope is a concept in *The Dialogic Imagination* (1981, pp. 84, 250) used to explore the relationship between time and space in artistic and literary texts. A key chronotope for Bakhtin is the "public square," which serves as the context of interaction for carnival and becomes a place where "high" and "low" elements in a text can symbolically interact.

Unlike a number of the thinkers surveyed in this book, there is no lack of sources on where Bakhtin's work fits in with classical scholarship and it is impossible to give a full treatment of these studies here. Bakhtin's theories of carnival and dialogism, in particular, have enjoyed considerable influence. Given Bakhtin's literary orientation, it is not surprising that he has been especially influential among scholars of ancient literature (from Homer to lyric poetry) and religion. While there is a truism that the classics are good to think with, R. Bracht Branham (in *The Bakhtin Circle*, p. xi) has suggested Bakhtin is good to "conjure with." Mystery religions, Dionysiac rituals, satire, comedy, the grotesque and scatalogical, the literary symbolism of food and drink, and Roman spectacle all have a place in Bakhtin's concept of carnival, though caution is urged lest these be trivialized. Carnival is an embodied experience where Susanna Morton Braund and Barbara Gold (in *Arethusa*, p. 248) observe that the description of bodily functions forms part of the language of satire. As an embodied experience, carnival might also be read from iconography, archaeological assemblages, and public gathering areas, further extending the unfinalizeability of the archaeological text as a literary genre.

In "The Bodily Grotesque in Roman Satire," Paul Allen Miller shows that even in the carnivalesque things are not always what they seem. Feasts can turn into grotesque exercises in excess rather than celebrations of conviviality. For example, the presentation of a pregnant lamprey at a feast, being served as if still alive, surrounded by swimming shrimp, is instead ended by the collapse of a dust-filled canopy in Horace's *Cena Nasidieni*. Miller compares the birth of Gargantua from a monstrous attack of diarrhea after a grotesque feast in *Rabelais* to a scene in Juvenal's *Satire 9*, where sex after a full meal is seen as more difficult than plowing a field. As Miller observes, "Bodies in question appear as open, leaking vessels; images of farming, food, or banqueting appear in close proximity; and sexuality is present" (p. 260).

In his Bakhtinian reading of Peter Rose's Marxist interpretation of Homer, John Peradotto (in "Bakhtin, Milman Parry and the Problem of Homeric Originality," p. 66) provides an example of how dialogism relates to classical studies. Peradotto observes that linking kingship to a divine genealogy in the *Iliad* not only serves as one of the ideologies that Peter Rose (in *Sons of the Gods, Children of the Earth*, see also chapter on **Marx**) identifies in the *Iliad*, it can also be viewed as an example of centripetal discourse (using language to establish hierarchy). In contrast, the claims to inherited leadership demonstrated through risk taking and success in battle as well as generosity to followers (see also, Rose in "Ideology in the Iliad," p. 192) represent the centrifugal discourses of decentralization within the *Iliad*. For Rose genealogy is as an emergent element in the *Iliad*, and along with "prowess on the field" and generosity, these elements represent competing discourses within the text (p. 186).

In "Petronius' Tale of the Widow of Ephesus," Daniel McGlathery explains how Petronius creates the ambience of the public square as a context for spectacle, from the widow's "ostentatious" display of her virtues as a faithful wife, to her exaggerated display of mourning upon the death of her husband, through to her later illicit affair with a soldier in the tomb of her dead husband. By placing events in the context of the tomb, McGlathery suggests that Petronius creates a Bakhtinian erasure of the normal boundaries structuring human existence. Elsewhere R. Bracht Branham (In "A Truer Story of the Novel") writes about Petronius' fascination with chronotopic motifs in *Cena Trimalchionis*, where numerous devices for measuring time such as calendars and sundials are gathered together at Trimalchio's excessive banquet.

With regard to the archaeology of the classical world, Bakhtin's work has important implications for the use of public space, interpretation of festivals and rituals, and interpretation of iconographic narratives. On a more contemporary scale, we might conceive of the discipline of classics, not monologically, in terms of pursuing a narrowly defined discourse, but dialogically, in terms of a dynamic and changing discipline including broad, interdisciplinary approaches to the study of the ancient Greek and Roman worlds.

Further reading

By Bakhtin

Art and Answerability: Early Philosophical Essays. Edited by Michael Holquist and Vadim Liapunov. Translated by Vadim Liapunov. Austin: University of Texas Press, 1986.
Speech Genres and Other Late Essays. Edited by Caryl Emerson and Michael Holquist. Translated by Vern W. McGee. Austin: University of Texas Press, 1986.
Problems of Dostoevsky's Poetics. Edited and translated by Caryl Emerson. Minneapolis: University of Minnesota Press, 1984.
* *The Dialogic Imagination: Four Essays.* Edited by Michael Holquist. Translated by Caryl Emerson and Michael Holquist. Austin: University of Texas Press, 1981.
* *Rabelais and His World.* Translated by Helene Iswolsky, Cambridge: MIT Press, 1968.

About Bakhtin

Branham, R. Bracht. "A Truer Story of the Novel." In *Bakhtin and the Classics*, edited by R. Bracht Branham. Evanston: Northwestern University Press, 2002.
* Branham, R. Bracht (ed.). *Bakhtin and the Classics.* Evanston: Northwestern University Press, 2002.
Branham, R. Bracht (ed.). *The Bakhtin Circle and Ancient Narrative.* Groningen: Barkhuis Publishing and Groningen University Library, 2005.
Braund, Susanna Morton, and Gold, Barbara K. "Introduction." In *Vile Bodies: Roman Satire and Corporeal Discourse. Arethusa.* 31.3 (1998) 247–56.
Kristeva, Julia. "Word, Dialogue, and Novel." Translated by Alice Jardine, Thomas Gora, and Leon Rudiez. In *The Kristeva Reader*, edited by Toril Moi. New York: Columbia University Press, 1986.
* McGlathery, Daniel. "Petronius' Tale of the Widow of Ephesus and Bakhtin's Material Bodily Lower Stratum." *Arethusa.* 31.3 (1998) 313–36.
Miller, Paul Allen (ed.). *Bakhtin and Ancient Studies: Dialogues and Dialogics. Arethusa.* 26.2 (1993).
Morris, Pam (ed.). *The Bakhtin Reader: Selected Writings of Bakhtin, Medvedev, and Voloshinov.* London and New York: E. Arnold, 1994.
Peradotto, John. *Man in the Middle Voice: Name and Narration in the Odyssey.* Princeton: Princeton University Press, 1990.
Peradotto, John. "Bakhtin, Milman Parry and the Problem of Homeric Originality." In *Bakhtin and the Classics*, edited by R. Bracht Branham. Evanston: Northwestern University Press, 2002.
Platter, Charles. *Aristophanes and the Carnival of Genres.* Baltimore: Johns Hopkins University Press, 2006.
Rose, Peter W. *Sons of the Gods, Children of the Earth: Ideology and Literary Form in Ancient Greece*, Ithaca, NY. Cornell University Press, 1992.
Rose, Peter W. "Ideology in the Iliad: Polis, *Basileus, Theoi.*" *Arethusa* 30.2 (1997) 151–99.
The Bakhtin Centre. http://www.shef.ac.uk/bakhtin/

8   Roland Barthes

> **Key concepts:**
>
> *   myths
> *   intertextuality
> *   the death of the author
> *   author-work vs. reader-text
> *   studium
> *   punctum

Roland Barthes (1915–80) was a French semiologist, literary critic, and cultural theorist. Born in 1915 in Cherbourg, France, he was raised in a bourgeois Protestant family. His early life is marked by long bouts with tuberculosis, which resulted in his being placed in a sanitarium for several months during his late adolescence. This experience of isolation turned Barthes inward and during the long hours spent alone he read a prodigious amount, including all of Michelet's volumes on French history. He went on to study French and Classics at the Sorbonne in Paris. There he was active in protests against fascism and wrote for leftist journals and magazines. During World War II he taught in Paris, having been exempted from military service because of his tuberculosis. After the war he taught in Romania, before continuing his studies at the University of Alexandria in Egypt, where he studied structural linguistics with A. J. Greimas in 1949–50. Barthes returned to Paris in the 1950s and worked at the Centre national de la recherche scientifique as a lexicographer and later as a sociologist. In addition to teaching at the École practique des hautes études from 1960 until his death, he was elected to a chair in literary semiology at the Collège de France in 1976. Along with several others, including Jacques **Derrida**, he was a member of the 1960s group organized around the literary journal *Tel Quel*. The traumatic death of his mother triggered the writing of one of Barthes' most famous texts, *Camera Lucida: Reflections on*

Photography (1980). This work was published shortly before Barthes' own death resulting from injuries suffered after being accidentally struck by a laundry truck as he was leaving the Collège de France in 1980.

From 1960 until his death, Barthes was arguably one of the most influential French intellectuals. His innovative, witty, and complex writings serve as a transition from structuralism to post-structuralism. Barthes' career can be divided into two main parts. The first consists of structuralist interpretations of literature and popular culture. This early work was informed by phenomenology and, particularly, the work of Ferdinand de **Saussure**. As a result of his studies with Greimas, Barthes based his work on the structuralist conception of the linguistic sign as an arbitrary signifier whose meaning is determined only within the differential structure of language (*langue*) as such. The apex of his structuralist research is undoubtedly his publication in 1957 of *Mythologies*, a semiotic study of the **myths** of popular culture and everyday life. Barthes submits wrestling, detergent advertisements, the iconography of the striptease, and even discussions about Einstein's brain to a structuralist analysis. He critiques the means by which ideology is naturalized in the twentieth century in mass cultural myths by analyzing the semiotics of mythic language (see also his *Elements of Semiology*, 1964).

The second part of Barthes' work begins in the late 1960s, when he turned away from structuralism with its scientistic conceits, embracing post-structuralism and deconstruction (see **Derrida**), and analyzing a discourse of desire. The focus here will be on Barthes' theoretical work during this second part of his career, with particular emphasis on two short, but important essays: "The Death of the Author" (1968) and "From Work to Text" (1971). This disruptive and anti-authoritarian position taken in these two inter-connected essays—along with post-structuralism itself—are themselves seen as products of the Parisian socio-political and cultural climate following the events of May 1968. These two texts present ideas that have thoroughly impacted the way we understand the nature of textuality and interpretation in general. Both are sustained critiques of the traditional role of the author and the conception of the work that undermine the Western cultural premise of an unbroken author–work corpus that grounds the meaning of any work in the notion of authorial intent. The significance of other key works: *S/Z* (1970), *Mythologies* (1957), and *Camera Lucida: Reflections on Photography* (1980), will also be touched upon.

"The Death of the Author" is Barthes' critique of traditional conceptions of the author, the literary work, and reading. It serves as a critique of the realist notion of representation, which views language as unproblematically providing an accurate depiction of reality. Barthes challenges the assumption that reality is more or less fixed, stable, and representable by language. In addition, he also challenges the privileged position of the author along with the notion of originary meaning.

Barthes questions the modernist strategy of looking at an author's life and body of work in order to discern the meaning of a particular text (visual or linguistic). In this, Barthes is also critiquing his own earlier work, as in *Mythologies*, which treated cultural forms primarily as distinct and isolated from the larger world. By opposing this tendency to locate the meaning of a text in the intentions of its author, Barthes argues that texts can only be understood in relation to other texts. This introduces the notion of **intertextuality**, a term originally coined by his student and colleague Julia **Kristeva** (see also **Bakhtin**'s concept of dialogism). For Barthes, as for Kristeva, every text is part of a larger field of texts that provides a broader referential context of meaning. Every text is in dialogue with other texts. The implication is that meaning is not derived solely from either authorial intention or authority, but from the network of relations between the reader, the text, and the larger conceptual networks suggested by that text. It is on this basis that he announces **the death of the author**, echoing Nietzsche's pronouncement of the death of God decades earlier: "The birth of the reader must be at the cost of the death of the Author" ("The Death of the Author," p. 148).

Barthes' declaration that the author is dead is not merely an obituary for the old way of understanding textual meaning. Rather it has important ramifications from where we understand meaning to reside. Remarking on the traditional understanding of the role of the author in transmitting textual meaning, Barthes observes: "The explanation of a work is always sought in the man or woman who produced it, as if it were always in the end, through the more or less transparent allegory of the fiction, the voice of a single person, the author 'confiding' in us" ("The Death of the Author," p. 143). With the death of the author a text becomes untethered from its author such that the author can no longer be considered the transcendent source of meaning of a text and the authority for how a text must be interpreted. Contrary to conventional views, texts do not transmit a singular, fixed meaning knowable by knowing the author's life history, cultural context, or intentions. Instead multiple, contextually determined meanings are produced in the reading of texts.

Referring to the author to obtain textual meaning serves to legitimate one's interpretation. As long as the authority of the author holds hegemonic sway, no other interpretation can be allowed or considered. But with the author symbolically dead, interpretation can move beyond the limitations of an author-centered way of reading. Barthes argues that "[o]nce the Author is removed, the claim to decipher a text becomes quite futile. To give a text an Author is to impose a limit on that text, to furnish it with a final signified, to close the writing" ("The Death of the Author," p. 147).

The death of the author means the intertextualizing of the text and the rise of the reader as the interpreter. The reader now has a more privileged role to play in generating textual meaning because the reader is now free to interpret a text regardless of authorial intention. We, as readers, have no access to what Barthes calls the "writer's interiority." In other words, we cannot know with any certitude an author's intentions in order to locate and fix a singular textual meaning, or in the case of material remains, a singular symbolic meaning. In addition, nothing says that these can be privileged as the "right" ones. The import of this is that it frees interpretation from the notion of a singular, authoritative meaning that has ideological and hegemonic implications. Textual interpretation shifts to the reader's interpretation of the meaning of the linguistic signs in the text.

Barthes argues that texts never convey a single meaning, but are subject to multiple meanings and interpretations. These different interpretations are not merely the result of different readers with different social and institutional perspectives, but rather are primarily the result of the unstable and shifting meanings of words and other categories of signifiers, as well as the presence of innumerable intertexts. Words are unstable because they are assigned their meaning only in relationship to other words and because the linguistic sign is arbitrary and differential or relational. It is this inherent instability of the sign that gives rise to multiple and competing interpretations of what text and material culture mean. This view of the sign is at once an assault on traditional views of representation because it repudiates the idea of a one-to-one relationship between word (signifier) and some external, fixed meaning in the world (signified). As interpretation shifts to the reader's interpretations of ancient linguistic signs and archaeological remains, some of which have been recirculated over lengthy periods of time and space, they accrue many layers of meanings in the past that continue to be added to as they are reinscribed into the present.

For Barthes, then, all texts are intertextual. That is, they are embedded in a larger system of interrelationships among multiple texts existing within a cultural context. All texts (including assemblages of material remains), then, whether fiction or nonfiction, scientific or religious, ancient or modern, whatever their textual genre, are part of every other text. And each text is "a multidimensional space in which a variety of writings, none of them original, blend and clash" ("The Death of the Author," p. 146). Further, the multiplicity of intertextuality is located in the reader:

> Thus is revealed the total existence of writing: a text is made of multiple writings, drawn from many cultures and entering into mutual relations of dialogue, parody, contestation, but there is one place where this multiplicity is focused and that place is the reader, not, as was hitherto said, the author. The reader is the space on which all the quotations that make up a writing are inscribed without any of them being lost; a text's unity lies not in its origin, but in its destination.
>
> ("The Death of the Author," p. 148)

In "From Work to Text," Barthes extends his post-structuralist, intertextual view of textuality by detailing the emergence of the contemporary "**text**" over and against the classical "**work**". He writes the term "text" with an uppercase "T"—Text—presumably to denote not a particular text, but the concept of "text" or "textuality" more generally. Although he does not put it this way, we might say that, for Barthes, the death of the author is also the death of the work. The birth of the reader as one who produces meaning in a text through his/her reading and interpretation as opposed to passively consuming the work of an author lies at the center of "From Work to Text." Barthes presents at least two important ideas here: his definition of a work as text and his suggestion that the reader's production of a text is an act of desire he terms "the pleasure of the text" (see also his *The Pleasure of the Text* (1976)).

The concept of the work can be understood as a counterpart of the living author. It reflects the traditional view of writing as the product of an individual who imbues the work with meaning. The work is a stable and contained entity that can be understood through knowledge of authorial intention and historical context. The work is also unproblematically representational. That is, its words point toward an external reality. It has a center that conveys a singular, stable truth; its meaning can be contained and controlled. The work is bounded—a thing that can be held in one's hands. Barthes defines an important distinction between the **author-work** and the **reader-text**. He contends that the text is a structure, but one that alludes to the structure of the Lacanian subject; it is both "decentered" and without "closure." Unlike what we find in the author–work model, where the author's life is the origin, a text is irreducible; it cannot be domesticated through the arbitrary application of any interpretive frame. Barthes writes:

> The Text is not a coexistence of meanings but a passage, a traversal; thus it answers not to an interpretation, even a liberal one, but to an explosion, a dissemination (...) since the text is that *social* space which leaves no language safe, outside, nor any subject of the enunciation in position as judge, master, analyst, confessor, decoder. The theory of the Text can coincide only with a practice of writing.
>
> ("From Work to Text," pp. 171, 174)

Unlike the work, the meaning of a text is unstable because it is subject to the play of meanings generated by the nature of language and intertextuality. The text is made up of what Barthes termed in "The Death of the Author," p. 146, "a tissue of quotations drawn from innumerable centres of culture." It is this understanding of a text that readers engage, in order to wrestle with its many possible interpretations. If the work is a tangible thing that can be placed on a shelf, the text is to be understood as something indeterminate, unfixable, and slippery; it is less a thing than a process of reading, experience, and interpretation, whereby the text simply explodes. A text is thus multivalent, contradictory, and ambiguous, and its meaning is uncontrollable. It has no center, just writing that generates more writing. It defers closure on a fixed truth or meaning (also **Derrida**). Post-structuralism denies the claim of a "one-to-one" relation between the signifier and the signified, privileging syntagmatic over paradigmatic readings (also **Saussure**). Moreover, a defining premise of post-structuralism is that a text always exceeds any interpretative frame; there is always something more that problematizes any structuralist claim to definitive meaning, i.e., any claim of being *dans le vrai*. Barthes' attention to this remainder is evident in his concept of the "pleasure of the text," which undermines the traditional notions of the author and the work. These factors have led some scholars to ponder the commodification of interpretation in post-structuralist critique.

An example of Barthes' style of post-structuralist reading appears in his book-length analysis of Honoré de Balzac's short story *Sarrasine*, in *S/Z* (1970). There, Barthes provides not only an enactment of his theoretical claims, but he presents some very clear statements on his notion of a productive reading of a text. He explains that "the writerly is our value" because "the goal of literary work (of literature as work) is to make the reader no longer a consumer, but a producer of the text" (p. 4). The act of reading, for Barthes, is "not a parasitical act," rather it "involves risks of objectivity or subjectivity" because "to read, in fact, is a labor of language" (*S/Z* pp. 10, 11). The labor of reading is to discern the construction of identities, social relations, and "reality" as such in and through language. Reading is not a passive act, but a performative and creative labor that "does not aim at establishing the truth of the text (its profound, strategic structure), but its plurality (however parsimonious)" (*S/Z*, p. 14).

Barthes is up front about the inexistence of the "writerly text" he theorizes, yet he suggests that certain works, usually canonical modernist ones like James Joyce's *Ulysses* (1922) but also some exceptional earlier texts like Sterne's *Tristram Shandy* (1759), signal the presence of the absent theoretical "writerly text" to come. These texts are "writerly" because they require a plural reading. "There cannot be," Barthes argues in relation to the "plural text," "a narrative structure, a grammar, a logic" (*S/Z*, p. 6). This absence of a predetermined reading and narrative logic is what allows for "the pleasure of the text." There are two French terms Barthes uses here: pleasure [*plaisir*], which signifies a reader being able to identify allusions in the text, etc., and the other is bliss or enjoyment [*jouissance*]. This kind of heightened pleasure [*jouissance*] has sexual connotations as well as a suggestion of the transformative power of "play" [*jou*] that Barthes desires. This "pleasure of the text" is an ecstatic [*ek-stasis*, breaking from the stasis, the status quo] one that unsettles a reader's historical, cultural, and psychological assumptions. In other words, the "pleasure of the text" undermines any claim to being given, to existing outside of the system of language. The productive reading of a text is "writerly" in that it substitutes any claim of authority, of grounding a text in something other than the instability of language, with plurality, contingency, and the potentiality to be rethought or "forgotten" as Barthes is fond of stating.

These concepts of pleasure, plurality, and desire imply a radical redefinition of the task of a classicist or archaeologist. This new task of interpretation is a "Nietzschean" one, implying an openness to the Dionysian characteristics of cultural production, which Barthes defines in the following: "To interpret a text is not to give it a (more or less justified, more or less free) meaning, but on the contrary to appreciate what *plural* constitutes it" (*S/Z*, p. 5).

Barthes was a prolific writer and another essay that has important implications for the study of the past is on the medium of photography. *Camera Lucida: Reflections on Photography* (1980) finds its justification in one of his earliest works. In *Mythologies*, Barthes explains how photography is perhaps the predominant text of mass culture. In *Camera Lucida*, he notes that the great portrait photographers are all "great mythologists" (p. 34).

The *studium* of a photograph is "the field of cultural interest" (p. 94). This includes its historicity (e.g. period clothes), representational strategy, its presentation of "reality," and so on. These are the elements that one can study and explicate; i.e., why one enjoys a certain photograph or how one can justify its historical importance. Barthes' text is weighted more toward the second and third concepts he develops.

The *punctum* is related to the "pleasure of the text"; it is the element of *jouissance* in the photograph. In *S/Z* Barthes describes a plural text as "the same and the new" (p. 16). This is precisely the language he uses to discuss the *punctum*: "It is what I add to the photograph and *what is nonetheless already there*" (p. 55). It is what wounds or cuts the viewer: an undialectical point that interrupts the passive reading of a photograph. Whether it is a boy's crooked teeth or a woman's pearl necklace, the *punctum* is a marginal element of a photograph that compels the viewer; it seizes the viewer in the act of reading as in "unexpected flash" that renders the viewer silent (p. 94). It is an ecstatic moment Barthes terms "the *kairos* of desire, which unravels any chronology" (p. 59). This leads to the indispensable aspect of time that marks the photograph for Barthes.

In looking for the distinct "photographic referent"—the essence or *noeme* of the photograph, what distinguishes it from other representational discourse—Barthes demands that it never forfeit its intimate relation to the past. It remains tethered to the "that-has-been" and renders it "a certificate of presence" in a form other than myth (p. 87). The founding order of photography is, therefore, not art nor communication, but *reference*, and this is the sense in which it is used in classical archaeology. The photograph is "an image without a code" because although "nothing can prevent the Photograph from being analogical, its *noeme* has nothing to do with analogy...The important thing is that the photograph possess an evidential force, and that its testimony bears not on the object but on time ... the power of authentication exceeds the power of representation" (pp. 88–9).

This relation defines what is unique to photography as opposed to cinema or painting. It simply states that the object in a photograph was there, before the camera, at one point in time. Barthes argues that "what I see is not a memory, an imagination, a reconstitution, a piece of Maya, such as art lavishes upon us, but reality in a past state: at once the past and real" (p. 82).

There are undoubtedly complications and paradoxes here, which have been and still need to be further addressed by classical archaeologists. It is the *studium* of a photograph that is privileged within classics, where it frequently serves as part of a particular rhetorical strategy whereby sites, objects, monuments, and hence the past are purported to "speak for themselves," yet this is a complete fiction perpetrated by particular scholar/authors, thus privileging a particular approach to the representation of the past.

The importance of Barthes' work is that he produces texts in which one can see him translating his theory into practice. His work, being thoroughly situated within the "linguistic turn," is insightful for the practice of classics because it demands that we ask questions about how we conceive and interpret authority, authorship, texts, art, objects, and monuments. Commenting on Barthes' work in relation to archaeology, Bjornar Olsen (In "Barthes: From Sign to Text") has observed, "archaeology exists only as text," in that the material and textual remains of the classical past are mediated through textual and visual representations, which become something both more and less than the original (see also **Benjamin**), and which are, themselves, open to interpretation. This self-reflexivity occurs not only because Barthes writes on these aspects of cultural production, but also because his conception of myth and his attention to representations of ideology refocuses our attention on the role of the past in contemporary Western culture. The major implication of Barthes' work for classics is that he decenters the privileged position of the original ancient authors and artists, as well as the idea that the excavator of a classical site has privileged insights into the character or significance of the remains. Writing the classics into the present has the potential to enliven the discipline through a greater engagement with contemporary culture.

Further reading

By Barthes

Elements of Semiology. Translated by Annette Lavers and Colin Smith. New York: Hill and Wang, 1968.
Mythologies. Translated by Annette Lavers. New York: Hill and Wang, 1973.
S/Z. Translated by Richard Miller. New York: Hill and Wang, 1974.
The Pleasure of the Text. Translated by Richard Miller. New York: Hill and Wang, 1976.
* "The Death of the Author" and "From Work to Text." In *Image-Music-Text*, translated by Stephen Heath. New York: Hill and Wang, 1977.

Camera Lucida: Reflections on Photography. Translated by Richard Howard. New York: Hill and Wang, 1981.

The Grain of the Voice: Interviews 1962–1980. Translated by Linda Coverdale. New York: Hill and Wang, 1985.

Empire of Signs. Translated by Richard Howard. New York: Hill and Wang, 1983.

About Barthes

Belsey, Catherine. *Critical Practice*. London and New York: Routledge, 1980.

* Culler, Jonathan. *Roland Barthes*. Oxford: Oxford University Press, 1983.

Knight, Diana (ed.). *Critical Essays on Roland Barthes*. New York: GK Hall, 2000.

Lavers, Annette. *Roland Barthes: Structuralism and After*. Cambridge, MA: Harvard University Press, 1982.

Moriarty, Michael. *Roland Barthes*. Cambridge: Polity Press, 1991.

* Olsen, Bjornar. "Barthes: From Sign to Text." In *Reading Material Culture*, edited by Christopher Tilley. Oxford: Basil Blackwell, 1990.

Shanks, Michael. "Archaeology and Photography." In *The Cultural Life of Images: Visual Representation in Archaeology*, edited by Bryan L. Molyneaux. London: Routledge, 1997.

Wiseman, Mary Bittner. *The Ecstasies of Roland Barthes*. London and New York: Routledge, 1989.

9   Georges Bataille

Key concepts:

- communication
- heterology
- accursed share
- order of intimacy vs. order of things
- the search for lost intimacy
- sacrifice
- base materialism
- *informe*

Georges Bataille (1897–1962) was born to a depressive, suicidal mother and a strict disciplinarian father in Puy-de-Dôme, France. At the outset of World War I, Bataille converted to Catholicism at the age of 17. The zeal with which he embraced his newfound faith is evident in his first published text, which laments the bombing of the Cathedral of Notre-Dame at Reims. Bataille joined a Benedictine seminary with the goal of becoming a priest, but was forced to serve in the French army from 1916 to 1917. His discharge from the army due to tuberculosis and his difficult personal life during this time caused him to abandon his faith. From 1918 to 1922 Bataille studied paleography and library science at the École des Chartes in Paris. The latter area of study led to his obtaining a position at the Bibliothèque Nationale. During the Nazi occupation of France, it was Bataille's position and his savvy that ensured the survival of Walter **Benjamin's** notes for his unfinished project on the Parisian arcades. When Benjamin decided to flee to Spain, he entrusted his working materials to Bataille, who hid them in the library. In a scholarly and artistic career spanning more than four decades, Bataille wrote on an impressive array of subjects, including autobiography, eroticism (he wrote erotic fiction as well as nonfiction on the subject of eroticism), literary criticism, numismatics, politics, philosophy, religion, sociology, and art. His thought is unclassifiable, a fact which led Roland **Barthes** to call Bataille a producer of "texts" rather than "works."

Bataille was involved in numerous and short-lived, radical antifascist groups throughout his life, including the Surrealist movement, which denounced him in the second Surrealist Manifesto in 1929. From 1931 to 1934 he was a member of the Democratic Communist Circle, which published the journal *La Critique Sociale*. Soon afterward he organized a group called Contre-Attaque (1935–6). Most important, perhaps, was his founding of a "secret society" that aimed to turn its back on politics and pursue goals that were solely religious—albeit "anti-Christian, essentially Nietzschean" ("Autobiographical Note," p. 115). The public face of this society was the now famous Collège de sociologie and its journal *Acéphale* ("headless"), which was published from 1936 to 1939.

In all of his work, Bataille acknowledges a debt to the work of Friedrich **Nietzsche**, especially in his discussion of the Dionysian aspects of artistic creation. In many ways, it is through Bataille that the key figures of post-structuralist thought in France—Jacques **Derrida**, Michel **Foucault**, and Jacques **Lacan**—were introduced to Nietzsche. Bataille's work evinces a long-standing interest in human experiences that reveal the limits of thought, experiences of a radical alterity beyond linguistic representation: the burst of laughter, erotic love, potlatch, sacrifice, mystical union. He sought to highlight those experiences that exceed independent self-existence, experiences of disorientation and unknowing that shatter the self. Bataille believed that such experiences make **communication** possible because they transcend the Cartesian self (thought of as a distinct body and mind), situating it in an inescapable relation with others. This disintegration of the self is a kind of self-transcendence that opens one up to the possibility of communion with others: It opens up the possibility of the "sacred." Bataille defines the sacred as that which originates and limits human behavior. Human experience, therefore, is conceived as an experience of limits (with death and its accompanying rituals and taboos being the absolute limit) and their transgression. For Bataille, transgression of the taboo or the forbidden both transcends and completes it. Transgression and taboo form the cultural order. In *On Nietzsche*, Bataille describes the Christian story of the crucifixion of Christ as a radical act of communication: a self-laceration of the divine that opens toward communion with all human beings.

In an early essay entitled "The Use-Value of D.A.F. de Sade (An Open Letter to my Current Comrades)," written in 1929-30, Bataille proposes a new academic program of study that focuses on this "other scene" of subversive excess, rupture, and self-transcendence. He calls this program **heterology**, defined as "the science of what is completely other" (*hetero* = "other") ("Use-Value," note 2). Indeed, heterology is an apt description of Bataille's entire body of work. Heterology attends to that which is irredeemably other—the "**accursed share**" within the dominant social order that cannot be assimilated into it. It deals with what is deemed useless in a world driven by use-value and that which is wasteful in a world driven by production; the "accursed share" names what is determined evil in a world that reduces the sacred to moral goodness.

What Bataille takes from Sade is the notion that sadistic eroticism lessens the anxiety caused by the constitutive human experience of limits. Through sexual degradation and humiliation, one can tap into an experience of the sacred and can regain an intimacy that has been lost through modernization. These types of sexual experiences are described in Bataille's early auto-biographical-fictional text *Story of the Eye* [*Historie de l'Oeil*] (1928). Bataille's argument that prohibition, taboo, revulsion, disgust, and the aura of death heighten desire and erotic pleasure has recently been used by Neal Walls (In *Desire, Discord and Death*) to underscore the eroticism in the Near Eastern myth of Nergal's coupling with Ereshkigal, the mistress of the underworld. Bataille's interest in sexual enjoyment [*jouissance*] is taken up in the work of Lacan.

Bataille's heterology has a strong orientation toward the religious. The "completely other" that is the focus of heterology is, for Bataille, closely related to notions of the "sacred"—but not as it is commonly associated in contemporary Western religious discourse with goodness (versus evil) and reverence. Rather, he understands the sacred as fundamentally ambivalent: on the one hand, set apart as holy and revered; on the other hand, set apart as accursed and dirty. In a footnote, he writes that *agiology*—from the Greek *agio*, "holy" or "sacred"—might be a more appropriate term than heterology, "but one would have to catch the double meaning of *agio* (analogous to the double meaning of *sacer* [sacred]), *soiled* as well as *holy*" ("Use-Value," note 2). Elsewhere in the essay he equates the "completely other" of heterology with the numinous, the wholly other, the unknowable, the sacramental, and the religious. He even considers whether his program should be called "religion" rather than "heterology," but is concerned that "religion" in modern Western society is too closely associated with institutions that regulate and prohibit access to the sacred.

In his work, Bataille formulated a fully developed theory of religion in *Theory of Religion* (first published in French in 1973, though written years earlier), which is closely related to his better known, three-volume *The Accursed Share*. In *Theory of Religion*, Bataille conceives of two radically opposed regions or "worlds": the order of intimacy and the order of things.

The **order of intimacy**—also described by Bataille as the sacred world—is the realm of undivided continuity and flow in which there are no distinct objects or individual selves, an "opaque aggregate" (p. 36) reminiscent of the primordial chaos described in many creation mythologies. (This is also reminiscent of **Lacan**'s prelinguistic stage before individuation and subject formation, the Imaginary.) In intimacy, there is no self-consciousness of oneself as an individual in relation to other individuals and objects.

Bataille associates this realm with animality, for animals are *"in the world like water in water* ... the animal, like the plant, has no autonomy in relation to the rest of the world" (p. 19).

The **order of things**, which he also calls the profane or ordinary world, is the order of discontinuity, individuation, division, and subdivision into subjects and objects. Whereas the order of intimacy is a realm of animality, the order of things is a realm of humanity. An early step out of the animal order of intimacy and into the human order of things was made when we began to use tools. A tool (i.e. a rock for hammering, a sharp stick for hunting) is something that we set apart and treat as an object, thereby positing ourselves as a subject. Thus the tool object and the tool-using subject are separated out of the undifferentiated continuity of intimacy and transformed into "things." We use the tool, moreover, to make and manipulate still other objects. In the process, we are self-objectifying, positing ourselves as an object in a world of other objects. The creation of art is also a product of the difference between the realm of humans and animals.

We experience this order of things, the "world of things and bodies," as the profane or ordinary world—"this world"—set over against a "holy and mythical world" of intimacy. The two worlds are incommensurable. "Nothing, as a matter of fact, is more closed to us than this animal life from which we are descended" (p. 20). So the order of intimacy, which is lost to us, is this world's wholly other, which is "vertiginously dangerous for that clear and profane world where mankind situates its privileged domain" (p. 36).

The privileged human domain of the order of things separates us from the order of intimacy and keeps it at bay—keeps it from breaking in and returning the order of things to primordial undifferentiated chaos.

> [Humankind] is afraid of the intimate order that is not reconcilable with the order of things .... [I]ntimacy, in the trembling of the individual, is holy, sacred, and suffused with anguish .... The sacred is that prodigious effervescence of life that, for the sake of duration, the order of things holds in check and that this holding changes into a breaking loose, that is, into violence. It constantly threatens to break the dikes, to confront productive activity with the precipitate and contagious movement of purely glorious consumption.
>
> (pp. 52–53)

What is religion in these two worlds? According to Bataille, religion is **"the search for lost intimacy"** (p. 57). While occupying the order of things, it reaches for contact with the order of intimacy. It operates according to the desire to commune with the wholly other sacred world of intimacy while remaining part of the order of things. It is in this world but not of it. In his characteristic heterodox way, Bataille also associates erotic desire with religious desire in many of his writings, especially *Eroticism* (first published in French in 1957). The lover's desire for intimate communion with another is, for Bataille, the desire to lose one's individual selfhood, to dissolve in intimacy.

With religion, Bataille presents **sacrifice** as an exemplary expression of this desire for lost intimacy. For Bataille, sacrifice is a failed effort at crossing over from the order of things to the intimate order. Rituals of sacrifice (*sacri-facere*, "to make sacred") take something with use-value within the order of things (a domestic animal, a person, a bushel of grain), removes it from that order, and passes it over to the order of intimacy, that is, to the realm of the sacred, through an act of wasteful consumption (burning, orgiastic feasting, destruction, deposition, etc.). Sacrifice is about wasting something that has use-value within the order of things, thereby sending it over to the other side, to the sacred realm of intimacy. That is why sacrificial animals are domestic rather than wild: A wild animal is already in the order of intimacy. There is identification on the part of the sacrificer with the object of sacrifice. Use-value has been used to explain why Prometheus' gift to the gods angers Zeus, has less value as a sacrifice than what is retained for mankind, and results in a continued reminder to humans of their mortality by requiring them to eat.

According to this idea of sacrifice, festival, carnival, and potlatch are also sacrificial practices. They are acts of sacred waste, removing valuables from the order of things by excessive (and therefore wasteful) consumption, and also, in the case of carnival, ruining social capital by mocking or otherwise subverting figures of public authority and law. Bataille's ideas about sacrifice have implications for understanding the deposition and/or breakage of prestige goods in Minoan culture such as bronze figurines and stone rhyta.

For Bataille, then, the religious violence of sacrifice must be distinguished from other kinds of violence, such as war. Contrary to patriotic proclamations that a soldier's death in battle is a sacrifice for a sacred cause (God, nation, capitalism), casualties of war are not sacrificial because they serve some cause deemed socially valuable. In war, the things and bodies that a people or nation expend are the price paid for advancing or maintaining some value within the order of things.

As in his earlier work on heterology, Bataille's description of the sacred world of intimacy as "vertiginously dangerous" leads to an understanding of religious experience—that is, experience of the sacred—as an irreducible combination of fascination and repulsion, fear and desire (vertigo: the experience of feeling simultaneously pulled over the edge and pulled back from it). As he writes in the second volume of *The Accursed Share*, "It is obviously the combination of abhorrence and desire that gives the sacred world a paradoxical character, holding one who considers it without cheating in a state of anxious fascination" (p. 95). Here we are reminded of Rudolph Otto's well-known characterization of religious experience as an encounter with the *Mysterium tremendum et fascinans*, a wholly other that is both terrifying and fascinating.

Despite the fact that Bataille rightly passes as a theorist of religion, his work has had relatively little influence on the study of ancient religion, especially among those working in English. This lack of influence is partly due to his unorthodox writing style, which often mixes traditional forms of academic argument with aphorism and autobiography, the scatological nature of some of his works, and partly due to the fact that many of his works on religion were not translated into English until the late 1980s.

Bataille's heterology was also the source of his rift with André Breton, leader of the Surrealist movement. Surrealism, as championed by Breton, aimed for a Hegelian sublation of the mundane and the fantastic, the conscious and the unconscious, dream and waking. Arrived at through Breton's quirky readings of **Freud** and his desire to unite **Marx**'s credo "To change the world" with the nineteenth–century French poet Arthur Rimbaud's intent "To change life," this sublation was supposed to unveil *surreality*. Bataille and others associated with Surrealism in its initial manifestation did not contest Breton's reliance on psychoanalysis, but rather his insistence that Surrealism be explicitly tied to the Communist Party. In contrast to Breton's historical materialism, Bataille posits a "base materialism." **Base materialism** is Bataille's attempt to undermine Breton's contention that Surrealism is a sublation of materiality into thought. In short, base materialism critiques the underlying Hegelian premise of Breton's notion of Surrealism. For Hegel, thought is materiality, but for Bataille, there is a base materialism—matter, mere things, filth, scatological elements—that exceeds thought. Its association with the surreal aspects of quotidian life exhibits a connection to the exotic aspects of ethnography, which has implications for the way we view the quotidian aspects of archaeological remains of the classical world. (Bataille's position is undeniably colored by the famous series of lectures Alexandre Kojève gave on Hegel from 1933 to 1939 in Paris.) Bataille's position is that base materialism, of which the *informe* (formless) is a primary element, indicates the possibility of transgression, the continued presence of an "accursed share" that one cannot frame or sublate into something socially acceptable. Base materialism is closely associated with Freudian desublimation. It signals a transgression of moral and political norms, a transgression of the boundaries of human values and their institutions.

In his "Critical Dictionary," published in the dissident Surrealist journal *Documents* in 1929–30, Bataille includes an entry on *L'informe*. In discussing this term, he writes:

> Thus *formless* is not only an adjective with a certain meaning, but a term serving to deprecate, implying the general demand that everything should have a form. That which it designates has no rights to any sense, and is everywhere crushed underfoot like a spider or a worm. For the satisfaction of academics, the universe must take shape ... To affirm on

the other hand that the universe does not resemble anything and is nothing but *formless* amounts to the claim that the universe is something like a spider or a gob of spittle.

(Bataille, "Critical Dictionary," p. 475)

The exclusion not only of idealism, but also of any claim to form or structure in the universe defines base materialism. Bataille's position breaks one of the fundamental premises of classical aesthetic thought. Namely, the contract, initially forwarded by Plato, that exists between artists and society: that art imitates life and vice versa. In the context of Plato's *Republic* breaking this contract results in expulsion from the ideal state. Thus, against Breton's teleological claim that Surrealism is the face of modernity as such—an authentic art for an existence radically redefined by Freud and Marx—Bataille counters with the *informe*, a transgression of the basic role of art in Western aesthetic thought. (**Kristeva** relied upon the *informe* in theorizing abjection.) The feral and scatological nature of the *informe*, which exceeds limits as well as any attempt to conceptualize and capture it as a style or as a paradigm of artistic practice, remains a concept in and through which artistic production and reception can be continually rethought.

In contrast, architecture, for Bataille, symbolizes order and authority, the violent imposition of social order upon disorder. As metaphor, architecture gives structure and order to language, where it "dominates and totalizes signifying productions" (Denis Hollier in *Against Architecture* (1989), p. 33). Purposeful formlessness for Bataille, represents the anti-architecture. The metaphor of the labyrinth, for Bataille, though architectural, represents a place where "oppositions disintegrate" by becoming complex.

Although not used widely in the study of the ancient world, Bataille's work has many potentially interesting implications for the study of it, particularly with regard to the study of religion, sacrifice, pollution and purity, conceptions of dirt and waste, other ancient conceptions of order, and the history of reception. In *Myth and Metamorphosis*, Lisa Florman analyzes Picasso's use of the *minotaur* in his various works, including the *Minotauromachy*, from the standpoint of Bataille's concept of sacrifice and its relationship to death and violence. Bataille's work has also informed Michael Shanks' study of Korinthian *aryballoi* in *Art and the Early Greek State*, in which he draws links between perfume, sacrifice, death, and eroticism. The value of the *aryballoi* deposited as gifts in graves is also invoked, while sometimes more valuable and exotic gifts such as bronze cauldrons are also deposited. The act of deposition forms a link between the living and the dead (p. 189). Perfume was associated with religion, sacrifice, *eros* (through anointment of the living body), stored clothes, *symposia* (drinking parties), was food based, and also used to anoint corpses (p. 174), while the use of perfume in religious rites may be seen as predicated on violence. If we take into account the embodied experience of sacrifice, we can consider the aromatic herbs and wood shavings, which were incorporated in animal sacrifice in ancient Greece and biblical Israel, while incense alone sometimes formed the sacrificial offering (as in the cult of Aphrodite on Cyprus). In my own experience of attending the Samaritan sacrifice of sheep for Passover on Mt. Gerizim, it became clear that the strong aromas of sacrificial activity permeates everything, mingling with the shedding of blood and cooking of the sacrificial offerings. The notions of danger and the formless in Bataille's writings have implications for the analysis of ecstatic and other altered states of consciousness as well as other performative (the raw, chthonic, and Dionysiac) aspects of religion in the ancient world, which help us to resist the "domestication" of the past through romanticized and idealist readings of texts and objects.

Further reading

By Bataille

Story of the Eye. Translated by Joachim Neugroschel. New York: Urizen Books, 1977.

Eroticism: Death and Sensuality. Translated by Mary Dalwood. San Francisco: City Lights, 1986.

Inner Experience. Translated by Leslie Anne Boldt. Albany: State University of New York Press, 1988.

The Accursed Share. Vol. 1, *Consumption*. Translated by Robert Hurley. New York, Zone Books, 1988.

The Accursed Share. Vol. 2, *The History of Eroticism*; Vol. 3, *Sovereignty*. Translated by Robert Hurley. New York, Zone Books, 1991.

"Critical Dictionary." In *Art in Theory, 1900–1990*, edited by Charles Harrison and Paul Wood. London, Blackwell, 1992.

On Nietzsche. Translated by Bruce Boone. New York: Paragon, 1992.

The Absence of Myth: Writings on Surrealism. Translated by Michael Richardson. London: Verso, 1994.

"Autobiographical Note" and "The Use-Value of D.A.F. Sade (An Open Letter to My Current Comrades)." In *The Bataille Reader*, edited by Fred Botting and Scott Wilson. Oxford: Blackwell, 1997.

* *The Bataille Reader*, edited by Fred Botting and Scott Wilson. Oxford: Blackwell, 1997.

About Bataille

Botting, Fred, and Scott Wilson (eds). *Bataille: A Critical Reader*. Oxford: Blackwell, 1998.

* Brown, Norman O. "Dionysus in 1990." In *Apocalypse and/or Metamorphosis*. Berkeley: University of California Press, 1991.

Campbell, Robert A. "Georges Bataille's Surrealistic Theory of Religion." *Method & Theory in the Study of Religion* 11 (1999) 127–42.

Clifford, James. "On Ethnographic Surrealism." *Comparative Studies in Society and History*. 23.4 (1981) 539–64.

Dean, Carolyn. *The Self and Its Pleasures: Bataille, Lacan, and the History of the Decentered Subject.* Ithaca: Cornell University Press, 1992.

Florman, Lisa. *Myth and Metamorphosis: Picasso's Classical Prints of the 1930s.* Cambridge, MA: MIT Press, 2001.

Gemerchak, Christopher. *The Sunday of the Negative: Reading Bataille, Reading Hegel.* Albany: State University of New York Press, 2003.

Hollier, Dennis. *Against Architecture: The Writings of Georges Bataille.* Cambridge, MA: MIT Press, 1989.

Jay, Martin. "The Disenchantment of the Eye: Bataille and the Surrealists." In *Downcast Eyes: The Denigration of Vision in Twentieth-Century French Thought.* Berkeley: University of California Press, 1993.

Richardson, Michael. *Georges Bataille.* London and New York: Routledge, 1994.

*Shanks, Michael. *Art and the Early Greek State: An Interpretive Archaeology.* Cambridge: Cambridge University Press, 1999.

Surya, Michael. *Georges Bataille: An Intellectual Biography.* Translated by Krzysztof Fijalkowski and Michael Richardson. London: Verso, 2002.

*Walls, Neal. *Desire, Discord and Death: Approaches to Ancient Near Eastern Myth.* Boston: ASOR Books Volume 8, 2001.

Yale French Studies 78 (1990): *On Bataille.*

10 Jean Baudrillard

Key concepts:

- simulation
- simulacrum
- postmodernity
- hyperreality

Jean Baudrillard (b. 1929) was born in Reims in northeastern France. His grandparents were peasant farmers and his parents worked in civil service jobs. At the University of Nanterre, Baudrillard studied sociology under the Marxist Henri Lefebvre. From 1966 until his retirement in 1987, Baudrillard taught sociology at Nanterre. His earliest work was written from the Marxist perspective, but in subsequent texts his intellectual mentors often became the objects of his critiques, including figures such as **Marx**, Lefebvre, and Jean-Paul Sartre. Baudrillard's early engagement with Marxist theory was later eclipsed by post-structuralist ideas in the 1970s. His work bears the traces of the theories and influence of both Roland **Barthes**, especially his work on modern mythologies, and of Marshall McLuhan's claim that the medium is more important than the message.

Baudrillard's first book, *The System of Objects* (1968) is a semiotic analysis of culture influenced by the post-structuralist concept of the indeterminate play of language, **Freud**'s notion of drive and desire, Marx's theory of commodity fetishism, and the French sociologist Marcel Mauss' work on symbolic exchange economies. Baudrillard is a controversial cultural theorist, particularly noted for his critiques of contemporary consumer society. He is one of the key theorists of postmodernity.

Baudrillard's work on postmodern culture—often simultaneously radical and hyperbolic in its claims—utilizes ideas drawn from various disciplines including linguistics, philosophy, communications, cultural studies, sociology, and political science. He addresses a wide range of issues, including mass media, mass consumption, travel, war, and terrorism. The best known of Baudrillard's reappraisals of modernity is *Simulacra and Simulation* (1981), in which he analyzes the constructed and fabricated nature of postmodern culture, asserting that contemporary culture can no longer distinguish image from reality. Baudrillard's basic contention is that the "conventional universe of subject and object, of ends and means, of good and bad, does not correspond any more to that state of our world" (*Impossible Exchange*, p. 28). There is a shift in Baudrillard's work from Marx to McLuhan, industrial production to consumption, wherein consumerism is the common denominator of contemporary Western society. What defines our society is the endless exchange and consumption of object-signs.

Within the context of his explorations of postmodern Western culture, Baudrillard is especially interested in representation. Drawing on the work of the French Situationist thinker Guy Debord's *The Society of Spectacle* (1967), Baudrillard examines the ways in which technology and media impact how we represent our experiences and what we can know about the world. He argues that contemporary culture is so saturated with images from television, film, advertising, and other forms of mass media that the differences between the real and the imagined, or truth and falsity, have become indistinguishable. Images no longer represent reality; instead, they have become the reality. Our lives are thus simulations of reality in the sense that **simulation** has no intrinsic or causal connection to what was previously considered reality. Images produced by mass media neither refer to reality nor harbor any independent meaning.

One of the central questions of Baurdillard's work is, what are the implications of living in an image-saturated, postmodern society? In effect, our experiences of the world are mediated through the many images that confront us everyday. These images frame how and what we see of the world. Notions of the perfect body, for instance, come about not because of some unmediated experience we have in the world, but largely through all the body images projected by consumer society and advertising technologies. Correspondingly, the past is also mediated through images, representations, and other forms of mediation.

Central to Baudrillard's understanding of the relationship between reality and representations of it are the concepts of "simulacrum" and "hyperreality." A **simulacrum** is an image or representation of something. Baudrillard uses this term to refer to an image that has *replaced* the thing it supposedly represents. In *Simulacra and Simulation*, and also in *Simulations*, he distinguishes three phases or "orders" of the simulacrum in the history of the sign. With each order, the simulacrum is increasingly alienated from that which it purports to represent. First order simulacra, or the counterfeit, which alter or mask reality and involve deconstructing the real into details, emerge prominently in the baroque period, with its privileging of artifice over realism. The second-order simulacra emerge with the modern age of mass production, where endlessly manufactured images diminish concern for uniqueness and origin. Here the importance of Walter **Benjamin**'s essay "The Work of Art in the Age of Its Technological Reproducibility" (1935–6) is especially felt: the idea that the "aura" of the original, the referent of the reproduction, withers. Third-order simulacra are the simulacra of the current postmodern age. In **postmodernity**, the simulacrum is severed from any relation to reality; it is a production of reality as such, not its imitation or representation hence, the counterfeit becomes confused with the original in the same "operational totality." With postmodernity, the simulacrum supersedes the real so that we live in a world of simulacra, representations of representations. Whether the object of study for the classicist is a text, an inscription, a building, or a pot, we are often left with a fetishized past that inhabits at least one and sometimes as many as all three of these orders. This especially becomes the case in the increasingly particularistic parsing of our objects of study into the minutiae of specialist reports.

Although images may appear to refer to or represent real objects in the so-called real world, "reflecting a preexisting reality," Baudrillard argues that in postmodernity images are the real. Thus, the simulated *is* the real. One characteristic of such a postmodern world is the proliferation of media for producing images that simulate reality, including film, television, the World Wide Web, and various forms of digital media, which are themselves becoming merged into one operational totality. Baudrillard claims that "[t]o simulate is to feign what one doesn't have" (*Simulacra and Simulation*, p. 3). In short, simulation no longer resembles or refers to reality, it constructs it.

In *Simulacra and Simulation*, Baudrillard provides us with an example of how an image becomes reality itself. He cites a story by Jorge Luis Borges (a writer whose work also plays a key role in Michel **Foucault**'s *The Order of Things*) in which "the cartographers of the Empire draw up a map so detailed that it ends up covering the territory exactly" (p. 1). The map, which is a representation of real space, becomes the reality, or to use Baudrillard's term, a **hyperreality**: "Simulation is no longer that of a territory, a referential being, or a substance. It is the generation by models of a real without origin or reality: a hyperreal" (p. 1). From this perspective, "[t]he territory no longer precedes the map, nor does it survive it. It is nevertheless the map that precedes the territory—*procession of simulacra*—that engenders the territory, and if one must return to the fable, today it is the territory whose shreds slowly rot across the extent of the map" (p. 1). A representation of an authentic past is what many academics strive for in classics and classical archaeology, yet the paradox remains that a 1:1 recreation like Borges' map remains a longed for, but impractical object of desire, while for Baudrillard, the map has become reality, not a representation of it.

A hyperreal world, then, is one in which the real and the imaginary have imploded and the boundaries separating them no longer stand, nor do boundaries separating previously autonomous spheres. For instance, 24 cable news networks blur distinctions between fact, opinion, sports, politics, and entertainment. The news does not describe or represent reality; *it is and it constructs reality.* Baudrillard goes so far as to argue that media and other imaginary constructs like Disneyland or the Getty Museum function to create America itself as nothing more than a hyperreal simulation of the real.

Simulation commonly refers to something fake or counterfeit, unreal, or in-authentic. But Baudrillard does not simply contrast simulation with the real; rather he sees these as having suffered a radical disconnection: "illusion is no longer possible, because the real is no longer possible" (*Simulations*, p. 38). Thus, we can no longer meaningfully inquire about the relative truth or falsity of images and representations. At the conclusion of *The Ecstasy of Communication* (1988), Baudrillard writes:

> And what if reality dissolved before our very eyes? Not into nothing-ness, but into the more real than real (the triumph of simulacra)? What if the modern universe of communication, of hyper-communication, had plunged us, not into the senseless, but into a tremendous saturation of meaning entirely consumed by its success—without the game, the secret, or distance?... If it were no longer a question of setting truth against illusion, but of perceiving the prevalent illusion as truer than truth.
>
> (pp. 103–4)

Reconstructed and ruined landscapes project a similar hyperreality whereby entire countries with rich archaeological heritages such as Greece and Israel become Disneyfied right down to the kitsch narratives, tchotchke stands, models, reconstructions, and sometimes even accompanying sound-tracks! The heavy reliance upon representations—in the form of images, artistic reproductions, casts, tourist paraphernalia, reconstructions, ruined landscapes, multimedia presentations, virtual worlds that blur the bound-aries between games and scholarship, graphic novels, weblogs (blogs), the lack of distinction between infotainment and information, decontextualized fakes passed off as the real thing enshrined in museums and authenticated by professional academics, slide lectures, and theatrical staging—give classics a certain importance because it is the discipline that not only educates people how to read images and narratives, but played a key role in the emergence of art history and archaeology as disciplines. And, despite claims of *Altertumswissenschaft* (science of antiquity) it both diminishes and exacerbates the impasse of truth and appearance.

Thus, the proliferation of images that, for Baudrillard, characterizes the postmodern is also characteristic of the challenges facing today's discipline of classics and the study of classical civilizations, particularly in an age of falling enrollments and the need to justify our value to university bureaucracies. The problem remains, however, especially now that central aspects of Baudrillard's theories have materialized in our global village of simulacra, of how to conceptualize the historical event that interrupts the transmission of simulacra. Rather than asking if it is possible to construct an authentic past, perhaps the question we now face is whether or not it is possible for a historical narrative to not be a simulacrum.

Further reading

By Baudrillard

Simulations. Translated by P. Foss, P. Patton, and P. Beitchman. New York: Semiotext(e), Inc, 1983.

The Evil Demon of Images. Translated by Paul Patton and Paul Foss. Sydney: Power Institute of Fine Arts, 1987.

America. Translated by Chris Turner. London: Verso, 1988.

The Ecstasy of Communication. Translated by Bernard Schutze and Caroline Schutze. New York: Semiotext(e), 1988.

The Transparency of Evil: Essays on Extreme Phenomena. Translated by James Benedict. London: Verso, 1993.

Simulacra and Simulation. Translated by Sheila Faria Glaser. Ann Arbor: University of Michigan, 1994.

The System of Objects. Translated by Chris Turner. London: Verso, 1996.

Impossible Exchange. Translated by Chris Turner. London: Verso, 2001.

Jean Baudrillard: Selected Writings. 2nd edn. Edited by Mark Poster. Stanford: Stanford University Press, 2001.

About Baudrillard

Durham, Scott. *Phantom Communities: The Simulacrum and the Limits of Postmodernism*. Stanford: Stanford University Press, 1998.

Eco, Umberto. *Travels in Hyperreality*. San Diego, London, and New York: Harcourt Brace and Company, 1986.

Gane, Mike. *Baudrillard's Bestiary: Baudrillard and Culture*. London and New York: Routledge, 1991.

Gane, M. (ed.). *Baudrillard Live: Selected Interviews*. London and New York: Routledge, 1993.

Hitchcock, Louise and Koudounaris, Paul. "Virtual discourse: Arthur Evans and the reconstructions of the Minoan palace at Knossos." In *Labyrinth Revisited: Rethinking 'Minoan' Archaeology*, edited by Yannis Hamilakis. Oxford and Oakville: Oxbow, 2002.

Horrocks, Chris and Jetvic, Zora. *Introducing Baudrillard*. Lanham: Totem Books, 1996.

Huyssen, Andreas. "In the Shadow of McLuhan: Baudrillard's Theory of Simulation." In *Twilight Memories: Marking Time in a Culture of Amnesia*. London and New York: Routledge, 1995.

*Kellner, Douglas. *Jean Baudrillard: From Marxism to Postmodernism and Beyond.* Cambridge: Polity Press, 1989.
*Lane, Richard. *Jean Baudrillard.* London and New York: Routledge, 2000.
Smith, M W. *Reading Simulacra: Fatal Theories for Postmodernity.* Albany: State University of New York.

11 Walter Benjamin

Key concepts:

- the task of the translator
- translation
- the work of art in the age of its technological reproducibility
- aura
- allegory
- profane illumination
- angel of history

Walter Benjamin was born in Berlin in 1892 to an assimilated German-Jewish family. He was educated at the universities of Berlin, Freiburg, Munich, and Bern. As a student he became involved in radical Jewish student movements and, along with his close friend Gershom Scholem, grew increasingly interested in Jewish mysticism. (Scholem went on to become a great scholar of Jewish mysticism.) Scholem unsuccessfully tried to convince Benjamin to migrate to Palestine and take up a position at Hebrew University of Jerusalem after Scholem's own migration there in 1923. In 1925 Benjamin submitted *The Origin of German Tragic Drama* as his *Habilitationsschrift* at the University of Frankfurt. It was rejected because of its unconventional, lyrical style and, as a result, Benjamin never held a formal academic post. He worked, instead, as an independent scholar, freelance critic, and translator.

In 1933, with the rise of Nationalist Socialism in Germany, Benjamin moved to Paris where he met Hannah Arendt and Georges **Bataille** along with many other intellectuals. In 1939 he was deprived of his German nationality and spent time in an internment camp for foreign nationals in France. In 1940, at the invitation of Theodor **Adorno** and Max Horkheimer of the Institute for Social Research (recently moved from Frankfurt to

New York to escape the Nazis), Benjamin attempted to flee the French Vichy regime for the United States. When he arrived in Portbou on the French–Spanish border, he was refused entry into Spain. To return to France would have meant certain death. He was found dead the next morning, apparently a suicide by morphine overdose.

Benjamin wrote on a wide range of topics—from literary tragedy to travel to messianism—and in a range of styles: from essay to commentary to aphorism. Artists, historians, archaeologists, literary critics and philosophers have all been drawn to his texts for their insight and provocation. With regard to the study of classics and classical archaeology, Benjamin's theoretical work raises significant questions and problems pertaining regard to reproduction, translation, and aura. While many of his essays are relevant, essential readings include "The Task of the Translator" (1923) and "The Work of Art in the Age of its Technological Reproducibility" (1935–6).

In **"The Task of the Translator"** (an introduction to his translation of Baudelaire's *Tableaux Parisiens*), Benjamin pushes the questioning of origins and foundations in a very different direction, exploring the relationship between an original literary work and its "afterlife" in **translation**. What is it that is being translated? With regard to any literary work worth translating it is not simply information but "the unfathomable, the mysterious, the 'poetic,' something that a translator can reproduce only if he is also a poet" (p. 70). Translation is an art by which a literary work becomes something more and something less than itself. In translation the work has an "afterlife," which is something more than it was originally: a "stage of continued life." Therefore, in the work of the translator, the original work must die to itself in order to live beyond itself in another language as a work of literary art. At the same time, the original calls for its translation because it, in itself, is incomplete and ultimately cannot reach the unfathomable mystery it seeks to attain. The task of the translator is not simply to convey the original's information to those who can't read the original's language. Rather, it is a task of "recreation" aimed at liberating the poetic power of the text from its imprisonment within a particular (and necessarily non-universal, impure) language (p. 80).

Related issues are explored in Benjamin's now classic essay, **"The Work of Art in the Age of its Technological Reproducibility"** (1935–6), which serves as a direct counterpoint to Martin **Heidegger**'s essay "The Origin of the Work of Art" written at the same time. Although Benjamin makes no reference to Heidegger's essay in his own, there is considerable evidence from Benjamin's correspondence and the notes for *The Arcades Project* that he considered his work as a direct response to Heidegger's work. Samuel Weber has dealt with this complicated threshold between Benjamin and Heidegger in his remarkable essay "Mass Mediauras; or, Art, Aura, and Media in the Work of Walter Benjamin" (1996).

Benjamin explores the origins of the work of art in relation to what he believes to be a radically new era in art history brought on by new methods of mass reproduction. Important here is the concept of "authenticity," by which Benjamin refers to the original work of art's unique existence in time and space, "the here and now of the original" that "founded the idea of a tradition which has passed the object down as the same, identical thing to the present day"; in other words its "historical testimony" (p. 103). This is the essence or "aura" of the work of art that cannot be reproduced. **Aura** is what gives the original work its *distance*, its historical otherness in relation to us. The technological reproducibility of art drives "the desire of the present-day masses to 'get-closer' to things, and their equally passionate concern for overcoming each thing's uniqueness by assimilating it as a reproduction" (p. 105). With every reproduction, the aura of the original is diminished because "the technology of reproduction detaches the reproduced object from the sphere of tradition. By replicating the work many times over, it substitutes a mass existence for a unique existence" (p. 104). Reproducibility depends on that original work's aura (otherwise there would be no interest in reproducing it) even while it uproots it from the historical time and space that gives it its aura.

Benjamin further argues that a work of art's aura, its being rooted in tradition, has its basis in ritual. This, he insists, was the work of art's first and original use-value. Long before beauty or some other aesthetic experience was the artist's goal, and long before the modern notion of "art for art's sake," the work of art was made for use in religious ritual. As artists increasingly created their works with the explicit aim of public exhibition rather than ritual or other ideological function, the work of art began to break free from its religious roots. Nonetheless, Benjamin argues, until this new age of technological reproducibility, those roots still cohered to the work of art and have implications for understanding ancient works as a kind of technology for the production of meaning and establishing communication with the realm of the divine.

Many more issues relevant to the study of classics than can be discussed here are raised by Benjamin's concepts of translation, aura, and reconstruction, which are also related to concepts of otherness (**Said, Spivak**). In "Black Feminist Thought and Classics" (1993), Shelley Haley illustrates how class, race, gender, and social context affect translatability, through contrasting her translation of a passage of an Augustan poem, the *Moretum*, of unknown authorship in Latin, with that of another African American classicist, Frank Snowden (p. 30):

> African in race, her whole figure proof of her country — her hair tightly curled, lips thick, color dark, chest broad, breasts pendulous, belly somewhat pinched, legs thin, and feet broad and ample...
>
> (Snowden)

> She was his only companion, African in her race, her whole form a testimony to her country: her hair twisted into dreads, her lips full,

her color dark, her chest broad, her breasts flat, her stomach flat and firm, her legs slender, her feet broad and ample ...

(Haley)

For archaeological remains and monuments, reconstructions and reproductions of various kinds can bring the public closer to a sense of the original, but at what cost to the actual remains? An extreme case in point is the Bronze Age "palace" at Knossos on Crete where the aura of the original is submerged in the concrete reconstructions of Sir Arthur Evans and the hyperreality of endless reproductions. In addition, there is ongoing fetishism of antiquities of dubious origin and authenticity. The creation of a fake is the construction of a simulacrum with a false aura, which is then "authenticated" through the projection of scholarly ego and desire onto the object. Many fakes have become "real" through such acts of academic sanctification. With regard to many ancient texts and works of art, their social and ritual meanings become lost to the particularistic analyses of linguistic study or emphasis on assigning objects to an artist's hand or workshop.

With the advent of photography and film, Benjamin posits that "for the first time in world history, technological reproducibility emancipates the artwork from its parasitic subservience to ritual" (in "Mass Mediauras; or, Art, Aura, and Media in the Work of Walter Benjamin," p. 106). In this new age, artists increasingly make their works with the conscious intention of reproducing them. The original is created for the purpose of its own reproduction. The work of art's reproducibility has become paramount, leading to a qualitative transformation of the nature of art: Breaking free from its original roots in ritual practice, it has the potential to serve an entirely new practice, namely politics: "But as soon as the criterion of authenticity ceases to be applied to artistic production, the whole social function of art is revolutionized. Instead of being founded on ritual, it is based on a different practice: politics" (p. 106).

In Benjamin's view film is the most important example of this new form of reproducible art. Film, he argues, has the power to "confront the masses directly" (p. 116), whether the goal is nationalism or revolution, acceptance or resistance. It does so by distracting spectators—by entertaining or enthralling them with spectacle—while at the same time reshaping their worldview, intervening in their conception of reality. Remember that Benjamin was writing "The Work of Art in the Age of its Technological Reproducibility" during the rise of Nazism—a movement particularly adept at using art as political propaganda. Benjamin's essay provokes new questions at the beginning of the twenty-first century, a time in which new technologies of representation proliferate with ever-increasing speed. Even if we accept Benjamin's argument, we must ask how art made in a digital age both continues and exceeds the revolutionary age of mechanical reproduction to which he refers, where artistic praxis is premised on the dialectic of authenticity and in-authenticity, the real and the copy. With digitization and use of the Internet as commonplace, images and text are not simply reproduced; they are viral, available almost anywhere at anytime, where anyone with a handheld digital device can instantly become a historian. Computer generated effects can recreate past spectacles on a previously unimagined and unimaginable scale, without much need to stay faithful to original texts or narratives (e.g. *Troy, The 300*). All of these technologies present new challenges not just to maintaining scholarly authority, but also to preserving the relevance and defending the value of academic scholarship.

In *The Origin of German Tragic Drama*, Benjamin takes German Baroque tragic drama as the pretext for a series of reflections on aesthetics, language, allegory, and redemption (a theme which occupies him through-out his work). Benjamin attempts to rescue the "mourning play" (*Trauerspiel*) from its debased position as a bankrupt form of classical tragedy. In doing so, he presents an utterly inimitable work of literary crit-icism that is simultaneously brilliant and esoteric. This study is unique precisely because while appearing to be a commentary on the historicity of the *Trauerspielen*, it is, in fact, an extended critique of cultural history, aesthetics, and politics embedded in a theological framework. The concept that connects this unique meditation on the intersection between concrete historical experiences and ontotheological issues is allegory.

Allegory is the *fils conducteur* of Benjamin's work—from his earliest essays on German Romanticism to his study of the French Symbolist poet Charles Baudelaire. For Benjamin, allegory signifies an ongoing dialectic between theological and artistic creation. In this way, it marks the affinity he reads between artworks in modernity and the seventeenth-century German Baroque 'mourning play', with its ambiguity, multiplicity of meaning, and fragmentary representations. On this crisis of meaning, Benjamin writes:

> Any person, any object, any relationship can mean absolutely anything else. With this possibility a destructive, but just verdict is passed on the profane world ... [which] is both elevated and devalued ... Allegories are, in the realm of thoughts, what ruins are in the realm of things. This explains the baroque cult of the ruin ... that which lies here in ruins, the highly significant fragment, the remnant, is, in fact, the finest material in baroque creation. For it is common practice in the literature of the baroque to pile up fragments ceaselessly, without any strict idea of a goal, and, in the unremitting expectation of a miracle.
>
> (*Origin*, pp. 175, 178)

In the theory of allegory Benjamin presents one of the most modern artistic means of dealing with a preceding tradition—that of citation, tearing a precedent out of context—as, in fact, a gesture that arose with German Baroque drama.

These issues are developed in relation to contemporary artistic practice and post-structuralist thought in Craig Owens' "The Allegorical Impulse: Toward a Theory of Postmodernism" (1980). Owens argues that allegory, while present in modernism, remains in potentia until it can be actualized in the activity of excessive reading that characterizes postmodernism. Postmodern art, he argues, transforms our experience of art from a visual to a textual encounter because it attempts to problematize historical reference and foreground the instability of meaning. This notion of transformation extends to ancient art and texts as well, because they become modern by writing about them in and into the present, while the concept of the "highly significant fragment" is central to translatability and historical reconstruction in both epigraphy and in archaeology.

Another essay "The Rigorous Study of Art" is a review of the first volume of *Kunstwissenschaftliche Forschungen* [Research Essays in the Study of Art], which was edited in 1931 by Otto Pächt, a leading figure in the "Viennese school" of art history. In addition to providing a critique of Heinrich Wölfflin, the author of *Renaissance and Baroque* (1888), *Classic Art* (1899), and *Principles of Art History* (1915), it also champions the work of Alois Riegl and more importantly it provides a summary of the approach to cultural history deployed in *The Arcades Project*—an approach which, as this essay makes clear, comes directly from Benjamin's long-standing contemplation of art and art history.

In his estimation of Riegl's work, especially *The Late Roman Art Industry* (1901), Benjamin praises his "focus on materiality" and his "masterly command of the transition from individual object to its cultural and intellectual function" ("Rigorous Study," p. 668). It is this combination that allows Benjamin to proclaim Riegl—and not the formalist Wölfflin—the "precursor of this new type of art scholar." The primary characteristic of this "new type of art scholar" is an "esteem for the insignificant" or "a willing-ness to push research forward to the point where even the 'insignificant'— no, *precisely* the insignificant—becomes significant" (ibid.). This focus on the insignificant recalls his statements on allegory and his unfinished *The Arcades Project*. In the work of his peers, these "new researchers" who are "at home in marginal domains" and thereby "the hope of their field," Benjamin sees reflected his own impetus to examine the Parisian arcades as an *ur-form* of capitalist modernity ("Rigorous Study," p. 670). Similarly, in turning to the margins of the material record and focusing more on quotidian objects, classical archaeology has been able to approach previously unstudied areas such as household economy, trade in certain commodities, and the lives of women and slaves.

The importance Benjamin gives to the Parisian arcades, which by the 1930s were nearly all destroyed, derives in large part from his fascina-tion with the Surrealists. Benjamin writes that it was this avant-garde group who "first opened our eyes" to "the ruins of the bourgeoisie" which "became for Surrealism, the object of a research no less impassioned than that which the humanists of the Renaissance conducted on the remnants of classical antiquity" (*The Arcades Project*, p. 898). More precisely, Benjamin's preoccupation with the arcades can be traced directly to Louis Aragon's observation on the arcades in *Paris Peasant*: "It is only today, when the pickaxe menaces them, that they have at last become the true sanctuaries of a cult of the ephemeral, the ghostly landscape of damnable pleasures and professions." Led by the mercurial André Breton, the Surrealists founded their work on the notion of the "encounter," i.e., a situation in which an immanent "surreality" is made manifest. This notion of "surreality" as a sublation of dream and reality, the fantastic and the mundane, the unconscious and the conscious are themes which are brought forth in the traveler's nostalgia for ruins and exotic landscapes as found in **Said's** orientalism, and which have shaped our interests in the classical past.

The similarities between the Surrealists' and Benjamin's desires to investigate the cultural and psychological origins of modernity are undeniable. They share an interest in liminal psychic states (the Surrealists were preoccupied with self-induced trances and the derangement of the senses as put forth by Arthur Rimbaud, one of their artistic precursors), politics, the fleeting experience of everyday life, fantasy, repression, and the outmoded commodity. Because of this constellation of common interests Benjamin sees a direct line between his line of inquiry and that of the Surrealists. This line of inquiry can be characterized as an attempt to identify and actualize the hidden possibilities of the past that remain latent in the present. Seizing these latent potentialities is the act Benjamin terms "profane illumination" in his essay on Surrealism. **"Profane illumination"** transforms the impoverished experiences of modernity into a revolutionary nihilism. The intimacy between the materiality of things (the detritus of nineteenth century capitalism) and redemption (a messianic interruption for Benjamin and the advent of "surreality" for Breton *et al.*) is premised on a radical, delimited notion of remembrance. This is a concept familiar to readers of Benjamin's *The Origin of German Tragic Drama*. All of these themes are replayed in classicists' enduring interest in the past, and the anthropologically oriented interest in trance and intoxication.

The importance of Benjamin's work for classics results from his ability to question modes of operation that are taken for granted: the situated context and multivalency of translation, the effects of reproduction on classical art works and monuments, the tension between beauty and materiality, the significance of ruins in our modern culture as images of memory, the role of and engagement with marginal categories of material culture, and the interstices between language and objects. In his *Theses on the Philosophy of History* (published in 1950), Benjamin's parable on the **"angel of history,"** which flies backward, staring at something left behind is an echo of still earlier Greek, Hittite, Akkadian, and Sumerian texts, which tell us that the future is that which is behind us, that we need to know the past in order to know ourselves.

Further reading

By Benjamin

"The Task of the Translator." In *Illuminations*, edited by Hannah Arendt and translated by Harry Zohn. New York: Harcourt, Brace and World, 1968.

"Theses on the Philosophy of History." In *Illuminations*, edited by Hannah Arendt and translated by Harry Zohn. New York: Harcourt, Brace and World, 1968.

The Origin of German Tragic Drama. Translated by John Osborne. London and New York: Verso, 1998.

The Arcades Project. Translated by Howard Eiland and Kevin McLaughlin. Cambridge, MA: The Belknap Press of the Harvard University Press, 1999.

"Author as Producer." In *Selected Writings Volume 2, 1927–1934*, edited by Michael W. Jennings, Howard Eiland, and Gary Smith and translated by Edmund Jephcott. Cambridge, MA: The Belknap Press of the Harvard University Press, 1999.

"Little History of Photography." In *Selected Writings Volume 2, 1927–1934*, edited by Michael W. Jennings, Howard Eiland, and Gary Smith and translated by Edmund Jephcott and Kingsley Shorter. Cambridge, MA: The Belknap Press of the Harvard University Press, 1999.

"Surrealism: The Last Snapshot of the European Intelligentsia." In *Selected Writings Volume 2, 1927–1934*, edited Michael W. Jennings, Howard Eiland, and Gary Smith and translated by Edmund Jephcott. Cambridge, MA: The Belknap Press of the Harvard University Press, 1999.

"The Work of Art in the Age of its Technological Reproducibility." In *Selected Writings Volume 3, 1935–1938*, edited by Howard Eiland and Michael W. Jennings and translated by Edmund Jephcott and Harry Zohn. Cambridge, MA: The Belknap Press of the Harvard University Press, 2002.

About Benjamin

Arendt, Hannah. "Introduction." In *Illuminations*, edited by Hannah Arendt and translated by Harry Zohn. New York: Harcourt, Brace and World, 1968.

* Assmann, Aleida and Assmann, Jan. "What is mechanical reproduction?" In The Work of Art in the Digital Age. Edited by Michael J. Marrinan. Stanford: Stanford University Press, 2003.

Buck-Morss, Susan. "Aesthetics and Anaesthetics: Walter Benjamin's Artwork Essay Reconsidered." *October* 62 Fall (1992).

Caygill, Howard. "Walter Benjamin's Concept of Cultural History." In *The Cambridge Companion to Walter Benjamin*, edited by David S. Ferris. Cambridge: Cambridge University Press, 2004.

Cohen, Margaret. *Profane Illumination: Walter Benjamin and the Paris of Surrealist Revolution*. Berkeley and Los Angeles: University of California Press, 1993.

* Haley, Shelley P. "Black Feminist Thought and Classics: Re-membering, Re-claiming, Re-empowering," In *Feminist Theory and the Classics*. Edited by Nancy S. Rabinowitz and Amy Richlin. New York and London: Routledge, 1993.

Hitchcock, Louise and Koudounaris, Paul. "Virtual discourse: Arthur Evans and the reconstructions of the Minoan palace at Knossos." In *Labyrinth Revisited: Rethinking 'Minoan' Archaeology*, edited by Yannis Hamilakis. Oxford: Oxbow 2002.

Pensky, Max. *Melancholy Dialectics: Walter Benjamin and the Play of Mourning.* Amherst: The University of Massachusetts Press, 1993.

Plate, S. Brent. *Walter Benjamin, Religion and Aesthetics: Rethinking Religion through the Arts.* New York and London: Routledge, 2004.

Rochlitz, Rainer. *The Disenchantment of Art: The Philosophy of Walter Benjamin.* New York and London: The Guilford Press, 1996.

Weber, Samuel. "Mass Mediauras; or, Art, Aura, and Media in the Work of Walter Benjamin." In *Mass Mediauras: Form, Technics, Media.* Stanford: Stamford University Press, 1996.

12 Pierre Bourdieu

> **Key concepts:**
> - habitus
> - doxa
> - hexis
> - cultural capital
> - field of cultural production
> - taste

Pierre Bourdieu (1930–2002) was a French sociologist whose work has been widely influential in both the social sciences and the humanities. He was born in rural southwestern France where his father was employed as a postal worker. Bourdieu received a scholarship that enabled him to attend the prestigious *lycée* Louis le Grand in Paris. He subsequently enrolled at the École normale supérieure where he studied with Louis **Althusser**. After graduating with a degree in philosophy, Bourdieu first taught at the high school level and then in 1959 he was appointed to a position in philosophy at the Sorbonne. He taught at the University of Paris from 1960 to 1964. In 1964 he was named director of studies at the École des hautes études en sciences sociales and founded the Center for the Sociology of Education and Culture. In 1982 Bourdieu was named chair of sociology at the Collège de France. He received the "Medaille d'Or" from the French National Scientific Research Center in 1993.

During Bourdieu's French military service in Algeria at the time of their war of independence, he also spent time teaching in the University of Algeria. This experience made him acutely aware of the racial and class chauvinism of French colonialism. He later conducted ethnographic field-work in Algeria employing an explicitly structuralist anthropology, which served as the foundation for many of his later concepts and theories. Bourdieu also conducted fieldwork in France where he studied the structures of social and class differences and marriage patterns in French society. He was interested in how systems of social inequality are embedded in cultural practices. He paid particular attention to the study of the French educational system and demonstrated how it reproduced class differences despite its claims to the contrary.

Like Jacques **Derrida**, Bourdieu was a publicly engaged intellectual. In 2001, he became a celebrity with the appearance of a popular documentary film about him entitled "Sociology is a Combat Sport" and despite his academic prose style several of his books were bestsellers in France. Bourdieu matched his status as a public intellectual with his political activism. He fought social injustice, publicly criticized the inequalities in the French class structure, and supported better conditions for the working classes, immigrants, and the homeless. He was also closely associated with anti-globalization movements. He succumbed to cancer in 2002 at the age of 71.

Bourdieu produced a large body of work, authoring more than 25 books, on a number of different areas, including the sociology of culture and taste, education, language, literature, and photography. Among his best-known texts are *An Outline of a Theory of Practice* (1972), *Distinction: A Social Critique of the Judgment of Taste* (1979), and *The Logic of Practice* (1980). Many of his key concepts (e.g., *habitus* and cultural capital) have had a significant and ongoing influence on the humanities as a whole.

Blending structuralist perspectives on social systems with a concern for human agency, Bourdieu sought to understand patterns of human behavior and how they are generated by and within society. His concept of practice, developed in *An Outline of a Theory of Practice*, strengthened his contention that social patterns of behavior reproduce structures of domination. By practice, Bourdieu is referring to the things that people *do* as opposed to what they *say*. This is related to his concern with agency: how do individuals contribute to the reproduction of social restrictions and what is possible and not possible to do in a particular cultural context? Bourdieu develops this notion of practice through the corollary concept of **habitus**. He defines *habitus* as a system of "durable, transposable *dispositions*, structured structures predisposed to function as structuring structures, that is, as principles of the generation and structuring of practices and representations which can be objectively 'regulated' and 'regular' without in any way being the product of obedience to rules" (*Outline of a Theory of Practice*, p. 72). In other words, a *habitus* is a set of dispositions or organizing principles, which generate and structure human actions and behaviors. It shapes all practice and yet it is not experienced as repressive or enforcing. As a mode of behavior, its effects on us typically go unnoticed as one's *habitus* is an unconscious internalization of societal structures.

A specific *habitus* comes into focus when social and cultural markers such as occupation, income, education, religion, and preferences of taste (food, clothing, music, and art) are juxtaposed. For example, a corporate executive with an advanced college degree, disposable income, season tickets to the opera, and a taste for fine wine, contrasts with the dispositions (*habitus*) of a "blue collar" worker with a high school diploma, significant debt, who watches sports on television, and prefers Budweiser to Bordeaux. Bourdieu locates *habitus* where these dispositions correlate to a particular social group or class. A specific set of such dispositions is what he means by the term *habitus*.

Knowing the *habitus* of a particular person—what social group or class they fit into by virtue of a set of dispositions—does not provide the social scientist with predictive power to know what practices a person will engage in. To claim this would be to remove individual agency and priviledge structure over practice. Bourdieu criticizes any method that would attempt to remove agency and practice from our understanding of social structure. Similarly, *habitus* is not a fixed or static system. Distinctions between one *habitus* and another, he asserts, are not rigidly set, but have a shared and processual quality. Moreover, dispositions are multiple—we may, for example, apply one set of dispositions in our home life and another while at work. They are also changeable over time; for example, retirement will result in a set of dispositions distinct from one's working life.

How does one acquire a particular *habitus*? Bourdieu describes this process as one of informal, unconscious learning rather than formal instruction. One learns to inhabit a *habitus* through practical means, such as using a particular space for a specific purpose, listening to music, cooking, drinking, wearing clothes, driving cars, and giving gifts. The *habitus* one occupies shapes the practices that one participates in. For Bourdieu, the notion of *habitus* reveals that while a person's behavior may be in part determined by formal social rules and mental ideas—which are to be uncovered and described by the social scientist—a significant determinant of behavior is hidden. This hidden factor is the implicit knowledge learned informally and embodied in specific social practices. Once internalized, the dispositions of *habitus* are taken for granted. Bourdieu uses the term **doxa** to refer to the taken-for-granted, unquestioned, unexamined (and, in fact, cultural) ideas about social life that seem to be common sense and natural to the one possessing these dispositions. In contrast, he uses the term **hexis** to refer to the active, embodied posture taken toward the world, which is engendered by *habitus*.

Bourdieu discusses *habitus* as a "system of dispositions—a present past that tends to perpetuate itself into the future by reactivation in similarly structured practices" (*The Logic of Practice*, p. 54). Although *habitus* may be understood as a result of inculcation, a product of repetition or routine, Bourdieu does not deny its potential reinscription by one of its members. Thus, *habitus* locates an individual in concrete social situations, which are spatially circumscribed, without foreclosing on his/her agency.

Central to this concept of *habitus* is how Bourdieu conceives of the relationship between the structure and the agent. He theorizes *habitus* as an alternative to concepts such as consciousness or subjectivity. Interestingly, one of his earliest uses of the term occurs in the 1967 "Postface" to his French translation of Erwin Panofsky's *Gothic Architecture and Scholastic Thought*, which includes Panofsky's famous essay on the Abbey Church of Saint-Denis. The use of the term *habitus* with regard to art and architecture demonstrates the importance of these fields to Bourdieu's work. Both serve to constrain and enable human action, and orchestrate daily routines, thus contributing significantly to the formation of social identity. The reconstruction of embodied experience through the analysis of material remains and texts from the classical past, can contribute much to the reconstruction of social history and identity.

Similar concepts have been articulated in Anthony Giddens' (In *The Constitution of Society*) theory of structuration whereby agents can either reproduce existing social structures or transform them through a change in behavior. To the extent that agents are capable of "making a difference" in a pre-existing state of affairs or course of events, they are said to be exercising power. Structure does not exist outside of social action, but is both constraining and enabling. Thus, social practices are constituted in the context of time–space relations and include the practical knowledge, which allows individual agents to "go on" with the routines of daily life. Agency, then, refers to those events of which an individual is the perpetrator, in the sense that the individual could, at any phase in a given sequence of conduct, have acted differently. The ability of social structures to both constrain and enable action is regarded as the duality of structure. Similarly, Bourdieu frequently referred to *habitus* as "practical sense" [*sens pratique*], which allows for strategy and the existence of agonistic positions. *Habitus* also allows Bourdieu to recuperate an element of individual agency through its implicit critique of Ferdinand de **Saussure**'s structuralism, which sacrifices agency to the structure of language as such.

In addition, Bourdieu's concept of *habitus* is not simply a process of socialization or enculturation into a set of practices; it also takes into account the power relations that exist between social classes, i.e., with how social inequality is perpetrated and maintained, thus it involves an ideological component. It contrasts the different sets of dispositions (social expectations, lifestyle choices, etc.) that exist between different classes. Class (and presumably gender) distinctions appear clearly in the complex of practices embedded in a particular *habitus*. This is socially powerful, according to Bourdieu, because class inequalities and the dominance of one class over another occur covertly. Symbolic power is deployed to maintain class distinctions and the appearance of their naturalness. Social class is defined by Bourdieu as "the unity hidden under the diversity and multiplicity of the set of practices performed" (*Distinction*, p. 101). Thus, money may have economic exchange value, but it also has symbolic exchange value in that its possession and manner of deployment in attempting to promote status, which may mark one as wealthy and upper class, poor and lower class, or even wealthy and *nouveau riche*. Although the economic system of exchange is controlled by the dominant class, it alone does not define social class because rather than the application of overt force there are a "diversity and multiplicity" of social practices at work that define social class.

In his later work, *Language and Symbolic Power* (a differently edited collection of essays based on *Ce que parler veut dire: l'économie des échanges linguistiques*, first published in French in 1982), Bordieu turns his attention to how language is used in the creation and maintenance of power relations. Among other things, Bourdieu looks at style of speaking as well as the personal vs. institutionally constrained and official use of language, in order to analyze the role of language use in establishing, reproducing, negotiating, or resisting power relationships. This project is of key significance for understanding how scholarly authority is constructed, disciplinary boundaries are established, maintained, or changed in classics as well as for analyzing the role of language use in the classical world.

In order to explain the relation between *habitus* and social class more fully, Bourdieu reinscribed the economic term "capital" as that which not only refers to financial assets but also to other resources that confer status and social class. Of course, financial capital matters for the establishment of class distinctions, but so does symbolic or **cultural capital**, which Bourdieu best defines in *Distinction* and elaborates further in *Language and Symbolic Power*. Cultural capital never forfeits its analogy with economic capital, but it refers to a familiarity with objects and practices in the cultural sphere determined by educational level, linguistic competence, and other forms of capital that mark a social class. Cultural capital is used to distinguish and maintain class distinctions and, by extension, social inequality.

Bourdieu defines the arena in which cultural capital flows and accrues value as the "**field of cultural production**." This concept of field [*champ*] is related to *habitus* in that it is a structural social formation. Each field— whether it is the academic field or the judicial field—has its own laws, codes of behavior, and standards. Thus, a field is not entirely independent of the economic, each field is however "structurally homologous" to every other, including the field of economic production and exchange value. Bourdieu develops this concept of field because it allows him to discuss an agent's actions, which are grounded in objective social relations—they occur in a field—without reducing them to strict determinism. In other words, the agent's actions do not merely passively reflect the larger underlying and determinate economic base, as in Marxist discourse for instance. Bourdieu breaks with the ideology of the transformative subject as well as socioeconomic determinism. His theory attempts to keep the strengths of each position through an elaboration of the refractive and prismatic means by which structural limitations and their potential inflections traverse a field. For Bourdieu, the logic of the field is structural and yet not conscious. It is defined by antagonism, challenges, threats, and discord. It is here that change and inflection become possible. The field of cultural production, which is central to any discussion of academic discourse, including classics, both produces and reproduces its origins, codes, rules, and values, yet it remains contingent and open to reinscription.

The field of cultural production and the wielding of cultural capital colored all of Bourdieu's sociological analyses. The roles of cultural production and capital can be analyzed in both the past and the present. Examples of how such analyses might shed light on the past include the role of material culture in the production of status and identity as well as what texts can tell us about cultural values, various types of identity construction, and social distancing. In the present and recent past, classics as a discipline is also bound up in the class distinctions analyzed by Bourdieu.

Bourdieu employs the category of **taste** to describe how distinctions between high and low culture are made and justified. In his own research, he found a correlation between French aesthetic preferences for the arts on one hand and "taste" preferences for such things as food and fashion on the other. He concluded that such tastes, like other forms cultural capital, serve to demarcate class differences. Because taste marks distinctions between different levels of socio-economic status and of cultural competence, it is also an ideological category. Thus, for Bourdieu, distinctions based on taste are part of the arsenal for differentiating social classes: "Taste classifies, and it classifies the classifier. Social subjects, classified by their classifications, distinguish themselves by the distinctions they make, between the beautiful and the ugly, the distinguished and the vulgar, in which their position in the objective classification is expressed or betrayed" (*Distinction*, p. 6). Historically, the study of classical art and languages has functioned as a significant "asset" in the "portfolio" of cultural capital, where it has served as a tool of social distancing and as an ideology to legitimize various forms of Western hegemony.

The manner in which the artistic field is laced with distinctions in social class and how it is premised on cultural competence is made evident in Bourdieu's studies of the modern museum. The founding of the modern museums of Europe and North America, which include large collections of Greek and Roman art, are clear examples of the "homology" between cultural and economic capital. Moreover, despite its pretense of democratic universalism, the modern museum does not erase but rather reproduces social class distinctions. While they may provide physical access to artworks (the repeated *raison d'être* of civic museums), there is a limiting factor: cultural competence. In *The Love of Art: European Art Museums and Their Public* (1990) and elsewhere, Bourdieu addresses the consequences of cultural competence as a code, acquired through one's *habitus* and education, that frames cultural knowledge and one's disposition toward art. He writes that "faced with scholarly culture, the least sophisticated are in a position identical with that of ethnologists who find themselves in a foreign society and present, for instance, at a ritual to which they do not hold the key" (*The Field of Cultural Production*, p. 217). An extension of this insight concerning the particularity and tendentious experience of classical art and texts makes evident the ramifications of one's social class in any experience of these.

To conclude, it is clear that Bourdieu's work has indelibly marked the discourse of the humanities in general and classics in particular, especially with his work on *habitus* and cultural capital. Bourdieu's work is widely applicable in both classics and classical archaeology, whether to understand the emergence, development, and maintenance of legal and social norms in classical Athens, analyzing behavior and adornment to create social distinctions in Republican Rome, the use of the Minoan past as symbolic capital in contributing to status and tourism in modern Greece, or to examine the role of material remains in reproducing social life. But perhaps the most important contribution Bourdieu's work makes to classics is his methodology itself. In the text *In Other Words: Essays Towards a Reflexive Sociology*, he argues:

> The theory of the field [leads] to both a rejection of the direct relating of individual biography to the work of literature (or the relating of the "social class" of origin to the work) and also to a rejection of internal analysis of an individual work or even of intertextual analysis. This is because what we have to do is all these things at the same time.
>
> (p. 147)

This exemplifies how Bourdieu raises the interpretative stakes for classics in terms of both archaeology and literary criticism. Rejecting any form of immanent analysis whether it is Jean **Baudrillard**'s fetishization of signs or Derrida's deconstructive practice, Bourdieu insists upon an interdisciplinary sociology of cultural production and the determinant structuralist readings given by psychoanalysis or Marxism. The simultaneity that defines the existence of art and text within a field of cultural production coupled with the understanding of *habitus* and the cultural competence of users, interpreters, readers, and other consumers demands nothing short of a total analysis of the production, circulation, and consumption of cultural capital.

Further reading

By Bourdieu

* *An Outline of a Theory of Practice*. Translated by Richard Nice. Cambridge: Cambridge University Press, 1977.

Distinction: A Social Critique of the Judgment of Taste. Translated by Richard Nice. Cambridge, MA: Harvard University Press, 1984.

In Other Words: Essays Towards Reflexive Sociology. Translated by Matthew Adamson. Stanford: Stanford University Press, 1990.

The Logic of Practice. Translated by Richard Nice. Stanford: Stanford University Press, 1990.

The Love of Art: European Art Museums and Their Public. Translated by Caroline Beattie and Nick Merriman. Stanford: Stanford University Press, 1990.

With Jean Claude Passeron. *Reproduction in Education, Society and Culture.* Translated by Richard Nice. London: Sage Publications, Inc., 1990.

The Field of Cultural Production: Essays on Art and Literature. Edited by Randal Johnson. Cambridge: Polity Press, 1993.

With Hans Haacke. *Free Exchange.* Cambridge: Polity Press, 1995.

Practical Reason: On the Theory of Action. Translated by Randal Johnson. Stanford: Stanford University Press, 1996.

Pascalian Meditations. Translated by Richard Nice. Stanford: Stanford University Press, 2000.

* *Language and Symbolic Power.* Edited by John Thompson and translated by Gino Raymond and Matthew Adamson. Cambridge, MA: Harvard University Press, 1999.

About Bourdieu

* Barrett, John. *Fragments from Antiquity: An Archaeology of Social Life in Britain, 2900–1200 BC.* Oxford, UK and Cambridge, MA: Blackwell, 1994.

Cohen, David. *Law, Sexuality and Society: The Enforcement of Morals in Classical Athens.* Cambridge: Cambridge University Press, 1991.

Corbeill, Anthony. "Political Movement: Walking and Ideology in Republican Rome." In *The Roman Gaze. Vision, Power and the Body.* Edited by David Frederick. Baltimore: The Johns Hopkins University Press, 2002.

* Giddens, Anthony. *The Constitution of Society: Outline of the Theory of Structuration.* Cambridge: Polity Press, 1993.

* Hamilakis, Yannis and Yalouri, Eleana. "Antiquities as symbolic capital in modern Greek society." *Antiquity*, 70.267 (1996) 117–129.

* Jenkins, Richard. *Pierre Bourdieu.* Rev. edn. London and New York: Routledge, 2002.

Johnson, Randal. "Editor's Introduction: Pierre Bourdieu on Art, Literature and Culture." In *The Field of Culture Production.* Cambridge: Polity Press, 1993.

Lane, Jeremy F. *Pierre Bourdieu: A Critical Introduction.* London: Pluto Press, 2000.

Robbins, Derek. *The Work of Pierre Bourdieu: Recognizing Society.* Buckingham and Philadelphia: Open University Press, 1991.

Rose, Peter W. "Divorcing Ideology from Marxism and Marxism from Ideology: Some Problems." *Arethusa* 39.1 (2006) 101–36.

Shusterman, Richard (ed.). *Bourdieu: A Critical Reader.* Oxford: Blackwell, 1999.

Swartz, David. *Culture and Power: The Sociology of Pierre Bourdieu.* Chicago: University of Chicago Press, 1997.

Webb, Jen. *Understanding Bourdieu.* London: Sage, 2002.

13 Judith Butler

Key concepts:

- gender
- performativity
- gender trouble
- paradox of subjection
- face of the enemy

Judith Butler (b. 1956–) is Maxine Elliot Professor in the Departments of Rhetoric and Comparative Literature at the University of California, Berkeley. She received her Ph.D. in philosophy from Yale University in 1984. Her interest in philosophy stems from her Jewish upbringing and the questions it raised concerning ethics and human life in the aftermath of the Holocaust. Her first major publication was a study of Hegel in contemporary French philosophy entitled *Subjects of Desire: Hegelian Reflections in Twentieth-Century France* (1987). After this her work became more focused on ethics, power, and identity, especially gendered identity. Butler is one of the most important feminist and political philosophers of her generation.

Her most influential work to date *Gender Trouble: Feminism and the Subversion of Identity* (1990), makes the powerful argument that neither **gender** nor sex are natural categories of human identity. At the time of its publication, this was a major challenge to the then-common position among feminists that gender (masculinity and femininity) is culturally constructed, whereas sex (male and female) is natural and pre-designated. Butler counters that "gender must ... designate the very apparatus of production whereby the sexes themselves are established. As a result, gender is not to culture as sex is to nature; gender is also the discursive/cultural means by which 'sexed nature' or a 'natural sex' is produced and established as ... prior to culture, a politically neutral surface on which culture acts" (*Gender Trouble*, p. 7). In other words, there is no male and female prior to the cultural engenderings of those two categories of identity. We cannot think outside our culture, so that "male" and "female" identities are culturally determined as are "masculinity" and "femininity." The idea that sexual identity is natural, that there are two sexes in nature, is a cultural construct.

Butler argues that these categories of identity take social and symbolic form in a culture through iteration. Thus, sexual identity is **performative**. "There is no gender identity," she writes, "behind the expressions of gender; ... identity is performatively constituted by the very 'expressions' that are said to be its results" (*Gender Trouble*, p. 25). Gender is not a category of ontology, rather a subject enacts its identity through language, actions, dress, and manner. It is not who you *are* but what you *do*. Gender is constructed through performative iterations. Butler's concepts of performativity and iteration also have implications for the formation of cultural and ethnic identity.

Butler is critical of forms of feminism that posit "women" as a group with a distinct identity, set of political interests, form of social agency, and so on. In making such assertions, she contends, feminism risks reinforcing a binary conception of gender, thereby reducing the possibilities of social identity for human beings to only two categories, man and woman, defined in opposition to one another. Here Butler's strained dialogue with Luce **Irigaray**, Julia **Kristeva**, and psychoanalytic discourse is most clearly felt. Writing from a historical context informed by post-structuralist thought, Butler calls for performances of identity that produce "**gender trouble**" within the social and symbolic order: i.e., drawing out the contradictions and excesses within oneself—the parts that do not "come together" into a simple, unified whole self—and acting out a multiplicity of gendered and sexual identities. The goal here is to undermine the binary oppositions that produce gender and sexual identity so as to open up new forms of social and ethical agency and ways of being in the world. Butler's engagement with Sophocles' *Antigone* entitled *Antigone's Claim* and heavily criticized for her lack of knowledge of Greek reads the character of Antigone on one level from the perspective of gender trouble: Antigone's death prevents her from marrying Creon and becoming a mother, thereby placing her outside the bounds of compulsory heterosexuality.

In developing her theory of performativity, Butler draws on Michel **Foucault**'s theory of power. Arguing against a reductive view of power as the dominant force of law, Foucault conceives of power as a "multiple and mobile field of force relations, wherein far-reaching, but never completely stable, effects of domination are produced" (*The History of Sexuality*, vol. 1: *An Introduction*, p. 102). Power takes form within society through ceaseless struggles and negotiations. It does not simply come down from on high but rather it circulates through society. In the process it materializes or takes a "terminal form" within a particular socio-political system of power/knowledge. Yet the "terminal forms" power takes are not entirely stable because they can never contain or totalize all the actual and potential forces within it.

Although they appear to us as terminal and fixed, they are, in fact, temporary and contingent. There are always points of resistance that cut across the social order and its stratifications of power and privilege, opening possibilities for subversion.

In *Gender Trouble* and *Bodies That Matter: On the Discursive Limits of "Sex"* (1993), Butler develops Foucault's insights into the formation and subversion of terminal forms of power into a psychoanalytically informed interpretation of gender and sexual identity politics. She conceives of every social and symbolic order as a regulatory consolidation of power in the Foucauldian sense. Such an order is established and maintained by prohibitions and repeated performances of identities within that order. Yet, as Butler puts it, to be *constituted* within such an order is not to be *determined* by it. There is always the possibility of agency, of acting out within the system in ways that are subversive and transformative of it, because there are always aspects of oneself that are "socially impossible," that cannot be reduced to the order of things, that exceed any particular identity within that order. Hence her serious interest in drag, cross-dressing, and other forms of gender trouble. As she states in *Bodies that Matter* (pp. 125, 139), "drag is a site of a certain ambivalence, one which reflects the more general situation of being implicated in the regimes of power by which one is constituted."

Butler's call "to recast the symbolic" is a *de facto* political gesture (*Bodies That Matter*, p. 22). Her thinking about performativity is inseparable from her political positions. These come across clearly in the dialogues she has with Ernesto Laclau and Slavoj Zizek collected in *Contingency, Hegemony, Universality: Contemporary Dialogues on the Left* (2000). Butler has argued that "[t]he incompletion of every ideological formulation is central to the radical democratic project's notion of political futurity. The subjection of every ideological formation to a *rearticualtion* of these linkages constitutes the temporal order of democracy as an incalculable future, leaving open the production of new subject-positions, new political signifiers, and new linkages to become the rallying points for politicization" (*Bodies That Matter*, p. 193). The intricacies of this position are best understood through her discussion of subjection.

In *The Psychic Life of Power* (1997), Butler engages **Foucault, Freud, Lacan, Althusser,** and others to explore further the issue of agency within the social and symbolic order, which she terms the **"paradox of subjection."** The paradox lies in the fact that subjectivity is founded on subjection. That is, in order to become an acting subject in a society one must be subjected to its order (its language, laws, values, etc.). Recall **Irigaray's** description of the social-symbolic order of patriarchy as "a certain game" in which a woman finds herself "signed up without having begun to play" (*Speculum of the Other Woman*, p. 22). So it is, in fact, with all forms of subjectivity. One acts *within* a certain social and symbolic order, a "game" with certain (and frequently unwritten) rules and codes to which and by which one is initially "subjected." Paradoxically, it is this subjection that makes subversion possible. Butler writes: "Subjection signifies the process of becoming subordinated by power as well as the process of becoming a subject ... A power exerted on a subject, subjection is nevertheless a power assumed by the subject, an assumption that constitutes the instrument of that subject's becoming" (*Psychic Life*, pp. 2, 11). Simply put, to be conditioned or formed by a certain terminal form of power is not to be determined by it. A subject's agency, she insists, one's exercize of power, is not "tethered" to the constitutive conditions. The subject is an effect of power and yet power itself can become the effect of the subject.

Butler has applied her theoretical interests in identity politics, subjectivity, and power to the issues of ethics and violence in the aftermath of September 11, 2001. In particular, she focuses on media representations of the "face of the enemy." How is it that America's enemies have been othered in such a way as to render them inhuman and their lives ungrievable, thereby turning us away from the reality of life as fragile and precarious? In exploring these issues, Butler draws on the work of Emmanuel **Levinas**, especially his concept of the face-to-face encounter with the other as the ultimate ethical situation, a moment of obligation to the other, whose pleas for clemency reverberate with the commandment "thou shall not kill." Media representations reduce the face of the other to the enemy (both as target and as victim of war) and thereby deny the possibility of a genuine face-to-face encounter. In a series of questions, Butler asks how one conceives of life in the aftermath of a trauma and, more importantly perhaps, how does one live up to the ethical possibility of bearing witness to the dehumanized face of alterity? Certainly such questions raise interesting implications about the representation of the "other" in the ancient world and for interpreting the traumas of ancient life, such as the violent destruction of entire cities.

The ethical and political implications of Butler's theory of identity politics have brought questions regarding the visual representations of the gendered subject into the foreground. Her importance to queer theory and feminist studies has made her work of key significance to those studying gender identity in classics and in classical archaeology. The insight that there is no gender-neutral historical knowledge adds another inflection to the intersection of classics and feminism. Feminist classicists, including Amy Richlin, Froma Zeitlin, John Younger, Nancy Sorkin Rabinowitz, Lisa Auanger, and Barbara Gold, have made many inroads into the resolutely gendered matrix of classical discourse, while the inclusion of Butler's work has influenced another generation of feminist classicists and classical archaeologists (including males). Stepping beyond the reified categories of male/female, the presence in text and material culture of hybrid and exotic beings provide an opportunity to explore their role in classical cultures from the aspect of Butler's concept of performativity. For example, Hitchcock (in "Knossos is Burning: Gender Bending the Minoan Genius") has used Butler to move beyond the binary iconographic categorizations of the Aegean genius, to interpret it as third gender, standing outside of traditional categories of gender identity, while wielding male symbols of power. Therefore, it is both in the discourse surrounding the interpretation of representations of gender and in the epistemological reinscription of the discipline of classics—a masculinist enterprise from its inception—that the weight of Butler's work is and will be felt.

Further reading

By Butler

Subjects of Desire: Hegelian Reflections in Twentieth-Century France. New York: Columbia University Press, 1987.

*Gender Trouble: Feminism and the Subversion of Identity. London and New York: Routledge, 1990.

Butler, Judith, and Joan W. Scott (eds). *Feminists Theorize the Political.* London and New York: Routledge, 1992.

*Bodies That Matter: On the Discursive Limits of "Sex." London and New York: Routledge, 1993.

Excitable Speech: A Politics of the Performative. London and New York: Routledge, 1997.

The Psychic Life of Power: Theories of Subjection. Stanford: Stanford University Press, 1997.

"Ruled Out: Vocabularies of the Censor." In *Censorship and Silencing: Practices of Cultural Regulation,* edited by Robert C. Post. Los Angeles: Getty Research Institute for the History of Art and the Humanitites, 1998.

"Subversive Bodily Acts." In *Spectacular Optical,* edited by Sandra Antelo-Suarez and Michael Mark Madore. New York: Trans/Art, Cultures, Media, 1998.

Antigone's Claim: Kinship between Life and Death. New York: Columbia University Press, 2000.

Precarious Life: The Powers of Mourning and Violence. New York: Verso, 2004.

The Judith Butler Reader. Edited by Sara Salih. Oxford: Blackwell, 2004.

About Butler

Benhabib, Seyla. *Situating the Self: Gender, Community and Postmodernism in Contemporary Ethics.* London and New York: Routledge, 1992.

*Hitchcock, Louise A. "Knossos is Burning: Gender Bending the Minoan Genius." In *Engendering Prehistoric 'Stratigraphies' in the Aegean and the Mediterranean,* edited by Katerina Kopaka. Rethymnon, Crete: University of Rethymnon (in press).

Jones, Amelia (ed.). *The Feminism and Visual Culture Reader.* London and New York: Routledge, 2003.

14 Hélène Cixous

Key concepts

- Jewoman
- the unconscious
- écriture feminine
- phallo(go)centrism
- white ink

Hélène Cixous (1937–) is professor of literature at the University of Paris VIII, an experimental university that she helped to found in 1968 and where she established a doctoral program in women's studies, the first and only one in France. Her childhood has been described as simultaneously Mediterranean and European. Raised in Oran, Algeria, her father's Sephardic Jewish family had fled Spain for Morocco and spoke French, Spanish, and Arabic. Her mother and grandmother were Ashkenazi Jews from Germany, and German was spoken in her home. She learned Arabic and Hebrew from her father, who died in 1948, and learned English as a student in London in 1950. She moved to France in 1955, where she became a student at the Lycée Lakanal, a preparatory school for boys.

Given her life story, it comes as no surprise that she has always had a sense of homelessness and otherness wherever she found herself, without legitimate place, without "fatherland." Cixous captures this sense of homelessness and hybridity in her self-description as **"Jewoman."** "This is a thought, that we Jewomen have all the time, the thought of the good and bad luck, of chance, immigration, and exile" ("We Who Are Free, Are We Free?" p. 204). She sees the same binary oppositions traditionally used to construct gender identity, as also applied to the construction of racial identity, which she seeks to break down. For Cixous, a groundless multiplicity of selves—this experience of fitting in anywhere and nowhere, without fatherland and without singular identity—becomes, in writing, the source of creativity. Writing allows her to create a "country of words," a home away from home. Indeed, it is precisely her sense of dislocation and perpetual immigration that, paradoxically, becomes the generative space of writing. Leonard (In "Creating a Dawn") observes that Cixous' engagement with classical texts places her beyond assimilation within a singular tradition.

Much of Cixous' writing also draws from the Hebrew Bible (e.g., "Coming to Writing" and *Veils*). In *Three Steps on the Ladder of Writing* (1993), she speaks directly about her understanding of the Hebrew Bible and why she so often returns to it for poetic inspiration. In these stories, she finds a wonderful crudeness, a shameless presentation of raw humanity that locates the Bible more with the **unconscious** than with states of repression that normally rule our conscious social lives. "The Bible's Moses," for example, "cuts himself shaving. He is afraid, he is a liar. He does many a thing under the table before being Up There with the other Tables. This is what the oneiric world of the Bible makes apparent to us. The light that bathes the Bible has the same crude and shameless color as the light that reigns over the unconscious" (p. 67).

In an endorsement that has appeared on nearly every book by Cixous since the early 1990s, her longtime friend Jacques **Derrida** has called her the greatest contemporary writer in the French language. Part of what makes her writing so great, according to Derrida, is that she is a "poet-thinker, very much a poet and very much a thinking poet." Cixous is a prolific writer of fiction and of theatrical texts, which have engaged Greek literary works, particularly Aeschylus' *Oresteia*. Productions of her plays have used casting (the same individual in different types of roles) and costuming (the Furies in *The Eumenides* as "bag ladies") to create counternarratives. Her writing represents a kind of thinking about writing, in which she follows her own creative process as it takes her into unfamiliar territories. "It's not a question of drawing the contours, *but what escapes the contour*, the secret movement, the breaking, the torment, the unexpected" ("Without End," p. 96). It is precisely this self-reflective—often autobiographical—thinking about writing, as she encounters the "unexpected" while pursuing "what escapes," which has made her such an important figure for scholars concerned with theory. If she "does" theory, it is toward a theory of writing.

Indeed, we might think of Cixous' writing as a kind of *poetics of deconstruction*. As it follows what escapes the main contours of thought, she watches those contours dissolve and new landscapes emerge. In this process, she and her readers become increasingly aware that the main contours have been keeping them from unknown worlds of possibility. Writing thus becomes a process of opening toward the mystery of the other. "The prisons precede me. When I have escaped them, I discover them: when they have cracked and split open beneath my feet" ("We Who Are Free," p. 203). In this respect, she does with her poetic writing what her contemporary Julia **Kristeva** looks for in her early semiotic analysis of literature, that is, a kind of revolutionary poetic language which can produce an "other" kind of subjectivity, capable of opening new possibilities for social relations and community that are subversive of the dominant patriarchal, capitalistic social-symbolic order.

A key concept in Cixous' early writings, such as "The Laugh of the Medusa" (1975) and *The Newly Born Woman* (first published in French in 1975), is that of **écriture féminine**, or feminine/female writing. Such writing has its source not just in post-structuralist Barthesian theory, but also in the embodied life experiences of women, and is closely related to a woman's speaking voice. The author of this kind of writing "signifies ... with her body." Contrasted against the univocal, authoritative, **phallo(go)centric** (language as a patriarchal-centered system) (see **Irigaray, Lacan**), and disembodied voice of the father identified with the symbolic order of things, *écriture feminine* is multivocal, "pregnant with beginnings," subversive, embodied, and resisting closure. In this kind of writing, moreover, there is a bond not only between the text and the body that wrote it, but also between that body and its original bond with the mother. The bond is symbolized in the concept of **white ink**, or writing in breast milk, conveying the ideal of the maternal bond. Literally, it is about women telling their own stories. There are echoes of Cixous in Nancy Sorkin Rabinowitz's frequently quoted Introduction to *Feminist Theory and the Classics* (p. 1): "If I decide to 'speak for myself,' which of my many voices would I adopt? ... I am a white, bourgeois, Jewish woman, who is 'married with children,' as well as a Hellenist ..." In the lyrical voice of *écriture feminine*, one can hear the mother's song as heard by the child before she could speak, that first voice which all women preserve in their own living voices.

Creating feminine subjectivities by writing through the body has the potential to disrupt masculinist discourse, which has dominated classical studies for so long. As Barbara Gold and others have pointed out, gender categories in antiquity are fluid rather than fixed, rendering the past an ideal milieu within which to explore the *écriture feminine*. For example, in "The House I Live in is Not My Own," Gold shows how Juvenal portrays the ideal character (male) as having an outward appearance that matches his inner character, whereas women conceal their outer and hence, their inner selves. Juvenal characterizes those persons who do not comfortably fit into one or the other gender category as females. And Gold goes on to elucidate how Juvenal also peoples his *Satires* with hybrid, gendered beings that resist easy categorization. Cixous' work has additional implications for considering identity with regard to migration as well as hybridity, which challenge us to work through her concepts in the study of texts and material culture. Miriam Leonard (In "Creating a Dawn") has viewed Cixous' engagement with classical antiquity through her translations of the plays of Aeschylus as a fusion of the traditionally opposed poles of Hebraism and Hellenism (also, **Levinas**), thus enabling her to examine the role of classical discourses within broader political and national agendas and stereotypes.

Further reading

By Cixous

"The Laugh of the Medusa." Translated by Keith Cohen and Paula Cohen of a revised version of "Le rire de la Méduse." *Signs* 1 (1975) 875–93.
With Catherine Clément. *The Newly Born Woman*. Translated by Betsy Wing. Minnesota: University of Minnesota Press, 1986.
"Coming to Writing" and Other Essays. Edited by Deborah Jenson and translated by Sarah Cornell, Deborah Jenson, Ann Liddle, and Susan Sellers. Cambridge: Harvard University Press, 1991.
Les Euménides/Eschyle: Théâtre du Soleil. Paris: Théâtre du Soleil, 1992.
"We Who Are We, Are We Free?" Oxford Amnesty Lecture, February 1992. Translated by Chris Miller. *Critical Inquiry* 19 (1993) 201–19.
"Without End No State of Drawingness No, Rather: The Executioner's Taking Off." Translated by Catherine A.F. MacGillivray. *New Literary History* 24 (1993) 91–103.
The Hélène Cixous Reader. Edited by Susan Sellers. New York and London: Routledge, 1994.
Three Steps on the Ladder of Writing. Translated by Sarah Cornell and Susan Sellers. New York: Columbia University Press, 1993.
Rootprints: Memory and Life Writing. Edited by Hélène Cixous and Mireille Calle-Gruber and translated by Eric Prenowitz. London and New York: Routledge, 1997.
With Jacques Derrida. *Veils*. Translated by Geoffrey Bennington. Stanford: Stanford University Press, 2001.

About Cixous

Armour, Ellen T. "Recent French Feminist Works." *Religious Studies Review* 17 (1991) 205–208.
Beal, Timothy K. "Subversive Excesses." In *The Book of Hiding: Gender, Ethnicity, Annihilation, and Esther*. London and New York: Routledge, 1997.
Bryant-Bertail, Sarah. "Gender, Empire and Body Politic as Mise en Scène: Mnouchkine's 'Les Atrides,' " *Theatre Journal* 46.1 (1994) 1–30.
Gold, Barbara K. "'But Ariadne was Never There in the First Place': Finding the Female in Roman Poetry." In *Feminist Theory and the Classics*, edited by Nancy Sorkin Rabinowitz and Amy Richlin. New York and London: Routledge, 1993.
Gold, Barbara K. "'The House I Live in is Not My Own,': Women's Bodies in Juvenal's *Satires*," *Arethusa*. 31.3 (1998) 369–86.
*Leonard, Miriam. "Creating a Dawn: Writing Through Antiquity in the Works of Hélène Cixous," *Arethusa*. 33.1 (2000) 121–48.
*Rabinowitz, Nancy Sorkin. "Introduction." In *Feminist Theory and the Classics*, edited by Nancy Sorkin Rabinowitz and Amy Richlin. New York and London: Routledge, 1993.

15 Gilles Deleuze and Félix Guattari

Key concepts:

- rhizome
- arborescence
- schizoanalysis
- body without organs
- deterritoralization
- desiring machines
- concepts

Gilles Deleuze (1925–95) was born in France in 1925 and, after a long and chronic battle with cancer, committed suicide in November 1995. He studied at the Sorbonne under Georges Canguilhem and Jean Hyppolite. He proceeded to teach philosophy at the Sorbonne, the University of Lyon, and, at the invitation of Michel **Foucault**, at the experimental University of Paris VIII at Vincennes. He retired in 1987. Deleuze was a prolific writer, penning individual monographs—which he termed a "philosophical geography"—on philosophy, literature, and art. This work includes important studies of the history of philosophy on Hume, **Nietzsche**, Bergson, Spinoza, Proust, Leibniz, as well as critiques of Kantian and Platonic thought. His work radically rethinks issues such as representation, linguistic meaning, subjectivity, and difference.

Félix Guattari (1930–92) was a practicing psychoanalyst and political activist. He embraced both radical psychotherapy or "anti-psychiatry," and Marxist politics, though he became disillusioned with the French Communist Party after the May 1968 strikes. He worked as a psychoanalyst at the Clinique de la Borde from 1950 until his death and was known for his use of alternative psychoanalytic therapies. Guattari received his training with Jacques **Lacan** at the École freudienne de Paris and underwent analysis with him from 1962 to 1969. Guattari later critiqued some of the central aspects of Lacanian psychoanalytic thought. In addition to his work with Deleuze, Guattari individually published works on psychoanalytic theory and collaborated with other Marxist thinkers and psychoanalysts.

Deleuze and Guattari met in 1969 and started working together soon after. Their collaborations include four books that are especially noteworthy for their dual critique of Marxist and Freudian thought: *Capitalism and Schizophrenia, volume 1: Anti-Oedipus* (1972), *volume 2: A Thousand Plateaus* (1980), *Kafka: Toward A Minor Literature* (1975), and lastly *What Is Philosophy?* (1991). In the two volumes of *Capitalism and Schizophrenia*, Deleuze and Guattari attempt to undermine essentialism and the grand narratives of **Marx, Freud,** and structuralism. A focal part of this attempt to undermine essentialist thought is made evident by their collaboration itself. Guattari's involvement at the Clinique de la Borde centered on experimentation aimed at ending the doctor/patient hierarchy through a collaborative and dynamic methodology. This can be seen as the model for their radical, multivocal writing efforts. Collaboration as a method of inquiry and multivocality define key strains of post-structuralist thought. At the beginning of *A Thousand Plateaus* they offer the following explanation of their work together: "Since each of us was several, there was already a crowd ... To reach, not the point where one no longer says I, but the point where it is no longer of any importance whether one says I. We are no longer ourselves. Each will know his own. We have been aided, inspired, multiplied" (p. 3). Echoing the French poet Arthur Rimbaud's famous declaration that "I is another [*Je suis un autre*]," Deleuze and Guattari present their work as an open system, as a discussion rather than an authoritative tract. It is the product of a multiplicity without unity because there is no author in the traditional sense, whose style or biography grounds the work. This only strengthens their insistent critiques of modernist ideas concerning the primacy of hierarchy, truth, meanings, subjectivity, and representation. The collaborative effort is designed to induce encounters and connections, a folding and unfolding of a line of thought so as to instigate another becoming—a "line of flight." Although the many neologisms they employ are more suggestive than definitive, there is one polyvalent concept that covers a lot of ground: the **rhizome.**

They refer to their collaborations as "rhizome-books." "We call a 'plateau' any multiplicity connected to other multiplicities by superficial underground stems in such a way as to form or extend a rhizome. We are writing this book as a rhizome, it is composed of plateaus," they write (*A Thousand Plateaus*, p. 22). A rhizome is a botanical term referring to a horizontal stem (a root or tuber such as ginger or a potato), usually underground, that sends out roots and shoots from multiple nodes. It is not possible to locate a rhizome's source root. The rhizome serves as a model for a particular type of thinking, for Deleuze and Guattari, which they contrast with an **arborescent** (tree-like) model of thinking that develops from root to trunk to branch to leaf.

Arborescent modes of thought, according to them, are especially characteristic of the grand narratives of modernist, capitalist thought (see **Lyotard**). Resisting these tendencies, their rhizomatic texts create concepts to describe ways of seeing and understanding both of individual subjects and of larger institutional entities. In order to destabilize what they refer to as fascist ways of acting in the world, they arm themselves with concepts like the rhizome, which demand that we think and conceptualize outside established, hegemonic, and naturalized modes of modern commonsense.

It is important to note that despite the tendency to associate Deleuze and Guattari with "postmodernism," they did not themselves see their intellectual project in this light. Guattari, for instance, repudiated postmodernism as "nothing but the last gasp of modernism; nothing, that is, but a reaction to and, in a certain way, a mirror of the formalist abuses and reductions of modernism from which, in the end, it is no different" ("The Postmodern Impasse," p. 109). From here we can see that, according to Deleuze and Guattari, their primary target is the arborescent mode that has dominated Western thought. This is the mode of thought that defines modernism and order: a "formalist abuse and reduction" in that it naturalizes hierarchic orders and gives priority to teleologic narratives of origin. Trees are rooted deep in their native soil, where they begin, branch outward and upward in a hierarchical manner, and don't go back. Deleuze and Guattari observe: "We're tired of trees. We should stop believing in trees, roots, and radicals. They've made us suffer too much. All of arborescent culture is founded on them, from biology to linguistics. Nothing is beautiful or loving or political aside from underground stems and aerial roots, adventitious growths and rhizomes" (*A Thousand Plateaus*, p. 15). According to Deleuze and Guattari, the arborescent mode, which has dominated Western thought, is hegemonic in that it naturalizes hierarchic orders and gives priority to narratives of origin.

Rhizomatic thinking, on the other hand, suggests non-linear and non-hierarchical, polyphonic narratives without origin or central root to serve as the source. "A rhizome," they argue, "has no beginning or end; it is always in the middle, between things, interbeing, *intermezzo* ... the fabric of the rhizome is the conjunction, 'and ... and ... and.' This conjunction carries enough force to shake and uproot the verb 'to be'" (*A Thousand Plateaus*, p. 25). The concept of the rhizome is not localizable; it is always between things, an "acentered, nonhierarchical, nonsignifying system" that, unlike a structure which is formed by points and positions, is composed of "lines of flight" or "deterritorializatons," i.e. "all manner of 'becomings'" (*A Thousand Plateaus*, p. 21). Thus, rhizomatic thinking is a philosophical concept premised on difference and chance, time and not space, becoming rather than being. Without beginning or end, rhizomatic thinking disrupts; it is a play of forces and forms.

To disrupt arborescent thought is to question the modern foundations of the human subject. Arborescence constructs the world in terms of freely choosing, autonomous, individual entities—like freestanding trees. In such a mode of thought, subject–object dichotomies are dominant. Deleuze and Guattari insist upon subverting this order through rhizomatic thinking, which privileges heterogeneity and syntagmatic or relational meaning (see **Sassure**). The rhizome is a conceptual force that undermines the dominant, transcendent interpretations of human subjectivity and history by cultivating heterogeneous relationships. They oppose these transcendent models (e.g. Freudian psychoanalysis) with an immanent mode of interpretation in which becoming is not foreclosed upon, but remains in play.

In *Anti-Oedipus*, Deleuze and Guattari take up the political nature of desire. In many ways this text broke the unquestioned bond that existed in France between psychoanalysis and leftist political parties. They attacked this alliance because it posed a new threat, an authoritative, centralized, fascism of reason—a "state philosophy" that inhibits becoming. Their critique of institutional psychoanalysis as well as their simultaneous creation of a post-Freudian materialism is accomplished with the concept of **schizoanalysis**. Schizoanalysis is a rhizomatic alternative to the arborescent thinking of psychoanalysis. In their schizoanalytic polemic against Freud (and by extension Lacan), they refute his negative notion of desire as lack, which the founder of psychoanalysis explained through the conceptual framework of the Oedipus Complex. For Freud, the Oedipus Complex is universal and ahistorical; it is a putatively natural human disposition. For Deleuze and Guattari, this framework is repressive because it subjects everyone to the same transcendent structure (mother-father-child). Rather than viewing the unconscious as characterized by desire as lack, they understand the unconscious as productive of desire and hence it falls victim to the repressive control of the capitalist state. In analysis, the immanent interpretation of individuals is recast into the transcendent interpretation of Freudian desire, the family triangle. The individual is thereby subjected to the repression and restraint of the psychoanalytic framework, and the patient is subjected to the interpretation of the powerful and authoritative analyst.

Libidinal impulses are instead to be understood as *desire-producing* and therefore potentially disruptive of a capitalist state, which wants to control desire and cast it in negative terms. By extension, culture, language, and other symbolic systems are also repressive because they subject people to their rules and codes. State and cultural institutions think in binary terms, thereby limiting multiplicity and becoming. In an interview conducted with Deleuze and Guattari in 1972, Deleuze explains:

> [*Anti-Oedipus*] is both a criticism of the Oedipus complex and psychoanalysis, and a study of capitalism and the relations between capitalism and schizophrenia. But the first aspect is entirely dependent on the second ... We're proposing schizoanalysis as opposed to psychoanalysis: just look at the two things psychoanalysis can't deal with: it never gets through to anyone's desiring machines, because it is stuck in oedipal

figures or structures; it never gets through to the social investments of the libido, because it's stuck in its domestic investments.

(Negotiations, p. 20)

A desiring machine is connected to a "**body without organs**" (often abbreviated BwO) a term borrowed from avant-garde playwright Antonin Artaud (1896–1948). This concept denies the idea that the person is to be found inside the body, composed of autonomous, self-sustaining, and organized internal forms. Instead, BwO suggests that the person-body is interconnected, exterior, open, multiple, fragmented, provisional, and interpenetrated by other entities. In their words: "There is no such thing as either man or nature now, only a process that produces the one within the other and couples the machines together. Producing-machines, desiring-machines everywhere, schizophrenic machines, all of species life: the self and the non-self, outside and inside, no longer have any meaning whatsoever" (*Anti-Oedipus*, p. 2).

In traditional psychoanalysis, the analysis is always predetermined. The analysand is subjected to the Oedipal framework. Schizoanalysis, on the other hand, is rhizomatic because it "treats the unconscious as an acentered system" and "the issue is to *produce the unconscious*, and with it new statements, different desires: the rhizome is precisely this production of the unconscious" (*A Thousand Plateaus*, p. 18). Deleuze and Guattari privilege the conceptual persona of the schizophrenic because it exemplifies fragmented subjectivity and "a desire lacking nothing, a flux that overcomes barriers and codes, a name that no longer designates any ego" (*Anti-Oedipus*, p. 131). It is the relation the schizophrenic has to desire that serves as the basis of schizoanalysis.

Desire is not conceived of as something to be repressed and/or contained, rather it is a flow that exists prior to any representation of desire in psychoanalysis, prior to any subject-object relation. In traditional psychoanalysis, desire is "territorialized" through political and ideological structures like family, religion, school, medicine, media, etc. What Deleuze and Guattari posit is a "deterritorialized" desire. **Deterritorialization** is desire as flow; it opens up possibility of multiple ways and directions at once, regardless of socially sanctioned boundaries that only seek to domesticate the flow of desire. Deterritorialized desire produces without structure because it is rhizomatic.

It is in the midst of this discussion of deterritorialization that Deleuze and Guattari forward their concept of **desiring machines**. This refers, in part, to the idea that desire stems from a moment prior to structure and representation. Bodies are desiring machines in which such things as ideas, feelings, and desires flow in and out of the body machine and into and out of other desiring machines. The desiring machine is an impersonal concept that serves to negate the personal, subjective representations of the unconscious given in Freud's domestic theatrical metaphor of *ein anderer Schauplatz* and even Lacan's contention that the unconscious is structured like a language.

Schizoanalysis, therefore, seeks to deterritorialize the structures of desire presented by psychoanalytic thought. It resists any discrete, hierarchical structuration, in favor of a fragmented, porous space in which boundaries are fluid, desire flows in multiple directions, and there is no "subject" (as in a being) other than becoming. Schizoanalysis is an attempt to construct a plane of immanence as a means to exit from the "mucky little kingdom" of "state philosophy" (*Negotiations*, p. 17).

Deleuze and Guattari's philosophy is an open system of concepts that relate to circumstances, situations—events—rather than essences. **Concepts** (e.g. the Cartesian *cogito*) are not given, but must be created and invented. In this fundamental act of philosophy—the creation of concepts—philosophers are creative and reflective. In this they are inextricably linked to scientists and artists. These connections are discussed in *What is Philosophy?*, which marks the final collaboration of these two men.

The work of Deleuze and Guattari shows several recurring strands of thought: difference, deterritorialization, distancing, folding and unfolding, non-linear or rhizome thinking, forgetting the status of the structure (whether it is visual or linguistic representation). As a discipline, classics is permeated with arborescent thinking: Whether it is the structure of Indo-European and classical philology with what Irad Malkin (in "Postcolonial Concepts and Ancient Greek Colonization," p. 358) refers to as its subsidiary branches of "languages and races," the genealogical stemma, or the Harris matrix of working out the stratigraphy of an archaeological site. How can it be possible to conceive of classics any other way? In *Experiencing the Past*, the classical archaeologist Michael Shanks has discussed the arborescent thinking that characterizes archaeology and classics in detail. As a way of promoting rhizomatic thinking as an alternative possibility for archaeologists, Shanks suggests "making connections, anarchic associations rather than hierarchical procedures of thinking, denial of final and definitive identities of things in reconstructions" (*Experiencing the Past*, p. 36). The ancient historian Irad Malkin (in "Networks and the Emergence of Greek Identity" and "Postcolonial Concepts and Ancient Greek Colonization") has used rhizomatic thinking to view Greece as relationally part of a pan-Mediterranean culture formed through the concept of the network or the rhizome, whereby there is a seemingly unlimited engagement through contacts in many directions facilitated by the seas and coastlines.

Further reading

By Deleuze and Guattari

Anti-Oedipus: Capitalism and Schizophrenia. Translated by Robert Hurley, Mark Seem, and Helen R. Lane. Minneapolis: University of Minnesota Press, 1983.
A Thousand Plateaus: Capitalism and Schizophrenia. Translated by Brian Massumi. Minneapolis: University of Minnesota Press, 1987.

Kafka: Toward A Minor Literature. Translated by Dana Polan. Minneapolis: University of Minnesota Press, 1986.

What Is Philosophy? Translated by Hugh Tomlinson and Graham Burchell. New York: Columbia University Press, 1994.

Deleuze, Gilles. *Negotiations, 1972–1990.* Translated by Martin Joughin. New York: Columbia University Press, 1995.

Guattari, Félix. "The Postmodern Impasse." In *The Guattari Reader,* edited by Gary Genosko. Oxford: Blackwell, 1996.

About Deleuze and Guattari

Badiou, Alain. *Deleuze: The Clamor of Being.* Translated by Louise Burchill. Minneapolis: University of Minnesota Press, 2000.

*Bogue, Ronald. *Deleuze and Guattari.* London and New York: Routledge, 1989.

Buchanan, Ian (ed). *A Deleuzian Century?* Durham, NC: Duke University Press, 1999.

Buchanan, Ian and Colebrook, Claire (eds). *Deleuze and Feminist Theory.* Edinburgh: Edinburgh University Press, 2000.

Hardt, Michael. *Gilles Deleuze: An Apprenticeship in Philosophy.* Minneapolis: University of Minnesota Press, 1993.

Malkin, Irad. "Postcolonial Concepts and Ancient Greek Colonization." *Modern Language Quarterly.* 65.3 (2004) 341–64.

*Malkin, Irad. "Networks and the Emergence of Greek Identity." *Mediterranean Historical Review.* 18.2 (2003) 56–74.

Massumi, Brian. *A User's Guide to Capitalism and Schizophrenia: Deviations from Deleuze and Guattari.* Cambridge, MA: MIT Press, 1992.

Olkowshi, Dorothea. *Gilles Deleuze and the Ruin of Representation.* Berkeley, CA: University of California Press, 1999.

*Shanks, Michael. *Experiencing the Past: On the Character of Archaeology.* London: Routledge, 1992.

Stivale, Charles. *The Two-Fold Thought of Deleuze and Guattari: Intersections and Animations.* New York: Guilford Press, 1998.

16 Jacques Derrida

Key concepts:

- *aporia*
- closure
- deconstruction
- *il n'y a pas hors-texte* (there is nothing outside the text)
- trace
- *différance*
- erasure
- trait
- *parergon*

Jacques Derrida (1930–2004) was born to a middle-class Sephardic Jewish family in the Algerian suburb of El-Biar. During World War II, when he was ten years old, he and other Jews were expelled from the public school system. Later, with the arrival of Allied forces, Derrida enrolled in a Jewish school. He moved to France when he was 19 years old and began his studies at the Grandes École preparatory program and studied phenomenology with Emmanuel **Levinas**. He went on to teach at the École normale supérieure and the École des hautes études in Paris; in addition he held teaching posts at several American universities, including Johns Hopkins, New York University, and the University of California at Irvine. Throughout his career Derrida demonstrated a strong commitment to public education, especially through his work with the Research Group on the Teaching of Philosophy, which advocates making philosophy a fundamental discipline in secondary school curricula. His social and political activism was associated more with particular causes than with party politics and matched by his unparalleled reputation and a critical style that has been often imitated but not reproduced. Derrida's passing in

November 2004 from pancreatic cancer marks a decisive loss for all those who knew him and who were compelled by his work.

It would be impossible to summarize Derrida's work and influence to date, even if we were to limit ourselves to his contributions to philosophy, literary theory, cultural studies, religion, and art history. Yet there is a consistent orientation throughout his many texts. This orientation could be described as a close and critical reading, giving relentless attention to how the fundamental presuppositions of Western thought are articulated. Derrida's attention to the paradoxes or **aporias** of Western thought is undertaken to reveal the uncertainties, instabilities, inconsistencies, and impasses implicit in our intellectual traditions, moving us to the edge of knowing, to a point at which "what once seemed assured is now revealed in its precariousness" ("An Interview with Derrida," p. 110). This is not, as his critics allege, done out of nihilistic contempt for all things Western or as a result of a masturbatory fascination with groundless intellectual free play. It is done to challenge our habitual assumptions about "how things are" so as to open up discursive space for continued reflection and the possibility of innovative and creative thinking, by keeping texts in "play." He treats the Western intellectual tradition as a living discourse and works to keep our intellectual disciplines and educational institutions from ossifying by resisting **closure**.

This is the proper context in which to understand the term **deconstruction**, a concept that has too often been alternatively misunderstood or misapplied by Derrida's readers. He first used the term in *Of Grammatology* (1967). (The English translation and accompanying introduction were done by Gayatri Chakravorty **Spivak**.) The term was developed and refined while Derrida was a member of the Yale School of Literary Criticism, along with Harold Bloom, Paul de Man, Geoffrey Hartman, and J. Hillis Miller in the late 1960s and early 1970s. Derrida's usage arose from his engagement with Martin **Heidegger**'s term *Destruktion* or *Abbau*. In French translation, Heidegger's term carried the sense of annihilation or demolition as well as destructuration. When Derrida published his text, the term "deconstruction" was seldom used in France, where its primary sense was mechanical, referring to the process of disassembly in order to understand parts in relation to the whole. For Derrida, deconstruction was conceived not as a negative operation aimed only at tearing down, but rather as a kind of close analysis that seeks "to understand how an 'ensemble' was constituted and to reconstruct it to this end" ("Letter to a Japanese Friend," p. 272). It is in the process of reading closely, with an eye for how a discourse is constructed and framed, that one also comes to see the points of potential instability as well as excluded elements within the structure of a text. Deconstruction is the event that happens within a close reading, and it is this devotion to and emphasis on critical analysis that places deconstruction both within and apart from a larger hermeneutic tradition (see **Gadamer**). In one of many statements in which Derrida asserts that deconstruction is not a method of analysis or a critique, we read:

> Deconstruction takes place, it is an event that does not await the deliberation, consciousness, or organization of a subject, or even of modernity. *It deconstructs it-self. It can be deconstructed* [*Ça se déconstruit.*]
> ("Letter to a Japanese Friend," p. 274).

Deconstruction happens to both the text at-hand, the one being closely read, and to the interpretation itself, thus, there is nothing outside the text (**il n'y a pas hors-texte**) (*Of Grammatology*, p. 158).

Deconstruction, then, is what happens when one works through a certain logic of thinking in such a way as to reach what that logic cannot admit, what it must exclude, the unthinkable upon which that very logic is premised. Terry Eagleton offers this summation:

> Deconstruction is the name given to the critical operation by which oppositions can be partly undermined, or by which they can be shown partly to undermine each other in the process of textual meaning ... The tactic of deconstructive criticism ... is to show how texts come to embarrass their own ruling systems of logic; and deconstruction shows this by fastening on the 'symptomatic' points, the aporia or impasses of meaning, where texts get into trouble, come unstuck, offer to contradict themselves.
> (*Literary Theory: An Introduction*, p. 132–4)

What is crucial to remember here is that Derrida does not pose deconstruction as a proper name, nor as a transcendent method of interpretation. The happening of deconstruction occurs in the situation of the text and its interpretation, both poles of which presuppose a limit, a border. "The deconstructive reading," as Barbara Johnson, one of Derrida's early English translators, puts it, "does not point out the flaws or weaknesses or stupidities of an author, but the *necessity* with which what he *does* see is symmetrically related to what he does *not* see" ("Translator's Introduction," *Dissemination*, p. xv). Thus, any text can be subjected to a close and critical reading, and the bounded nature of every text implies that all texts contain the seeds of their own deconstruction (see also **Barthes, Kristeva**).

Throughout his career, Derrida was criticized for writing texts that are too difficult for many readers to understand. Such texts are sometimes referred to as producer texts, in that the reader is required to actively engage with, and reflect upon the text in order to understand it, rather than passively absorbing an already digested body of information. He defended himself by insisting that his texts require so much from the reader because they are fundamentally concerned with questioning precisely those things we think we understand. Derrida's texts are not mere expositions of his ideas, but—in an attempt to undermine even this notion of a representation of ideas—they are performances of his arguments. This performance takes the form of writing, but a writing that does not claim to represent ideas. "No one gets angry with a mathematician or with a doctor he doesn't understand at all, or with someone who speaks a foreign language, but when somebody touches your own language ..." ("An Interview with Derrida," p. 107). The tendency to not critique obfuscation in these other fields can be seen as bound up in our modern reverence for science.

Derrida first articulates this position in 1967, with the simultaneous publication of three books: *Speech and Phenomena*, a treatise on Edmund Husserl's phenomenology; *Of Grammatology*, a critique of how Western theories of language and communication have privileged speech over writing; and *Writing and Difference*, a collection of essays (some written as early as 1959) offering close readings of major contemporary thinkers including Claude Lévi-Strauss and Georges **Bataille**. With the publication of these texts Derrida emerged as a major force in contemporary philosophy and literary studies. Five years later, in 1972, he published three more texts: *Dissemination*, also on writing with attention paid to Plato, Mallarmé, and Sigmund **Freud**; *Positions*, a collection of interviews with him; and *Margins of Philosophy*, readings of and in the margins of philosophical texts. The fact that many of Derrida's writings engage the work of other theorists and philosophers in a detailed manner, frequently limits the accessibility of the work of Derrida and other theorists to the casual reader as these works contain numerous references to the works of earlier scholars. The less familiar the reader is with the works being discussed, the less s/he will be able to understand, requiring a major investment of time and effort on the part of the reader or reliance on a mediating text to begin to understand many of the issues under discussion. Thus, understanding is gradual and comes in stages, rather than through an "add theory and stir" approach.

In 1967, a year before his first set of texts was published, Derrida gave a lecture at Johns Hopkins University entitled "Structure, Sign, and Play in the Discourse of the Human Sciences" (later published in *Writing and Difference*). More than any other, it is this essay that led to the widespread association of Derrida with "post-structuralism," a term coined not by Derrida but by American literary scholars who appropriated his theories for their own research. However, if post-structuralism is to be regarded as a critique of structuralism, the association is relevant, with many scholars frequently using the terms deconstruction, post-structuralism, and postmodernism interchangeably to the extent that they may seem meaningless without some kind of contextualization.

In this lecture, Derrida situates his work in the aftermath of the intellectual revolution of structuralism, which he views as a transformative moment that destabilized the inherited understandings about the stability of language and meaning in Western thought. He describes this complex transformation as the "moment when language invaded the universal problematic, the moment when, in the absence of a center or origin, everything became discourse ... that is to say, a system in which the central signified, the original transcendental signified, is never absolutely present outside a system of differences" ("Structure, Sign, and Play," p. 280, see also **Barthes**). Here Derrida expresses his appreciation for the discourse inaugurated by Ferdinand de **Saussure** while simultaneously pressing the implications of structuralism. Rather than limiting Saussure's model to written or even visual texts, Derrida argues for a "generalized text" in which "reality" as such exists as a kind of indeterminate linguistic flux. This absence of a structural center or ordering (first) principle ("God," "Being," or some other transcendental signified) in language, one that would guarantee meaning and coherence within its system of signification, "extends the domain and the play of signification infinitely," he insists (p. 280). Derrida is not simply undermining Saussurean structuralism in the name of an infinite and unstable play of meaning; rather he is calling attention to the radical implication identified by structuralism, namely that *there is nothing outside language* to control, limit, or direct the play of signification, which is deferred. This reading posits that if signs are not inherently stable, then neither is meaning. It is an ultimate "undecidability" that pervades all language. Contra to the either-or of paradigmatic meaning associated with structuralism, the ever presence of these undecidable elements poisons any oppositional logic.

Derrida proceeds to consider what our options are in the wake of the crisis in meaning he has just described. He identifies two responses, two "interpretations of interpretation." On the one hand, there is a melancholic, remorseful nostalgia for origins, a longing for "archaic and natural innocence" that "seeks to decipher, dreams of deciphering a truth or an origin which escapes play ... and which lives the necessity of interpretation as exile" (p. 292). Derrida reads Lévi-Strauss' search for the foundational, structural, elements of myth as an example of this mode of interpretation. On the other hand, there is the exuberant affirmation of play in a world without center or ground or security, as exemplified in the work of Friedrich **Nietzsche**. Both are responses to the modern Western experience of being ungrounded and dislocated. While one longs with nostalgia for that which is forever lost, the other gets lost in limitless, deracinated play.

Perhaps one of the clearest examples of the change brought about by this argument is the visual and textual arrangement of Derrida's performative text *Glas* (1974). This text comprises two vertical columns, which are interrupted by quoted statements in different fonts to represent the voices of different authors. The left-hand column is about G. W. F. Hegel; the-right hand column is about the French writer Jean Genet. Derrida desires to open the discourse of philosophy to literature by challenging the traditional notions of authorship and even what constitutes a "literary" work. His method of composition—at the time, a kind of radical collage self-consciously copied by some archaeologists, though now, rather dated—is taken from artistic practice. The title *Glas* functions as an undecidable. In French the word means "knell" (like the ringing of bells in a "death knell"), but when spoken it sounds like *glace*, meaning ice, mirror, or window. Here, the multiple meanings expressed through speech and writing may be constructed as a "hinge" [*brisure*] between literature and philosophy so as to suspend any sense of an impervious border between two disciplines founded on "writing." All of these meanings remain in play in this and in Derrida's other texts as puns, which enhance the performative aspect of his work, but which are frequently lost in the English translations.

The argument Derrida performs in *Glas* stems from his discussion of speech and writing in his earlier work, especially *Of Grammatology*. Derrida's early work is an extended meditation on how the boundaries of philosophical discourse are created and sustained, as well as how philosophy conceives of language as a means to arrive at concepts such as "truth" and "presence." Beginning with the privileging of speech over writing that Derrida reads in one of the founding texts of Western philosophy, Plato's *Phaedrus*, he proceeds to cast a rather large net over various categories of meaningful expression that ensnares everything from poetry to architecture. Derrida argues that speech is conceived as closer to thought, and thus writing is considered derivative, supplemental to speech as thought. Western philosophy is characterized by this logocentrism: a history of speech as presence, or a repression of writing. Derrida displaces the "origin" [*arche*] of both speech and writing in a concept of "arche-writing," a trace. This is meant to undermine metaphysical thinking by challenging its notion of presence. It is speech that has been given this task of carrying full presence, whereas writing is associated with distance, delay, and ambiguity. By writing a letter to a friend, for instance, the writer is absent and yet the trace of his/her presence is conjured. Neither simply present, nor absent, the trace is undecidable: a play of presence and absence at the very "origin" of any system of meaning, and hence an apt concept to employ in the study of classical texts and material culture.

Beyond addressing the inherent instability of language, Derrida's reinscription of "writing" as an undecidable play at work in both speech and writing challenges any discursive structure premised on presence and, by extension, traditional notions of "truth" or "being." Writing, for him, must be iterable—repeatable but with difference. This marks the entrance of Derrida's famous concept of *différance*, a pun indicating that the meaning(s) signified by signifiers are always different and deferred to their relationships with other signifiers. Thus the meaning of a signifier is always partly deferred or partially inscribed in other signifiers, rendering all signifiers incomplete and hence under **erasure** or *sous rature*, yet carrying **traces** of deferred meanings. Such deferrals take place in space and time. Writing, for Derrida, signifies an event: the *an-archic* deconstruction of Western philosophy.

By turning his attention to iterability and how meaning is construed as *différance*, Derrida proceeds to argue that not even context can ensure the reception of intent in language. No context can enclose iterability. This does not eradicate context, but it can no longer entirely govern or guarantee meaning. Recall how Derrida's texts are not outside of the texts he reads. Rather than being in a transcendent position of authority, his texts are implicit within the host text he explicates. His strategy, therefore, is one of rehearsal (*répétition*). Derrida rehearses or reiterates the texts he reads; he enacts them again in order to deconstruct them. Therefore, as Derrida acknowledges, his texts bear the "traits" of the others. The performances Derrida enacts in his "writerly texts" (see **Barthes**) aim only at the deconstruction of presence; his work is an extended meditation on the presence-absence of the trace. This meditation is extended to his commentaries on artworks and aesthetics, which may be understood on another level as metaphorical meditations on signification, distanciation, and interpretation. Derrida's famous discussion of the frame (*parergon*, that which is extrinsic to the work, what is by-the-work) is an extension of his thinking on the "hinge" between speech and writing, philosophy and literature.

> This hinge [*brisure*] of language as writing, this discontinuity ... marks the impossibility that a sign, the unity of a signifier and a signified, be produced within the plenitude of a present and an absolute presence ... Before thinking to reduce it or to restore the meaning of the full speech which claims to be truth, one must ask the question of meaning and of its origin in difference. Such is the place of a problematic of the *trace* (...) To recognize writing in speech, that is to say difference and the absence of speech, is to begin to think the lure. There is no ethics without the presence of *the other* but also, and consequently, without absence, dissimulation, detour, difference, writing. The arche-writing is the origin of morality as of immorality. The nonethical opening of ethics. A violent opening.
>
> (*Of Grammatology*, pp. 69–70, 139–40)

In his later writings Derrida examines ethics, hospitality, and forgiveness (texts where the importance of **Levinas** is especially felt), but before he turns to these concepts his work encounters aesthetics. In this sense, the hinge between his notion of writing and ethics passes through the creation and reception of art.

Derrida's interest in what he terms the "spatial arts" receives its most extended discussion in *The Truth in Painting* (1978). Here he engages the Italian artist Valerio Adami's "Drawings After *Glas*," a work that participates in a dialogue with Derrida's performative text. Through his reading of the fragmented, phonetic symbols that pervade Adami's drawings—gl, tr, +R—Derrida argues that this decomposed language signifies the very materiality of language and questions concerning the inherent instability of meaning return in Derrida's discussion of Adami's work.

One of the tasks Derrida sets himself in *The Truth in Painting* is to interrogate the fundamental concepts of aesthetics. He situates his text in "a matrix of inquiry" that asks "what defines the limits of my domain, the limits of a corpus, the legitimacy of questions, and so on" (*Deconstruction in the Visual Arts*, p. 9). Derrida focuses on the ways in which aesthetic discourse is written, equally shifting between its two disciplinary frames—art history and philosophy. In doing so he extends the scope of deconstruction beyond what is traditionally thought of as "textual." He insists that "the most effective deconstruction, and I have often said this, is one that deals with the nondiscursive, or with discursive institutions that don't have the form of written discourse" (*Deconstruction in the Visual Arts*, p. 14). However, what Derrida proceeds to do, as suggested by his reading of Adami's work, is to reveal how and why aesthetics is a discursive practice and what the epistemological and ethical consequences of this *ekphrasis*—the verbal description of an artwork—are. There is always already something that exceeds the border—or frame—of the context.

Derrida situates *The Truth in Painting* amid three of the most important texts of aesthetics: Immanuel Kant's *Critique of Judgment*, Hegel's *Lectures on Aesthetics*, and Heidegger's essay "The Origin of the Work of Art." Derrida begins by simply re-asking the basic questions of aesthetics. What is a work of art? How has our experience of the work of art been described? What are the criteria by which it can be judged or evaluated? These are questions that are just as much, if not more relevant to classical archaeology as they are to art history.

It is a discourse, however, not on the work of art itself [*ergon*], but rather on its frame, the **parergon**, that which encloses and defines an inside while creating an outside that is of equal if not greater significance in the *Truth in Painting*. *Parergon* in Greek signifies what is incidental, what is "by-the-work." The frame of a work of art is what separates the work from what is extrinsic to it, and yet the frame maintains a discourse between this interior and its exterior. In Kant's work, the frame, the room in which a work of art is to be found, and any ornament (e.g., drapery) whatsoever constitute the *parerga*. Derrida divulges that there is no way we can be sure about these imposed limits or borders; the frame functions not as a barrier but as a "hinge" that simultaneously breaks with all that is extrinsic to the work and yet remains connected to it. The initial attempt by aesthetics to define its object of study falls into disarray because without a clearly defined object, the "science of aesthetics" cannot guarantee its concepts of aesthetic experience, judgment and/or truth. The frame also serves as another opportunity for Derrida to forward his theory of the "generalized text" because there is no object of study specific to aesthetics; there is no frame that defines and polices the borders between philosophy and other disciplines. The ironic status of both disciplinarity and defining a context is thus, called into question.

This situation allows Derrida to return to a statement made by Cézanne in a 1905 letter to Emile Bernard: "I owe you the truth in painting and I will tell it to you" (cited in *The Truth in Painting*, p. 2). Derrida plays with this notion of "rendering" the truth: It is what is owed as much as what is represented ("rendered"). Derrida does not simply come out and announce the "truth in painting." In his thinking, this would be to fall victim again to the logic of presence that he attempts to deconstruct. Rather, he states: "I write four times here, *around* painting" (*The Truth in Painting*, p. 9). The first pass "around painting" follows the frame, the *parergon* that, which is neither inside nor outside the work—the determining limit of the work of art. This is where he deals with Kant, Hegel, and Heidegger. The second iteration is his reading of the "*graphic* traits" in Adami's work. The third pass allows Derrida to extend his discussion of the signature and to develop the concept of the "countersignature," which brings into play the entirety of the exhibition-reception system of a work of art. In the final "writing around" Derrida turns his attention to *ekphrasis*, particularly how Heidegger and Meyer Shapiro write about as well as *overwrite* a painting by Vincent Van Gogh entitled "Old Shoes" (1886–7). Derrida refers to this final section as a "polylogue," where he critiques the appropriation of the painting by means of language.

This situation characterizes not simply aesthetics, but also archaeology and literature, where writing and commentary mediates the object, for unknown present and future readers. One way that Derrida deals with this situation is to reject the authorial, magisterial voice of the art historian who translates the visual into text. On the contrary, he suggests that any writing on or around a work of art is a refracted self-portrait, a ruin of presence (see the work of Walter **Benjamin**). Derrida's ideas here operate on (at least) two levels. First of all, material culture is always textually mediated through description, photographs, and drawings, so that the result is always something more and something less than the original, and a product of scholarly authority. On another level, Derrida's discussion of the frame is a metaphor for the limits or rules of exclusion placed on discourse. A frame circumscribes every text: whether it is a lecture, a book, an article, or a thesis, and thus, all are subject to deconstruction by virtue of what they exclude.

The importance of Derrida's work lies not in the answers he gives to the fundamental questions of understanding text or material culture (there is no unified post-structuralist approach), but in its uncanny ability to present those same questions in a new light and to keep fundamental questions in play. How does classics constitute its object of study? Where does the discipline locate meaning(s)? How, where, and why does it construct its frameworks of interpretation and disciplinary practice? Why does the discipline resist theory? What forms do the arguments take that bridge the gap between past and present? How is the past written in and into the present? These questions will continue to haunt classics as long as the *traits* that Derrida drew through epistemology, aesthetics, and politics are taken as discrete structures rather than as an ensemble that must be rehearsed. Whenever these questions are posed, in the margins of that text, Derrida will have been a presence-absence.

Further reading

By Derrida

Writing and Difference. Translated by Alan Bass. Chicago: University of Chicago Press, 1978.

* *Positions*. Translated by Alan Bass. Chicago: University of Chicago Press, 1981.

Dissemination. Translated by Barbara Johnson. Chicago: University of Chicago Press, 1981.

"An Interview with Derrida." Translated by David Allison. In *Derrida and Difference*, edited by David Wood and Robert Bernasconi. Warwick: Parousia Press, 1985.

* *The Truth in Painting*. Translated by Geoff Bennington and Ian McLeod. Chicago: University of Chicago Press, 1987.

Glas. Translated by John P. Leavey, Jr. and Richard Rand. Lincoln: University of Nebraska Press, 1986.

"Letter to a Japanese Friend." In *A Derrida Reader: Between the Blinds*, edited by Peggy Kamuf. New York: Columbia University Press, 1991.

Memoirs of the Blind. Chicago: University of Chicago Press, 1993.

"The Spatial Arts: An Interview with Jacques Derrida." In *Deconstruction and the Visual Arts*, edited by P. Brunette and D. Wills. Cambridge: Cambridge University Press, 1994.

* *Of Grammatology*. Translated by Gayatri Spivak. Baltimore: Johns Hopkins University Press, 1976; corrected edition 1998.

Acts of Religion. Edited by Gil Anidjar. New York and London: Routledge, 2002.

About Derrida

Arac, Jonathan *et al.* (eds). *The Yale Critics: Deconstruction in America*. Minneapolis: University of Minnesota Press, 1983.

Beardsworth, Richard. *Derrida and the Political*. London and New York: Routledge, 1996.

Benjamin, Andrew. (ed.). *Post-Structuralist Classics*. London and New York: Routledge, 1988.

Brunette, Peter and David Wills (eds). *Deconstruction in the Visual Arts*. Cambridge: Cambridge University Press, 1993.

Culler, Jonathan. *On Deconstruction: Thought and Criticism After Structuralism*. London and New York: Routledge, 1983.

Duro, Paul (ed.). *The Rhetoric of the Frame: Essays on the Boundaries of the Artwork*. Cambridge: Cambridge University Press, 1996.

Eagleton, Terry. *Literary Theory: An Introduction*. Minneapolis: University of Minnesota Press, 1989.

Hamacher, Werner. "The End of Art with the Mask." In *Hegel After Derrida*, edited by Stuart Barnett. London and New York: Routledge, 1998.

Hitchcock, Louise, and Koudounaris, Paul. "Virtual discourse: Arthur Evans and the reconstructions of the Minoan palace at Knossos." In *Labyrinth Revisited: Rethinking 'Minoan' Archaeology*, edited by Yannis Hamilakis. Oxford and Oakville: Oxbow, 2002.

Maharaj, Marat. "Pop Art's Pharmacies." *Art History*, 15 (1992).

Melville, Stephen. "Aesthetic Detachment: Review of Jacques Derrida, *The Truth in Painting*." In *Seams: Art as a Philosophical Context*, edited by Jeremy Gilbert-Rolfe. Amsterdam: G+B Arts, 1996.

Menke-Eggers, Christoph. *The Sovereignty of Art: Aesthetic Negativity in Adorno and Derrida*. Cambridge, MA: MIT Press, 1998.

Spivak, Gayatri. "Appendix on Deconstruction." In *A Critique of Postcolonial Reason: Toward a History of the Vanishing Present*. Cambridge, MA: Harvard University Press, 1999.

Wigley, Mark. *The Architecture of Deconstruction: Derrida's Haunt*. Cambridge, MA: MIT Press, 1993.

Wood, David (ed.). *Derrida: A Critical Reader*. Oxford: Blackwell, 1992.

Yates, Timothy. "Jaques Derrida: 'There is Nothing Outside of the Text'." In *Reading Material Culture*, edited by Christopher Tilley. Oxford: Blackwell, 1990.

17 Michel Foucault

Key concepts:

- discipline
- biopolitics
- archaeology of knowledge
- discourse
- genealogy
- rupture
- translation
- ethics
- resemblance/similitude

Michel Foucault (1926–84) was a French philosopher, social and intellectual historian, and renowned cultural critic. He was born in Poitiers, the son of upper-middle-class parents. He went to Paris after World War II where he was admitted to the esteemed École normale supérieure in 1946. There he received his *agrégation* in philosophy in 1952 under the guidance of Georges Canguilhem. Like many other French intellectuals in the 1940s and 1950s, Foucault, at the suggestion of Louis **Althusser**, became a member of the French Communist Party in 1950, but he left the party in 1953.

During the 1950s and early 1960s Foucault held teaching positions at various European universities while conducting research and writing his first widely influential books, including *Madness and Civilization* (1961), *The Birth of the Clinic* (1963), and *The Order of Things* (1966). This last became a bestseller in France and made Foucault a celebrity.

In response to the May 1968 strikes and student demonstrations, the French government opened the University of Paris VIII at Vincennes. Foucault, who had been working at the University of Tunis since 1966, was immediately named chair of its philosophy department. In 1970 Foucault was elected to the Collège de France, the country's most prestigious academic institution. This permanent appointment as professor of the history of systems of thought provided him with a position in which he could devote nearly all his time to research and writing. His only teaching-related responsibility was to give an annual sequence of a dozen or so public lectures on his work. Among these lectures was the famous "What is an Author," delivered in 1969.

During this period Foucault also became increasingly involved in social and political activism. His advocacy of prisoner rights, for example, influenced his history of the prison system, *Discipline and Punish* (1975). Around this same time he turned his attention to sexuality, publishing the first of three volumes on *The History of Sexuality* in 1976. He completed the other two volumes shortly before his death from AIDS-related complications in 1984.

Although classical scholarship has actively participated in the critique of Foucault's exclusion of the feminine or their treatment as objects in his research on sexuality, which he links to a broader discourse of patriarchal power and ideology, there is little doubt that the questions and issues he raises have permanently affected the way we understand the humanities and social sciences. In addition, classicists have roundly criticized Foucault for glossing over and ignoring ancient sexuality and the relevance of his categories, thus contributing to a misleading view of sexuality in the ancient world. Still, his work has inspired what James Porter (In "Foucault's Antiquity" p. 171) calls the "Foucault effect," the proposition that "subjects/sexuality are culturally constructed, not naturally given." Despite its shortcomings, Foucault's scholarly output is impressive for its quantity as well as for its breadth of interests and insight. His work relentlessly challenges what counts as commonsense knowledge about human nature, history, and politics, identifying it as culturally constructed and historically situated. Moreover, he questions the assumptions of thinkers such as Sigmund **Freud** and Karl **Marx** whose ideas underlie Western intellectual thought.

Foucault's theories are developed out of his concepts of biopolitics, discourse, subjectivity, and knowledge power. These concepts can be positioned within three areas that were central to Foucault's cultural analysis: (1) the archaeology of knowledge, (2) the genealogy of power, and (3) ethics. Underlying all three areas is a concern with the notion of the subject and subjection, i.e., the process by which a human subject is constructed. (Judith **Butler** elaborates on the paradoxes of subjection, in relation to Foucault.)

Foucault's work explores the parameters of what he calls the "human sciences," that academic field in which humanistic and social science discourses construct knowledge and subjectivity. He analyzes how various institutions (psychiatric clinics, prisons, schools, hospitals, etc.) produce bodies of knowledge in and through which people are **disciplined** into becoming modern subjects. In this process Foucault has brilliantly shown how bodies of disciplinary knowledge and power co-construct each other and are thus, inextricably bound together and wielded in what he calls **biopolitics.**

He explains that power in modernity is biopolitical; it is not merely about a simple top-down subjugation, rather biopolitics exceeds the traditional juridical-political order by pervading bodies through defining the lives of its subjects. The concept of biopolitical power is also relevant to the study of the past. For example, the study of Romanization in both text and material culture provides a unique opportunity to study how subjects were constituted in the past through the imposition of certain regimes, such as Roman forms of hygiene, which were introduced into the provinces.

The **archaeology of knowledge** is both the title of Foucault's 1969 book and the name he gives to his method of historical and epistemological inquiry. There, the concept of archaeology is used metaphorically, to uncover the history of **discourses**, that is, institutionally defined and constrained statements of knowledge about a particular topic. His concern is not with historical "truth," but rather with understanding how discursive formations—for example, the medical discourse on sexuality—come to be seen as natural and self-evident, accurately representing a body of knowledge. His attempt to uncover the structures and rules through which regimes of knowledge are constructed and implemented is informed by, but not limited to, structuralist thought. In the preface to *The Order of Things* Foucault explains his method: "... what I am attempting to bring to light is the epistemological field, the *episteme* in which knowledge, envisaged apart from all criteria having reference to its rational value or to objective forms, grounds its positivity and thereby manifests a history which is not that of its growing perfection, but rather that of its conditions of possibility" (p. xxii). It is discursive knowledge that determines the "conditions of possibility" that Foucault desires to reveal.

Institutionally constrained discourses or bodies of knowledge regulate what can be said and done, what constitutes right and wrong, and what counts for knowledge in the first place. In other words, institutions establish and control the production of, and access to, knowledge. Foucault's archaeological method regards discourse as fluid yet systematic, as well as mutable yet stable. For instance, the medical discourse of the Renaissance bears no necessary similarity to contemporary medical discourse, yet each has a distinctive historical archive. The goal of Foucault's work is not to uncover the "quasi-continuity" between these periods, which, in his mind, is the misguided work of traditional historiography. On the contrary, he insists that the goal of his work "has not been to analyze the phenomena of power, nor to elaborate the foundations of such an analysis. My objective, instead, has been to create a history of the different modes by which, in our culture, human beings are made subjects" ("The Subject and Power," p. 208). Thus, he has examined discourses of madness, reason, and mental asylums in *Madness and Civilization* and discourses of medical practices and the medical "gaze" in *The Birth of the Clinic*.

During the 1970s Foucault devoted his attention to what he described as the genealogy of power, a history of the meanings and effects of power and how discourse and other "technologics of power" are employed to discipline human behavior. The term **genealogy** is used by Foucault to refer to a mode of historical analysis that he develops in texts such as *Discipline and Punish* (1975) and the first volume of *The History of Sexuality: An Introduction*. The concept of genealogy is borrowed from Friedrich **Nietzsche**, who published *On the Genealogy of Morals* in 1887. Foucault addresses his debt to Nietzsche in his 1971 essay "Nietzsche, Genealogy, History."

In this essay Foucault advances an alternative to the traditional narration of history. He critiques the teleology of traditional historiography, wherein historical events are narrated as a simple relation of causes and effects that produce human events. In this scheme events can be traced, in a linear and logical fashion, backward to origins. To counter this epistemic structure, Foucault posits that historical narrative is fragmented, nonlinear, discontinuous, and hence **ruptured**. Thus, historical narratives exist without being grounded in the certitude of cause and effect. His concept of genealogy, which is a refinement of his notion of archaeology, does not rest on any point of origin, whether it is an active human subject or the authoritative voice of the historian. "Genealogy," he writes, "is gray, meticulous and patiently documentary. It operates on a field of tangled and confused parchments, on documents that have been scratched over and recopied many times" ("Nietzsche, Genealogy, History," p. 139). For Foucault, then, history is a sometimes ambiguous and often conflicting textual narrative. History bears the marks of repeated emendations—additions, deletions, embellishments, **translations** (see **Benjamin**) and other textual manipulations—that makes it impossible to follow a cause-and-effect lineage back to an origin. A historical origin is thus something at once obscured and unrecoverable. Historical truth suffers a similar fate in this critique. Following Nietzsche, Foucault interprets any claim to historical truth, any claim by a historian or cultural critic of being *dans le vrai*, as an error and as yet another instance of knowledge power. His critique opposes the conception of history as an unbroken continuum, such as the one implied in the view of Greece as the ethnically pure childhood of European democracy, a teleology again promoted in the opening ceremonies of the Olympic ceremonies in Athens.

Genealogy as a method underscores the interpretive nature of any narration of the past. Moreover, it presents the past as always and inevitably read through contemporary interests and concerns. Objectivity is abandoned in favor of acknowledging the historian's political and ideological investment in the narrative being told. Even if historical truth exists, Foucault argues, historians have no particular or privileged access to it. He is most interested in understanding historical documents as discourses of knowledge, and hence, power, that foreground some perspectives while suppressing others. He wants to reread the past and narrate the story from other perspectives; from perspectives that disrupt the fiction of the unitary and originary historical past as such. In this desire to narrate a counterpractice, Foucault concentrates on minor elements, "accidents," and other elements of discourse that exceed their ideological emplacement in the order of things. This genealogical approach interrupts any idea of history as relating the "truth" of past events—of telling what "actually" happened. Rather than chasing after some ephemeral grand narrative that silences any discontinuities, Foucault seeks to interpret the past in ways that will not deny the ambiguity, contingency, and struggle that must accompany any genealogical analysis. (There is a clear tie to Walter **Benjamin**'s philosophy of history here.) Because the historian must admit the place from which s/he enunciates any narrative of history, the myth of history as a unified and transcendental story fragments into a multiplicity of narratives about the past. For example, histories of ancient Greece written from the perspective of women, Persians, and/or archaeological remains would be multivalent and privilege different ideas and groups of individuals. Thus, we begin to understand the historical past not as static, fixed, and transcendental—as a reified object placed before us—but as a continually changing narrative discourse contingent upon and written in terms of the present. Additionally, Foucault's methods can also be applied to the study of discourses of power and regimes of representation in the past.

Foucault applies his genealogical analysis to the history of power, exploring how power operates to produce particular kinds of subjects. For him, power is not a monolithic, unchanging force; instead, it has a genealogy and a context. For instance, a Marxist view of power as the force wielded by governments, corporations, and others who control the economic means of production is very different from a feminist view of patriarchal power. Resisting these totalizing systems of thought, Foucault's genealogy of power is multivalent. In "The Subject and Power" (1982), he insists that the concept of power must always include the possibility of resistance to power. Power, therefore, is always a relationship that creates subjects, but it can always be resisted. In other words, we can oppose the subject positions that discourses and material practices consign us.

It has been said that Foucault's work forecloses upon the very possibility of change because he rejects the liberal humanist ideology of agency, but the challenge his work presents lies in being able to discern the underlying thesis of all his work: the possibility of biopolitical discursive change. As he stated in a lecture at Dartmouth College given in 1980: "I have tried to get out from the philosophy of the subject through a genealogy of this subject, by studying the constitution of the subject across history which has led us up to the modern concept of the self. This has not always been an easy task, since most historians prefer a history of social processes, and most philosophers prefer a subject without history" ("About the Beginning of the Hermeneutics of the Self," p. 160). A genealogical view of subjectivity is Foucault's attempt to abandon the idealized and essentializing conceptions of the human subject as a singular, transcendent entity.

Foucault's later work is devoted to the issue of the "ethics of self." **Ethics** here, however, does not simply refer to moral behavior of the individual.

Instead, Foucault is interested in identifying the "technologies" of the self, i.e., the constitution of a particular human subject resulting from regulated forms of behavior. Such technologies, which include sexual, political, juridical, educational, and religious patterns of behavior, may be taken for granted, going completely unnoticed by the subject who is constituted by them. Nonetheless, they function to *discipline* the body and mind, constituting the subject within a larger order of power knowledge. Technologies of the self are subjugating practices that create and shape one's sense of self. These practices are not universal, but are cultural and/or institutional, varying over time and place. Foucault demonstrates that these technologies of the self are also practices "which permit individuals to effect by their own means, or with the help of others a certain number of operations on their own bodies and souls, thoughts, conduct, and way of being, so as to transform themselves in order to attain a certain state of happiness, purity, wisdom, perfection, or immortality" ("Technologies of the Self," p. 146). Significant here is the ethical idea that individuals can attempt to resist power and transform their own subjectivity.

Foucault's discussion of ethics thus contrasts the Greek notion of ethics as simply a matter of personal choice that emphasizes the rational control of deviant desires with his call for an "ethics of the self" that challenges the presupposed benefits of the discourse of mastery, control, and repression. However, what he suggests in its place is a more general view of the Greek notion of ethics as "an aesthetics of existence." "What strikes me," Foucault explained in an interview from 1983, "is the fact that in our society, art has become something which is related only to objects and not to individuals, or to life. That art is something which is specialized or which is done by experts who are artists. But couldn't everyone's life become a work of art? Why should the lamp or the house be an art object, but not our life" ("On the Genealogy of Ethics: An Overview of Work in Progress," p. 350). What Foucault calls for here is not a blind utopian project, but rather an "aesthetics of existence" that does not transcend discourse as much as it explores the limits and the possibility of difference within the same.

Foucault's work on the "technologies of the self" is devoted to understanding how various systems of representation construct individuals as subjects. This and the ethical question of an "aesthetic of existence" intersect with the discipline of classics in numerous ways. As a collection of discursive practices, the discipline of classics prescribes our modern relation to ancient texts and material culture. Much of a student's time is spent undertaking the study of difficult languages, while passively assimilating and mastering a large body of textual material. The heavily footnoted text upholds the tyranny of the discipline, which is kept in place by referencing a long genealogy of scholarly authority, a trope of homage to the ancestors of the discipline. It is a system of learning, which students are discouraged from questioning. Although most classics programs have one individual that focuses on literary criticism, and sometimes even gender, discursive practices have been re-enforced through the elitism, sexism, and racism which in the past have privileged white male patriarchal modes of discourse in classics (e.g., Attic history and topography), and is frequently re-enforced through gender imbalance in departments of classics. Although gender imbalance may be more of a problem outside of North America, structural changes are merely cosmetic if female classicists conform to and uphold masculinist forms of discourse, codes of behavior, and power structures. To deviate from the established scholarly norm means to risk being denied access to academic rewards such as scholarships, jobs, and a forum to present one's ideas.

The tyranny of the text also permeates classical archaeology, where large bodies of data are disciplined according to typologies, which privilege order and categorization over meaning and interpretation, yet their status is also ironic and historically contingent. At the beginning of *The Order of Things* (p. xv–xxi), Foucault describes Borges' Chinese encyclopedia, which appears odd to the Western observer with its unusual categories such as sirens and sucking pigs. The categories vary from the embalmed to the frenzied and the fabulous, thus illustrating the arbitrary, cultural, and subjective nature of typologies. In his discussion of the Chinese encyclopedia, Foucault (1992: xix) warns us that taxonomies lead us "to a kind of thought without space, (reduced) to words and categories that lack all life and place." He explains that the exotic charm of the system of thought that produced the Chinese encyclopedia is that it demonstrates the limitations of our own system of thought in its unlikeliness to make such distinctions. They are symptomatic of an archaeological project rooted in the ceremonial space of a disciplinary discourse in which description and classification frequently passes for knowledge and explanation.

Foucault's engagement with the work of the Belgian Surrealist Magritte in *This is Not a Pipe* (1973), explores the meanings of Magritte's famous *Ceci n'est pas une pipe* (1926) in which a visual representation of a pipe is seemingly negated by a handwritten script. The inclusion of text within the painting challenges the discursive code that prohibits the inclusion of the linguistic within the visual. In the short text Foucault posits two principles that dominate painting from the fifteenth to twentieth century: "the separation between plastic representation (which implies resemblance) and linguistic reference (which excludes it)" and "an equivalence between the fact of resemblance and the affirmation of a representative bond" (*This is Not a Pipe*, pp. 32, 34). Foucault acknowledges the absence of a common ground, a commonplace, between the visual and the linguistic, but it is precisely within this threshold that Magritte creates his works. The argument hinges on Foucault's distinction between resemblance and similitude. "To me," he writes, "it appears that Magritte dissociated similitude from resemblance, and brought the former into play against the latter" (p. 44). **Resemblance**, for Foucault, has a "model," a referent or an "origin" that "orders and hierarchizes the increasingly less faithful copies that can be struck from it ... [it] serves representation, which rules over it" (p. 44). On the other hand, **similitude** develops in series that have neither beginning nor end, that can be followed in one direction as easily as in another, that obey no hierarchy, but propagate themselves from small differences among small differences ... similitude serves repetition, which ranges across it. Resemblance predicates itself upon a model it must return to and reveal; similitude circulates as an infinite and reversible relation of the similar to the similar.

(p. 44)

What Foucault argues here is that similitude is not a mimetic representation, but it is a series, an open-ended exchange. In Magritte's work there is a rejection of resemblance ("This is not a pipe"), and in its place there is sketched only "an open network of similitudes" (p. 47). Magritte severs the system of representation from the thing itself. Furthermore, Foucault argues that modern and contemporary art are systems of similitude—simulacra in much the same way Jean **Baudrillard** discusses the term—wherein text and image ceaselessly circulate around "the ghost of the thing-itself" (p. 49). This argument can easily be extended to include ancient art and its reproductions, representations, and endless catalogs because they are interpreted and written about in and into the present. What Magritte's painting inaugurates, thus allows Foucault to conclude that "the 'This is a pipe' silently hidden in mimetic representation has become the 'This is not a pipe' of circulating similitudes" (p. 54).

The equivalences of the similar, the repetition of the same, allow us also to conceive of the opposite, and hence, the "possibility of change" Foucault sought throughout his work. A change Foucault here terms difference. From out of the repetition of the same, it is possible that difference can present itself. Foucault's work provides us with the opportunity to rethink and reconfigure our regimes of representation in order to both make change possible and remain viable.

Further reading

By Foucault

The Order of Things: An Archaeology of the Human Sciences. Translated by Alan Sheridan. New York: Vintage, 1970.

Madness and Civilization: A History of Insanity in the Age of Reason. Translated by Richard Howard. New York: Vintage, 1973.

The Birth of the Clinic: An Archaeology of Medical Perception. Translated by A. M. Sheridan-Smith. New York: Pantheon, 1973.

*The Archaeology of Knowledge. Translated by A. M. Sheridan-Smith. London: Tavistock, 1974.

"Nietzsche, Genealogy, History" and "Theatrum Philosophicum." In *Language, Counter-Memory, Practice: Selected Essays and Interviews*, edited by Donald F. Bouchard. Ithaca: Cornell University Press, 1977.

132   *The Theorists*

The History of Sexuality, vol. I: An Introduction. Translated by Robert Hurley. New York: Vintage, 1978.

*"The Subject and Power." Afterword to *Michel Foucault: Beyond Structuralism and Hermenuetics*, edited by Hubert L. Dreyfus and Paul Rabinow. Chicago: University of Chicago Press, 1983.

This is Not a Pipe. Translated by James Harkness. Berkeley: University of California Press, 1983.

"On the Genealogy of Ethics: An Overview of Work in Progress." In *The Foucault Reader*, edited by Paul Rabinow. New York: Pantheon, 1984.

Foucault Live: Interviews, 1961–84. Edited by Sylvere Lotringer. New York: Semiotext(e), 1996.

"About the Beginning of the Hermeneutics of the Self." In *Religion and Culture*, edited by Jeremy R. Carrette. London and New York: Routledge, 1999.

"Technologies of the Self." In *The Essential Foucault*, edited by Paul Rabinow and Nikolas Rose. New York: The New Press, 2003.

About Foucault

Bennett, Tony. *The Birth of the Museum: History, Theory, Politics*. London and New York: Routledge, 1995.

Carroll, David. *Paraesthetics: Foucault, Lyotard, Derrida*. New York: Methuen, 1987.

Danaher, Geoff, Tony Schirato, and Jen Webb. *Understanding Foucault*. London: Sage Publications, 2000.

Deleuze, Gilles. *Foucault*. Translated by Seán Hand. Minneapolis: University of Minnesota Press, 1988.

Dreyfus, Hubert L. and Rabinow, Paul. *Michel Foucault: Beyond Structuralism and Hermeneutics*. 2nd edn. Chicago: University of Chicago Press, 1983.

Greene, Ellen. "Sappho, Foucault, and Women's Erotics," *Arethusa* 29.1 (1996) pp. 1–14.

Gutting, Gary (ed.). *The Cambridge Companion to Foucault*. Cambridge: Cambridge University Press, 1994.

Halperin, David M. "Forgetting Foucault: Acts, Identities, and the History of Sexuality." *Representations* 63 (1998) 93–120.

McNay, Louis. *Foucault: A Critical Introduction*. New York: Continuum, 1994.

Mills, Sara. *Michel Foucault*. London and New York: Routledge, 2003.

*Morris, Ian. "Archaeologies of Greece." In *Classical Greece: Ancient histories and modern archaeologies*, edited by Ian Morris. Cambridge: Cambridge University Press, 1994.

O'Leary, Timothy. *Foucault: The Art of Ethics*. New York: Continuum, 2002.

Porter, James I. "Foucault's Antiquity." In *Classics and the Uses of Reception*, edited by Richard Thomas and Charles Martindale. Oxford: Blackwell, 2006.

Richlin, Amy. "Zeus and Metis: Foucault, Feminism, Classics." *Helios* 18 (1991) 160–80.

Shapiro, Gary. *Archaeologies of Vision: Foucault and Nietzsche on Seeing and Saying*. Chicago: University of Chicago Press, 2003.

*Tilley, Christopher. "Michel Foucault: Towards an Archaeology of Archaeology," in *Reading Material Culture*. Edited by Christopher Tilley. Oxford: Blackwell, 1990.

18 Hans-Georg Gadamer

Hans-Georg Gadamer (1900–2002) was born in Marburg, Germany and moved to Breslau (now Wroclaw, Poland) in 1902. His father was a professor of chemistry at the University of Breslau and later directed a pharmaceutical institute. He began his study of philosophy and classical philology at the University of Breslau in 1918 and moved to University of Marbug in 1919, completing his Ph.D. there on Plato in 1922. Although his life was marked by personal tragedies, including the loss of his mother at an early age, caring for a disabled brother, and suffering from polio, he earned his *Habilitation*, entitled *Interpretation of Plato's Philebus*, under the direction of Martin Heidegger in 1928 (published in 1931). He held posts at the universities of Marburg, Leipzig, Frankfurt, and moved to Heidelberg in 1949, where he remained until his death. Despite his retirement in 1968, Gadamer remained active in research and writing until his death in 2002.

Along with Heidegger and the philosopher of religion Paul Ricoeur, Gadamer is one of the most important twentieth-century scholars of **hermeneutics** (from Greek, *hermeneutice* and connected to the name of the Greek god Hermes, the messenger), the science and art of interpretation, a field of study that has its ancient beginnings in Platonic philosophy and in biblical exegesis. In Gadamer's work, hermeneutics is transformed from the science of interpretation to the science of *understanding*. As such, it replaces metaphysics and epistemology as lords of the human sciences, addressing how humans find meaning and understand themselves and the world.

Although prolific, with ten volumes of collected works, Gadamer's best-known and most influential work is *Truth and Method*, published in German in 1960 and translated into English in 1975. There he develops a theory of understanding that is both linguistic and historical. Understanding takes form in language, and its form would be different if it were to develop in another semiotic field or according to other terms. Language is not simply a tool one uses to communicate, but the medium in which one lives and moves and has one's being. There is no understanding of oneself or of another without language. One is born and raised and formed as a subject within a language. Indeed, language is "the house of being." Likewise, there is no such thing as understanding that is not rooted in a particular historical context. Following Heidegger's concept of Being as *Dasein*, "there-being," Gadamer insists that a human being is always already located, that is, "here." Human existence is always being-in-the-world, and there is no way for a human being to eradicate its historical-cultural situatedness from its understanding of anything. Gadamer describes this historical and linguistic situatedness of the human being as a person's *Wirkungsgeschichte*, or "**effective history.**"

Yet there is another side to the hermeneutical event, another horizon or range of possibilities. There is something—a work of art, a text, a cultural artifact, an idea—that is "other," that the human encounters and seeks to understand. Understanding is the process in which that "other" thing or idea or person is made meaningful, that is, understood. Gadamer describes this process of understanding as a **fusion of horizons**. On the one hand, there is the horizon of the one who wants to understand, located within that person's particular historical and linguistic context and shaped by its pre-existing traditions, its effective history. On the other hand, there is the thing or person or text that someone is trying to understand. And that other horizon emerges from its own more or less unfamiliar historical, cultural, and linguistic context. In the hermeneutical process, that is, the process of interpretation, the horizon of the interpreter fuses with that other horizon, creating a new meaning through dialogical interaction that is not identical to the monologue of the interpreter. Gadamer can be regarded a theorist of dialog, influenced by Platonic tradition. In practice, hermeneutics takes place through a careful **reading** of the aspects (text or material culture) of the past one is dealing with and through "conversation" or a process of question and answer. It is a productive activity that requires both being immersed in context and moving between contexts. There is an aspect of **contemporaneity** (*Gleichzeitigkeit*) in this process, whereby the relevance of ancient texts is recognized as speaking in the present; thus, Gadamer resists the of historicism of relegating the past to the past.

Although the historian, R. G. Collingwood, whose work has heavily influenced contemporary archaeological practice (most notably Ian Hodder), influenced Gadamer's hermeneutics, there are key differences. Collingwood's approach emphasizes reenactment and empathy, reconstructing the past as an experience lived through the mind of the historian. Critics who regard Collingwood's approach seriously treat it as more of an internalized process that privileges past meanings and is thus historicist, standing in contrast to the attempt to fuse the horizons of past and present.

Gadamer's theory of understanding as historical and linguistic involves a critique of Enlightenment thought, with its ideal of the objective interpreter who remains detached from all cultural influences that threaten to **prejudice** one's understanding and thus, can be said to stand outside of history. Understanding always involves pre-understanding. We are always already historically situated, shaped by our cultures (e.g., social, ethnic, institutional, disciplinary, and gendered) and language, and that situatedness or context shapes our understandings of everything. We bring our own horizon, our own effective history, as a prejudice to any moment of understanding. For Gadamer, "the prejudices of the individual, far more than his judgments constitute the historical reality of his being" (*Truth and Method*, p. 245). Gadamer's critique of objectivity and acknowledging of infinite possibilities in the back and forth of interpretation between past and present places him in the discourse of postmodernism. However, hermeneutics differs from deconstruction, which also engages in a careful reading, in having a goal in mind in terms of assigning meaning to a body of data, rather than privileging critique.

Gadamer's rehabilitation of prejudice by an interpreter's cultural context put his theory of hermeneutics in direct conflict with the tradition of ideological critique, insofar as it suggested that there is no non-ideological position from which to critique an ideology. This made Gadamer appear to some that he was returning to a precritical position and led to a now-famous series of debates with Jürgen Habermas, who contended that Gadamer's position does not adequately recognize the ways ideology can distort communication through the hidden, underlying expression of force masked by ideology (see Ricoeur, "Hermeneutics and the Critique of Ideology"). He also argued that Gadamer places too much weight on the power of our historical and linguistic context as that which constitutes us. Habermas, by contrast, called for more of an orientation toward the future, with an emancipatory interest in what ought to be rather than what was and is. This raises the issue of how the study of the past can be used to improve the future, by writing about it in a way that engages with or is relevant to the present. It has been suggested that one way to go about this is to emphasize the "otherness" of the past, which sits on a continuum alternating between strangeness and familiarity. Cultural relativism is held in check by the evidence of the past. One of the implications of the notion of prejudice is that an objective past cannot be recovered, and even limiting oneself to the practice of documenting the past (text or objects) is interpretive, as well as historically and culturally situated.

Despite being a philosopher and philologist, Gadamer frequently applied his theory of hermeneutics to the study of religious myths and scriptures (see, for instance, the essays collected in *Hermeneutics, Religion, and Ethics*). Late in life, at 92, he made a particularly significant contribution to a small symposium on religion organized by the philosopher Jacques **Derrida** and Gianni Vattimo. A central topic for the conference was "Religion and the Religions," that is, the relation between universal ideas and theories of religion on the one hand and actual, historical religions as they are practiced on the other. Can we talk about "religion" in general? Is there such a thing as "religion?" In his contribution to the conference, "Dialogues in Capri," Gadamer makes a point that merits our attention here.

Regarding the search for a universal theory of religion (which often characterizes an anthropological approach), Gadamer suggests that the one thing that all religions have in common is the "ubiquitous knowledge of one's own death and at the same time the impossibility of the actual experience of death" (p. 205). On the one hand, I know I will die. On the other hand, I cannot actually experience that death, because my death is the end of me as a sentient, experiencing being. Religion, Gadamer proposes, is always in some sense about negotiating that tension, which is at the very core to be human. The centrality of death is at the core of ancient society and religion, with the presence of grave goods suggesting to many that belief in an afterlife is among the earliest identifiable evidence of religious belief.

Within the fields of classics and classical archaeology, Gadamer's work has been and has the potential to be extremely influential, particularly in its application to Aegean iconography and architecture. In particular, his theory of hermeneutics has provided a central conceptual framework for exploring how ancient life, tradition, and culture can be reimagined and reconstituted in relation to new horizons of interpretation. It is also beginning to play a key role in reception studies, that is, the role of the past in the present. Hermeneutics is well-suited to the classics as careful reading has always characterized classical scholarship. In addition, hermeneutical approaches have played a key role in identifying the problems involved in interpreting the past, namely that an academic community within the humanities is an interpretive community and that its interpretations are always unique fusions of horizons. Historical traditions (in the past and present) are always a dynamic of interpretation and hermeneutics emphasizes these practices as dynamic and dialogic interpretive processes, thus challenging the study of the past as a fixed set of ideas and institutions.

Further reading

By Gadamer

Philosophical Hermeneutics. Edited by David E. Linge. Berkeley: University of California Press, 1976.

Dialogue and Dialectic: Eight Hermeneutical Studies on Plato. Translated by P. Christopher Smith. New Haven: Yale University Press, 1980.

Plato's Dialectical Ethics. Translated by Robert M. Wallace. New Haven: Yale University Press, 1991.

Truth and Method. 2nd rev. edn. Translated by Garrett Barden and John Cumming. Revised translation by Joel Weinsheimer and Donald G. Marshall. New York: Crossroad, 1993.

About Gadamer

Dostal, Robert J. *The Cambridge Companion to Gadamer.* New York: Cambridge University Press, 2002.

Grondin, Jean. *Hans-Georg Gadamer: A Biography.* Translated by Joel Weinsheimer. New Haven: Yale University Press, 2003.

*Johnsen, Harald and Olsen, Bjornar. "Hermeneutics and Archaeology: On the Philosophy of Contextual Archaeology." *American Antiquity* 57.3 (1992) 419–36.

*Morgan, Livia. "Idea, Idiom and Iconography." In *L'Iconographie Minoenne.* Edited by Pascal Darque and Jean-Claude Poursat. *Bulletin de correspondance hellénique Supplement* 11 (1985) 5–19.

Palmer, Richard. *Dialogue and Deconstruction: The Gadamer-Derrida Encounter.* Albany: State University of New York Press, 1989.

*Ricoer, Paul. "Hermeneutics and the Critique of Ideology." In *Hermeneutics and Modern Philosophy*, edited by Brice R. Wachterhauser. Albany: State University of New York Press, 1986.

Vardoulakis, Dimitrios. "The Vicissitude of Completeness: Gadamer's Criticism of Collingwood." *International Journal of Philosophical Studies.* 12.1 (2004) 3–19.

19 Martin Heidegger

Key concepts:

- Being
- Dasein
- aletheia
- clearing
- the work of the work of art
- world and earth

Martin Heidegger (1889–1976) is one of the most influential and contro-versial thinkers of the twentieth century. Born in 1889 to a Catholic family from Messkirch in Baden, Germany, Heidegger's early life was marked by an intense interest in religion. From a young age he wanted to become a priest. This culminated in two years of theological study at Freiburg University, but Heidegger ultimately changed paths. In 1911 he began studying natural science and mathematics, which led to a doctorate in philosophy with a dissertation entitled *The Doctrine of Judgment in Psychologism* (1913). Heidegger's goal was to be appointed as Freiburg's professor in Catholic philosophy. His qualifying dissertation [*Habilitationsschrift*] on John Duns Scotus, a medieval philosopher and theologian, did not get him the post and so in 1915 Heidegger began his teaching career as a lecturer at Freiburg. It is at this time that Heidegger developed a personal relationship with Edmund Husserl, the founder of phenomenology. Heidegger's work on Duns Scotus had been influenced by Husserl's thought, but it was not until this time at Freiburg before and after World War I that Heidegger shifted his interests from Catholic philosophy to phenomenology.

In 1919, Heidegger turned his attention to the work of Aristotle, Sören Kierkegaard, and Friedrich **Nietzsche**, but his major influence continued to be Husserl, with whom Heidegger worked closely. Heidegger's own growth as a thinker owes much to his close reading of his mentor's *Logical Investigations* (1900–01). Eventually, Heidegger broke away from the phenomenology of Husserl with its attendant notion of the transcendental consciousness in order to develop his own system of thought, resulting in the publication of *Sein und Zeit [Being and Time]* in 1927. During the interwar period, Heidegger married Elfride Petri, a Lutheran, and they had two sons, both of whom served in Hitler's *Wehrmacht*. In addition, Heidegger began a year-long affair with Hannah Arendt, the German-Jewish philosopher, in 1925. Arendt was one of Heidegger's most promising students, but their affair was unable to withstand the strain caused by Heidegger's support for Nazism. Arendt and Heidegger did, however, maintain a friendship through correspondence and occasional visits that lasted until Arendt's death in 1975.

Heidegger's engagement with Nazism during the 1930s has been the source of warranted unease regarding his thought. When the Nazis rose to power, Heidegger deluded himself into eliding his philosophy with the ultimate aims of Hitler—most problematically, that of the fulfillment of the destiny of the German people. Heidegger's biography and especially the work completed during this period of Nazi affiliation (including his essay "The Origin of the Work of Art") are marred by many unanswered questions regarding Heidegger's avowed conservative and nationalistic support for Hitler's policies, which resulted in his joining the Nazi party and being elected director of Freiburg University in 1933. Heidegger was forced to resign from his post in 1934 when the Nazis determined his lectures and his desire to integrate the goals of Nationalist Socialism into the life of the university were of no direct use to the party. After the war, Heidegger was not allowed to teach in Germany due to his support of the Nazis. In 1950 he was allowed to resume lecturing at Freiburg and elsewhere. He died in 1976 at his home in Zähringen.

Heidegger's work is central to any discussion of post-structuralism, post-Marxism, and identity politics. He has been especially influential in France, on the writings of Jean-Paul Sartre, Jacques **Derrida**, Michel **Foucault**, Jacques **Lacan**, and Gilles **Deleuze**, despite the fact that many of these thinkers are Jewish. Perhaps this paradox is best demonstrated by the Romanian poet Paul Celan's 1967 visit with Heidegger in Todtnauberg. Celan survived a Nazi labor camp, but his parents were less fortunate. His poetry is driven by an attempt to interrogate the threshold between language and experience. The question arises Why did Celan accept Heidegger's invitation and why did he describe the three-day visit as "most happy and productive?" What remains especially problematic, as Celan himself discovered, is Heidegger's silence: his refusal to discuss, explain, or even attempt to justify (if that is at all possible) his support of Nazism. In spite of this silence, Heidegger's work has received a critical reading that does not foreclose upon the potentiality of his thought. It is crucial that the issue of Heidegger and Nazism be addressed in the starkest of terms, but the conclusion of this address must not be a complete rejection. As Jürgen Habermas has stated, the goal is "to think Heidegger against Heidegger." This is a question of ethics and politics, a question of critical reading—one of the primary lessons of theory as such. It is for this reason that Derrida argues: "Why isn't the case closed? Why is Heidegger's trial never over and done with? ... we have to, we've *already* had to, respect the possibility *and* impossibility of this rule: *that it remains to come*" (Derrida, *Points*, pp. 193–4).

Heidegger's *Being and Time* is one of the more difficult texts in the history of philosophy. This is in no small part because of his ambition to enact a radical "destructuring" [*Destruktion*] of the entire metaphysical tradition. Toward this end, Heidegger redefines the normative terms of philosophical discourse: "subject", "object", "being", "thought", etc. This is the first step because he sets out to "destruct" the structures and semantics that have accrued around and over the sole subject of his work: **Being** [*Sein*]. By Being, Heidegger does not mean the traditional concern of metaphysics, the being of beings, i.e., the essence of an entity [*Seiend*], whether a dog or a hammer. Rather, Heidegger is after an un-presupposed Being, an intransitive Being, the meaning of Being as such. This is what he terms "fundamental ontology." In many ways, his primary question is "what is 'is'?" *To be* rather than *to be something*, this is Heidegger's starting point, one he claims has been neglected and forgotten throughout the history of Western metaphysics. In order to begin addressing these issues Heidegger first has to "destruct" metaphysics: the meaning of existence, the duality of thought and matter since Descartes, and even Husserl's phenomenology. For Heidegger, the history of metaphysics is the history of the concealment of Being. In contrast, he posits "thinking" as that, which can take into view *Being as Being*, Being as such. Many of the central elements of this "thinking" are found in *Being and Time*.

Heidegger posits that the human being [*Dasein*] is defined by a process of becoming; **Dasein** is disclosive because it always already has an understanding of Being. Dasein is not subjectivity or rationality, but describes the specificity of human being as an entity. This process of becoming being is a movement of disclosing and understanding Being, whether it is that of Dasein or other entities. Therefore, Dasein is defined by its very openness to itself (as the becoming disclosedness of Being) and its openness to other entities. Heidegger terms this openness "the there" [*das Da*] because Dasein makes possible the disclosure of its own existence as openness. In addition, this self-disclosure (Being related to itself) allows for the disclosure of other beings: the being there [*Da-sein*] of other beings.

He also argues that the meaning of Dasein is "being-in-the-world." Contrary to the *ego cogito* of Descartes and even the concept of the ego forwarded by Sigmund **Freud**, each of whom construct their respective worlds, Heidegger argues that Dasein is thrown into a pre-existing world of historically constituted situations, moods, and a determinate use of language. Dasein, he insists, is defined by its "thrownness" [*Geworfenheit*]—it's always already being-in-the-world. In other words, there is never a moment when

Dasein is not absorbed in the world, i.e., absorbed in social discourse. At the same time, however, Dasein is also constructed in time. In fact, the essence of Dasein is temporal. While Dasein is beleaguered with the being thrown into the world and the demands made upon it by *das Man* ["the They"], the anonymous field of the other, it is also a projection into the future. Thus Dasein is a "thrown projection" [*geworfener Entwurf*]. This becoming-absent of Dasein—its being-unto-death, its mortality—opens up the field of significance for Being as such because the temporality of Dasein is the horizon for any disclosure of Being. The temporality of Dasein is central to the realm of disclosure Heidegger terms "the Open," i.e., the very "topology of Being" that his work sets out to think ("The Thinker as Poet," p. 12).

To describe the temporal situation of Dasein in relation to Being, the becoming present of what one already is—*the being there that defines Dasein*—Heidegger recuperates a Greek term, *alethia*. The term means disclosure or unconcealment. Heidegger's interest in this term stems from its prefix *a-* (un- or dis-), which indicates a privation or an absence at the heart of this concept of unconcealment. This prefix shelters the root of the term and, by extension, the root of truth—the presence of Being: *lethia*, concealment. *Alethia* was the ancient Greek word for truth, but Heidegger reclaims and redefines the term neither as the truth of metaphysics nor as the designation of a correct proposition, but as the truth of thinking. His conception of *aletheia* defines the very process of the becoming present of Being. This becoming present is determined by disclosure, the anticipation of absence. *Aletheia* is a central term in Heidegger's thought because it indicates the play of absence and presence that organizes any thinking about Being. In *aletheia*, what was concealed comes to presence, by being drawn out of secrecy and darkness, but never completely. This coming to presence is partial and discursive because every presence of Being is predicated on the absence of Being. It is this structure of disclosure that delimits the field of significance. In other words, the topology of Being is a presence-absence—an *aletheia*—in which all entities are defined in their being as becoming "the there" of Da-sein. In his early work, Heidegger is insistent that disclosure never happens except in Dasein as Da-sein. In *Torture and Truth*, Page du Bois gives a darker reading of Heidegger's conception of *aletheia*, likening it to a fascination with secrecy and violence congruent with his animosity to democracy. Truth, whether in the mind of a philosopher or of a slave, can only be motivated by coercion and interrogation.

For Heidegger, disclosure-as-such occurs in a certain place. In *Being and Time*, the place was Dasein, which is defined as a being that held itself open to beings as Da-sein. However, Heidegger's thought undergoes a change in the 1930s. It is important to recall that *Being and Time* represents only one-third of Heidegger's initial project. His inability to shift from the analytic of Dasein to the interrogation of Being as such caused him to rethink the place of disclosure. Heidegger ultimately proposes the concept of the "**clearing**" [*Lichtung*] as the place of disclosure. The "clearing" is a threshold beyond

Dasein. In fact, Dasein exists (*ex-sists* as Heidegger writes it to denote its constitutive lack of immanence), along with all other entities, in the "clearing." What is made present in the "clearing" is the disclosure of Being. In the "clearing" a being (e.g. a hammer) appears in a certain way, as a tool or as something dangerous. Appearing in one aspect of its being conceals another. Every unconcealing is predicated on a concealing and what is concealed are other possibilities. "Each being we encounter," Heidegger writes, "and which encounters us keeps to this curious opposition of presence in that it always withholds itself at the same time in a concealedness" ("The Origin of the Work of Art," p. 52). In abandoning his thesis that one must account for one particular entity (Dasein) before one can talk about being as such, Heidegger turns to other paradigms that allow him to discuss Being. The primary and related ones are poetry, art, and technology. Although the means of discussing the disclosure of Being changes, Dasein remains a central character, less in its essence than in its use of language and in its productions.

Influenced by Heidegger's notion of "Being-in-the world," Julian Thomas, (*Time, Culture and Identity*) views monuments as the outcome of a process of transformation whereby social relations are established or negotiated. Similarly, the occurrence of new styles in the production of ancient objects structure experience and performance in the creation of social identities. Furthermore, knowledgeable individuals draw on different traditions to create distinct identities. Thus artifacts and texts acquire multiple layers of meaning in the temporal process of being used in the past and read and re-read in the present.

Among Heidegger's most important later works is "The Origin of the Work of Art" (1935–6), which includes an "Addendum" written by Heidegger in 1956. The draft of this essay was written as early as 1931, and in November of 1935 he lectured publicly on the subject. The long essay is divided into three sections: "Thing and Work," "The Work and Truth," and "Truth and Art." Each of these sections is organized around a single example: Vincent Van Gogh's "Old Shoes" (1886–7), the fifth century BCE Doric Temple of Hera II in Paestum (Italy), and the poetry of Freidrich Hölderlin.

Heidegger's interest lies in understanding "**the work of the work of art.**" What "work" does the work of art accomplish? In attempting to answer this pressing question he distinguishes between the work of art as a specific entity (a particular painting or poem) and art itself. Art itself here means the essence or the origin of all art. Art is important to Heidegger because, for him, it is a unique kind of disclosure: The work of art is able to disclose not merely an entity but the disclosure-as-such of that entity's being. The work of the work of art, Heidegger argues, is the "installation"—the setting-into-work [*Sich-ins-Werk-setzen*]—of *aletheia*, the "fixing into place" and "letting happen" of truth.

The work of art reveals the happening of **world** and **earth**. The world, as discussed above, is the realm of human activity and relations into which

Dasein is thrown. But in this essay Heidegger expands his understanding of this concept of world. "There is only 'world' where there is language, that is, understanding of being," he insists (In *Four Seminars*, p. 32). Earth refers not only to nature and natural entities, a mass of matter, or an astronomical idea of a planet; instead it is that "on which and in which man bases his dwelling ... that which comes forth and shelters ... effortless and untiring" ("Origin," pp. 41, 45). The world as "the self-disclosing openness of the broad paths of the simple and essential decision in the destiny of a historical people" and the earth as the realm of concealment, sheltering and preserving, are inextricable from one another ("Origin," p. 47). These two concepts, Heidegger explains, are bound in "strife" [*Steit*]. This "strife" is not disorder; rather Heidegger conceives it in a way that is very similar to Hegel's original understanding of the term "sublation" [*Aufhebung*]. Heidegger writes that in "strife" "the opponents raise each other into the self-assertion of their natures" not to indicate their contingency, but so that each "surrender[s] to the concealed originality of the source of [its] own being. In the 'strife', each opponent carries the other beyond itself" (translation slightly modified, "Origin," pp. 47–8).

The work of art belongs to both realms—world and earth—at once. It is the work of the work of art to allow the "strife" between the world and the earth to remain undecided; it is not to reconcile them. The work of the work of art holds open the Open of the world by setting it into the earth. Thus, this place of strife, of pain, is what Heidegger calls the "clearing" or the Open.

Heidegger's two art historical examples, Van Gogh's shoes and the Temple of Hera II, are chosen precisely to foreground the "strife" between the world and the earth. By extension, they reveal the relation between the work of art and disclosure-as-such. Art is a way of unveiling or discovering a means to put *aletheia* into a work. The truth erupts in the work of art in the form of the "strife" between world and earth. Here we can see that the "strife" is what illuminates [German, *Lichtung* for "clearing" has this connotation as well] the contours of the "clearing."

Heidegger explains: "In the midst of beings as a whole an open place occurs. There is a clearing, a lighting ... Only this clearing grants and guarantees to us humans a passage to those beings that we ourselves are not and access to the being that we ourselves are ("Origin," p. 51). In this manner, the representation of a peasant's shoes by Van Gogh indicates being-in-the-world: more than a mere thing and yet in and of themselves unable to presence their being. In their contact with the earth, the shoes present the happening of truth in the work of art—the *aletheia* of Being—disclosed in the primal conflict between world and earth within the "clearing." This is the "nature of truth" for Heidegger. He explains that it happens in Van Gogh's painting, but that its fullest expression—its destiny so to speak—is more pressing in the Greek temple and in Hölderlin's poetry because in these instances the work of the work of art is tethered to a "native ground" and the historical destiny of a people. Heidegger's assertion that the work of art (whether text, object, or monument) founds a people, a community in its "origin" is of key significance for all historical disciplines, particularly with the role philology and archaeology have played and continue to play in the interpretation of ethnic identity.

Heidegger concludes his meditation on the work of art by turning to poetry. His argument has two key steps. He claims that "art breaks open an open place, in whose openness everything is other than usual" ("Origin," p. 70). This is how he describes the happening of truth, i.e., the setting-itself-into-work of truth. The second step follows from the first: "Art, as the setting-into-work of truth, is poetry ("Origin," p. 72). Art is never gathered from ordinary things at-hand, nor is poetry merely everyday language; instead, Heidegger conceives both as exemplary."

This displacement of art (both plastic and architectonic) under the aegis of poetry evinces Heidegger's position that it is language which first brings Being into appearance as word. It is poetic language that first conceals Being, not visual or spatial representation. He privileges the originary power of "saying" and "naming," which is why Heidegger ends his essay on the work of art with a discussion of Hölderlin's poem "The Journey." However, this does not diminish the importance of classical archaeology. On the contrary, the history of objects is historical because it "preserves" the happening of truth in the work. This is given added significance because art, for Heidegger, "is history in the essential sense that it grounds history" ("Origin," p. 75). Heidegger foregrounds the work of the work of art—the setting-into-work of truth—because it is authentically historical [*geschichtlich*], i.e., it presences the history of Being, the oblivion of metaphysics. In short, objects and monuments counteract the oblivion of Being he sees in the history of metaphysics.

Heidegger's philosophy has been subjected to many critical readings. The responses it elicits have run the gamut from dismissive to celebratory, but his basic contention remains that different historical periods are defined by their different understandings of Being. These understandings account for different preoccupations when it comes to history and material culture. Further, our study of the classical past continues to play a key role in bringing the self into existence, and this is why the study of the past remains relevant.

Further reading

By Heidegger

Being and Time. Translated by Joan Stambaugh. Albany: State University of New York Press, 1996.

"The Thinker As Poet," "The Origin of the Work of Art," and "Addendum." In *Poetry, Language, Thought*, translated by Albert Hofstader. New York: Perennial Classics, 2001.

Four Seminars. Translated by Andrew Mitchell and François Raffoul. Bloomington: Indiana University Press, 2003.

The Question Concerning Technology. Translated by William Lovitt. New York: Harper and Row, 1977.

Introduction to Metaphysics. Translated by Gregory Fried and Richard Polt. New Haven: Yale University Press, 2000.

On the Way to Language. Translated by Peter D. Hertz. New York: Harper and Row, 1972.

About Heidegger

Biemel, Walter. "Elucidations of Heidegger's Lecture 'The Origin of the Work of Art' and the Destination of Thinking." In *Reading Heidegger: Commemorations*, edited by John Sallis. Bloomington: Indiana University Press, 1993.

Clark, Timothy. *Martin Heidegger.* London and New York: Routledge, 2002.

Derrida, Jacques. *Points ...: Interviews 1974–1994.* Translated by Peggy Kamuf, et al., edited by Elisabeth Weber. Stanford: Stanford University Press, 1995.

*du Bois, Page. *Torture and Truth.* New York: Routledge, 1991.

Fóti, Véronique. "Heidegger and 'The Way of Art': The Empty Origin and Contemporary Abstraction." *Continental Philosophy Review* 31 (1998) 337–51.

Gadamer, Hans-Georg. "The Truth of the Work of Art." In *Heidegger's Ways*, translated by John W. Stanley. Albany: State University of New York Press, 1994.

Guignon, Charles (ed.). *The Cambridge Companion to Heidegger.* Cambridge: Cambridge University Press, 1993.

Harries, Karsten, and Christoph Jamme (eds). *Martin Heidegger: Politics, Art, and Technology.* London and New York: Holmes and Meier, 1994.

Lacoue-Labarthe, Phillipe. *Heidegger, Art and Politics.* Translated by Chris Turner. Oxford: Blackwell, 1990.

*Thomas, Julian. *Time, Culture and Identity: An Interpretive Archaeology.* London and New York: Routledge, 1998.

Vattimo, Gianni. *The End of Modernity.* Translated by Jon R. Snyder. Baltimore: The Johns Hopkins University Press, 1991.

Wolin, Richard (ed.). *The Heidegger Controversy: A Critical Reader.* Cambridge, MA: MIT Press, 1993.

20 Luce Irigaray

Key concepts:

- sexual difference
- specul(ariz)ation
- phallo(go)centrism
- *écriture féminine*

Luce Irigaray (b. 1930) was born in Belgium. She earned her master's degree from the University of Louvain in 1955 and taught high school in Brussels until 1959. She then moved to Paris to continue her studies, receiving a psychology diploma in 1962 from the University of Paris. She attended Jacques **Lacan**'s seminars, became a member of his École Freudienne, and trained to become an analyst. In 1968 she earned her doctorate in linguistics with a work entitled "*Le langage de déments.*" This led to a teaching post at the University of Paris VIII at Vincennes (1970–4). Upon publishing *Speculum of the Other Woman* (1974), which argued that psychoanalysis was a phallocentric discourse, she was expelled from the École Freudienne by Lacan and lost her faculty position as a result of his actions. Throughout her career, Irigaray has been an active leftist political thinker as well being involved in many women's groups and struggles. Her work has established her as one of the most prominent feminist philosophers in the postwar period. She has received several honorary degrees and visiting appointments and serves as director of research at the Centre National de la Recherche Scientifique in Paris.

Unlike some other French feminists with which she is frequently identified (especially **Kristeva**), Irigaray has consistently held that there is in fact such a thing as **sexual difference** and that female sexual identity is autonomous and unique, grounded in women's specific embodied experiences (a position sometimes called "difference feminism").

In *Speculum of the Other Woman* and other early works such as *This Sex Which is Not One* (collected essays published in 1977), she argues that the

Western intellectual tradition has essentially elided the feminine, positing it not on its own terms but rather in relation to, or over against, the masculine as the normative or default human identity. "Woman" in Western discourse has often been defined as man's other. To demonstrate this, Irigaray enacts a critical mimicry of the discourses of **Freud**, Plato, and other male intellectuals "about women"—what are they? where do they come from? what are they for?—that demonstrates how "woman" functions primarily as a vague idea that only serves to clarify the concept of "man," that is, as man's other/opposite. She describes this in terms of a process of **specul(ariz)ation**, that is, a process of male speculation about woman as man's other that associates her with a series of othered terms and concepts within a larger set of oppositions that organize the Western patriarchal symbolic order (see **Lacan's** definitions of the symbolic and imaginary orders in this volume). Within this set of structural oppositions or "interpretative modalities" that shape our understanding of the world, "woman" and the "feminine" are associated in each pairing with the negative term, the term of lack or absence: light–dark, in–out, heavens–earth, rational–illogical, clear–confused, order–disorder, culture-nature, and especially phallus-lack, original-derivative, and active-passive. It is important to note that similar associations are applied to non-Western cultures, which are frequently associated with the feminine. Irigaray (*Speculum*, p. 30) suggests that the phallus has an implicit association with the penis so that within discourse as it is conceptualized through dichotomies, the masculine is the norm while the feminine is an excess, which is silenced thus, it is reduced to sameness.

In a chapter entitled "The Blind Spot of an Old Dream of Symmetry" Irigaray writes:

> All these are interpretative modalities of the female function rigorously postulated by the pursuit of a certain game for which she will always find herself signed up without having begun to play .... A hinge bending according to their exchanges. A reserve supply of *negativity* sustaining the articulation of their moves, or refusals to move, in a partial fictional progress toward the mastery of power. Of knowledge. In which she will have no part. Off-stage, off-side, beyond representation, beyond selfhood.
>
> (*Speculum of the Other Woman*, p. 22)

Irigaray situates her critique of the primary structures of Western cultural and political discourse as **phallocentric** (and with **Cixous, phallo(go)centric**) in a psychoanalytic register. This provides her with a discourse that she uses to construct a female imaginary that undermines its authority to speak for women and abuse difference in general. However, psychoanalytic discourse itself must be critiqued in the process. In psychoanalytic discourse, the "phallus" occupies a primary place of symbolic significance, since Freud and Lacan privilege the boy–mother relationship. In theorizing the castration complex, for instance, female genitalia are inscribed as a lack or absence. Furthermore, Lacan will translate this constitutive lack into language itself. Here the constitution of the male subject in and through language remains a question of the phallus and dispossession. The "phallus" here becomes the signifier of a pre-Oedipal relation with the mother and symbolizes the primary repression that constructs an individual's unconscious. Thus, the discourse and the scopic regime of psychoanalysis is phallocentric; the role played by the phallus as visual index and master signifier within language is that on which the discourse is founded.

Irigaray's desire to posit a female imaginary, which exists prior to the acquisition of a subject position within the phallocentric symbolic order (language), is undertaken in order to end the state of affairs in which the "'feminine' is always described in terms of deficiency, lack, or atrophy, as the other side of the sex that alone holds monopoly on value: the male sex" (*This Sex Which is Not One*, p. 69). Working against this symbolic reduction of woman to the "other side" of man, Irigaray asserts the non-oppositional difference of a real and embodied other woman. Here woman is not reducible to a commodified object of exchange within the male sexual economy. This is an otherness with agency that is unpredictable and irreducible to the male economy. As such, her voice, actions, and ways of seeing (not simply talked about, acted upon, and seen) have an active and subversive power within that economy. The aim of Iragaray's project is a "destruc(tura)tion" of the privileged male/masculine subject of Western discourse and society: "A fantastic, phantasmatic fragmentation. A destruc(tura)tion in which the 'subject' is shattered, scuttled, while still claiming surreptitiously that he is the reason for it all" (*Speculum*, p. 135). The woman's subjectivity, therefore, can bring about a collapse of the binary logic of the phallocentric symbolic order, thereby opening up new possibilities for social relations.

This post-structuralist philosophy that Irigaray forward has been charged with biological essentialism; however, her primary goal is not the definition of a feminine essence, but a radical ethics of sexual difference. She articulates this female imaginary not through a proscriptive polemic style, but rather through an immanent deconstruction of the primary texts of the phallocentric order (See Jacques **Derrida**). Examples of Irigaray's praxis—the action of theory in practice—can be found in her innovative close reading of Maurice **Merleau-Ponty** in "The Invisible of the Flesh: A Reading of Merleau-Ponty, 'The Intertwining – The Chiasm'" (1982), where she claims that Merleau-Ponty's phenomenology, with its distinction between sight and touch as well as its insistence on embodied experience, actually constitutes a feminist epistemology. This line of argument is continued in discussions of *écriture féminine*. This feminist experimental-deconstructive praxis of writing arises in the 1970s with Hélène **Cixous'** text "The Laugh of Medusa" (1975). *Écriture féminine* is a kind of hysterical–mystical and metaphorical writing with the body that privileges the tactile over the visual; it denotes a radical subject position that resists a simple engendering by the symbolic order, thereby remaining in an indeterminate threshold between "male" and "female." Irigaray is often included in discussions of *écriture féminine* because of the open structure of her texts, which strive to undermine the patriarchal, authoritative voice of the symbolic order.

Feminist writing in the classics has sought to deconstruct the phallocentric discourse. Shelly Haley (in "Black Feminist Thought and Classics") has likened the discipline to a family, noting that it is constructed as European, white, and patriarchal, where race and women are either invisible or submerged within a masculinist discourse. It has historically been a discipline of white male privilege. Marilyn Skinner (In "Woman and Language in Archaic Greece" p. 128) embraces Elaine Showalter's (*The New Feminist Criticism*) concept of *gynocritics*, the investigation of "history, themes, genres, and structures of literature by women" as opposed to a feminist critique of male-authored texts. While elsewhere criticizing Irigaray's (in *This Sex Which is Not One*) assertion that history is just another hom(m)osexual construct, as a result of exclusively male and hence, patriarchal exchange, Skinner (in "Woman and Language in Archaic Greece") focuses on the woman-centered discourse of Sappho and her group, which served as a strategy for perpetuating women's culture. Ellen Greene (in "Sexual Politics in Ovid's *Amores*," p. 346) has focused on Irigaray's observations on the commodification of women in Western patriarchal culture as an overlooked theme in Ovid (*Amores* 2.19), whereby the narrator claims his desire is evoked in imagining his mistress is held captive by her husband. In *This Sex Which Is Not One* (and also in *Speculum*), Irigaray proposed to teach a history of engagement with Sophocles' *Antigone*, who she reads as a symbol of maternal power and law based upon kinship, caught up in the transition to a rule of law based on patriarchy.

These brief examples show that the importance of Irigaray's work to our understanding of the ways in which the phallocentric economic, cultural, aesthetic, and libidinal economy perpetuates the unequal exchange of women in a patriarchal society that is undeniable. Even at their most difficult and, at times frustrating, moments her texts evince a commitment to an ethics of sexual difference that has not only influenced feminists in classics (beginning in the 1980s), but is slowly beginning to make itself felt in the discursive practices of the broader discipline. The manner in which women are written about and the ways in which the construction of gender occurs in the discourse are and will be marked by Irigaray's texts.

Further reading

By Irigaray

Speculum of the Other Woman. Translated by Gillian C. Gill. Ithaca: Cornell University Press, 1985.

This Sex Which Is Not One. Translated by Catherine Porter. Ithaca: Cornell University Press, 1985.

Je, Tu, Nous: Toward a Culture of Difference. Translated by Allison Martin. London and New York: Routledge, 1990.

The Irigaray Reader. Edited by Margaret Whitford. Oxford: Blackwell, 1991.

Marine Lover of Friedrich Nietzsche. Translated by Gillian C. Gill. New York: Columbia University Press, 1991.

"The Invisible of the Flesh: A Reading of Merleau-Ponty, 'The Intertwining – The Chiasm'." In *An Ethics of Sexual Difference*, translated by Carolyn Burke and Gillian C. Gill. Ithaca: Cornell University Press, 1993.

Sexes and Genealogies. Translated by Gillian C. Gill. New York: Columbia University Press, 1993.

About Irigaray

Berg, Maggie. "Luce Irigaray's 'Contradictions': Poststructuralism and Feminism." *Signs* 17.1 (1991) 50–70.

Butler, Judith. *Bodies That Matter: On the Discursive Limits of "Sex."* London and New York: Routledge, 1993.

Greene, Ellen. "Sexual Politics in Ovid's *Amores*: 3.4, 3.8, and 3.12." *Classical Philology* 89.4 (1994) 344–50.

*Haley, Shelley P. "Black Feminist Thought and Classics: Re-membering, Re-claiming, Re-empowering." In *Feminist Theory and the Classics*, edited by Nancy S. Rabinowitz and Amy Richlin. New York and London: Routledge, 1993.

*Jay, Martin. "'Phallogocularcentrism': Derrida and Irigaray." In *Downcast Eyes: The Denigration of Vision in Twentieth Century French Thought*. Berkeley: University of California Press, 1993.

Showalter, Elaine. *The New Feminist Criticism: Essays on Women, Literature, and Theory*. New York: Pantheon, 1985.

Skinner, Marilyn. "Woman and Language in Archaic Greece, or, Why is Sappho a Woman," In *Feminist Theory and the Classics*, edited by Nancy S. Rabinowitz and Amy Richlin. New York and London: Routledge, 1993.

Whitford, Margaret. *Luce Irigaray: Philosophy in the Feminine*. London and New York: Routledge, 1991.

21 Julia Kristeva

Key concepts:

- Semiotic/*chora*
- symbolic
- signifying process
- intertextuality
- abjection

Julia Kristeva (b. 1941) is a psychoanalyst and feminist theorist of language and literature. Born in Bulgaria, she moved to Paris in 1965 on a doctoral research fellowship. There she quickly became involved in the leftist intellectual movement that congregated around the literary journal *Tel Quel*, which also included Jacques **Derrida**. Her most influential teacher during that time was Roland **Barthes**. Her doctoral thesis, *Revolution in Poetic Language*, published in 1974, led to her appointment as chair in linguistics at the University of Paris VII, where she has remained throughout her academic career. Since 1979 she has also maintained a practice as a psychoanalyst.

Kristeva situates her work at the intersection of linguistics, psychoanalysis, and feminist theory. She has written on an impressive array of topics, including horror, love, and depression. Overall, her interests lie less in the formal structures of language and meaning, than in what escapes and disrupts them—the unrepresentable, inexpressible other within language, within the self, and within society. There, she sees the possibility for revolutionary social transformation.

In *Revolution in Poetic Language*, Kristeva refers to the revolutionary alterity (otherness) within language as the **semiotic**, or *chora* (place), which exists in relation to the **symbolic**. The semiotic is decipherable within language (especially in poetic language), yet it is in tension with the dominant symbolic order that governs language (see Jacques **Lacan**).

Kristeva's semiotic, however, differs from the standard meaning of semiotics as the science of signs. What Kristeva forwards here is a "semanalysis," a combination of semiotics and psychoanalysis that aims at revealing how the laws of the symbolic are resisted. In psychoanalytic terms, the semiotic is associated with the pre-linguistic phase and the mother's body. Indeed, Kristeva associates this semiotic element in poetic language with the mother, the child, pre-linguistic babbling, the pre-Oedipal maternal space, and so on. It exists within language, especially within poetic language, as a potentially subversive, eruptive force. The semiotic, then, can never be entirely constrained by the symbolic; it perpetually infiltrates the symbolic construction of meaning, reintroducing fluidity and heterogeneity within the speaking/writing subject. It reopens the process of creation. Kristeva describes it as the "very precondition" of the symbolic order (*Revolution in Poetic Language*, p. 50). Insofar as the symbolic order of language is identified with consciousness, we can think of the semiotic as language's unconscious. The infiltration of the semiotic within language indexes the continual presence of archaic drives, the loss of relation with one's mother.

Throughout her works, Kristeva focuses on the **signifying process** more than its product. She reads a text in order to discover not only the processes by which it comes to have meaning (*signify*), but also what it is within the text that resists and undermines that process (see also "Semiotics" and "The System and the Speaking Subject"). In this respect, we can think of her method of literary analysis as a kind of psychoanalysis of texts that does not take their final fixed state for granted but reads them in order to explore how they came into being, how they came to say what they say, as well as to indicate what was repressed in the process, i.e., what within them that keeps them fundamentally unstable (see also **Derrida**). In this manner, we can refer not only to the signifying process, but also to the *signifying economy*, a term Kristeva borrows from **Freud**'s metapsychology. Her analysis seeks those places in language that open the possibility of individual and social transformation, "the production of a different kind of subject, one capable of bringing about new social relations, and thus joining in the process of capitalism's subversion" (*Revolution in Poetic Language*, p. 105). In this way, psychoanalysis takes on a more socio-political aspect in her work.

In *Strangers to Ourselves* (1998), for example, she calls for open national borders and an ethics of the neighbor whereby immigrants and foreigners are treated with respect. Her argument is premised on the proposition that ethics necessarily begins with the psychoanalytic realization that we are all "strangers to ourselves." Applied to the study of the past in both text and archaeology, her call encourages embracing rather than suppressing alterity, colonization as a process, creolization, and hybridity.

Kristeva's theory of **intertextuality** has had a tremendous influence on literary studies, less so on philosophy and religion. This theory was developed in relation to Mikhail **Bakhtin's** concept of dialogism. The idea of intertextuality first appears in her 1969 essay, "Word, Dialogue, and the Novel" as part of a larger critique of modern conceptions of texts as discrete, self-enclosed containers of meaning. Contrary to this conception, intertextuality draws attention to the fact that every text is "constructed as a mosaic of quotations" ("Word, Dialogue, and Novel," p. 66). It is a "field of transpositions of various signifying systems (an inter-textuality)" (*Revolution in Poetic Language*, p. 60), an "intersection of textual surfaces rather than a point (a fixed meaning)" ("Word, Dialogue, and Novel," p. 65).

Within classics, intertextuality offers a way of conceiving of texts and traditions that challenges their categorization into the canonical and noncanonical. To recognize texts such as the Homeric poems, ancient plays, rhetoric. as well as the great art works of classical civilizations as an inter-textuality, is to recognize that they cannot be separated from the various textual fields—ancient as well as contemporary—that are their contexts. For example, from the presence of prehistoric elements such as boar's tusk helmets in the Homeric poems, to the references to Homer in later Greek plays or in Roman literature, to their effect of the lives on modern soldiers; and from the role of the classical Greek canon whether inspiring, Renaissance humanism as a rebirth of classical antiquity or postmodern art as a reaction against it—there is no such thing as a closed canon. The term has not been consistently applied in the sense it is used by Kristeva, and more often it has been used to compare and contrast similar texts or to identify allusions.

Another key concept in Kristeva's work that has obvious implications for classics is **abjection** (see especially *Powers of Horror*, first published in French in 1980). The abject is that which does not fit within or disturbs the social and symbolic order of things, and which therefore must be excluded from that order, declared unclean or impure and pushed outside the boundaries. Always threatening to break back into that order and contaminate it, the abject must be kept at bay. Abjection, then, is the process by which a society identifies the abject and excludes it from its order through various prohibitions and taboos. As such, abjection serves to define the boundaries of the social-symbolic order.

In *Powers of Horror*, and later in her essay on "Reading the Bible" (first published in French in 1993), Kristeva finds the laws and prohibitions of the Book of Leviticus to be particularly revealing as a process of abjection. Leviticus, she argues, is a "logicizing of what departs from the symbolic" (*Powers of Horror*, p. 91). It begins with the foundational opposition of humanity and God, and develops from there a "complete system of logical oppositions" (*Powers of Horror*, pp. 98–9). Within this system, "the pure will be that which conforms to an established taxonomy" and the impure, or abject will be "that which unsettles it, establishes intermixture and disorder" (*Powers of Horror*, p. 99).

Kristeva's analysis does not simply interpret the symbolic order in Leviticus as patriarchal and xenophobic, it also delineates how divinely sanctioned commands and prohibitions subordinate "maternal power" to its rule (*Powers of Horror*, p. 91). Religion is thus concerned with purifying the abject and associated rituals and art can be studied as a catharsis for purifying it. She similarly uses the concept of the abject to understand Odysseus' defilement. Thus, abjection also becomes a way to conceptualize how pollution and purity served to structure the cultures of classical civilizations and to uphold patriarchal institutions in relationship to a feminine other.

In "Giotto's Joy," Kristeva attempts to construct a theory of material culture that, while informed by linguistics, can grasp the ecstasies of creating and presenting signs, which precisely exceeds the mode of semiological analysis. She is speaking of *jouissance* here (see Barthes' *Camera Lucida* for a different version of this discussion). Giotto's joy, his *jouissance*, is "the sublimated jouissance of a subject liberating himself for the transcendental dominion of One Meaning (white) through the advent of its instinctual drives, again articulated within a complex and regulated distribution ... This chromatic joy is the indication of a deep ideological and subjective transformation; it discreetly enters the theological signified, distorting and doing violence to it without relinquishing it" (*Desire in Language*, p. 224). Nothing less than the potential ecstatic transformation of the individual as well as the collective is what Kristeva desires from art: the irruption of the semiotic into the tyranny of the symbolic.

In an ambitious reading of the entire history of Western painting from Giotto to Piet Mondrian, Kristeva forwards a theory of color that aids in explicating the transition from figurative realism to abstraction in art. She writes:

> By overflowing, softening, and dialectizing lines, color emerges inevitably as the "device" by which painting gets away from the identification of objects and therefore from realism (...) Color is the shattering of unity. Thus, it is through color—colors—that the subject escapes its alienation with a code (representational, ideological, symbolic, and so forth) that it, as conscious subject, accepts. Similarly, it is through color that Western painting began to escape the constraints of narrative and perspective norms (as with Giotto) as well as representation itself (as with Cézanne, Matisse, Rothko, Mondrian).
>
> (*Desire in Language*, p. 221)

Kristeva's point here is that the translation of the plastic arts into linguistic categories (the triad of signifier, signified, referent) fails to account for certain aspects of the visual arts such as color. Her examination of color is an interpretative strategy that reveals the limitations of the traditional semiological analysis of art. To correct this myopic focus, she supplements the structure of the sign with the psychic economy Freud develops between perception and thought processes, where thought denotes conscious activity and "thing presentations" are aligned with perception (the unconscious). Thus, to the semiological definition she adds the "triple register of exterior drives, interior drives, and signifier"—the Freudian economy that problematizes both representation and language (*Desire in Language*, p. 218). Attempts to more fully incorporate the senses into the study of classical art and archaeology, are rare, but have increased in recent years through an increased emphasis on embodiment and phenomenology.

Further reading

By Kristeva

Desire in Language: A Semiotic Approach to Literature and Art, edited by Leon S. Roudiez. New York: Columbia University Press, 1980.

*"Word, Dialogue and the Novel." In *Desire in Language: A Semiotic Approach to Literature and Art*, edited by Leon S. Roudiez. New York: Columbia University Press, 1980.

* *Powers of Horror: An Essay on Abjection*. Translated by Leon S. Roudiez. New York: Columbia University Press, 1982.

Revolution in Poetic Language. Abridged and translated by Margaret Waller. New York: Columbia University Press, 1984.

*The Kristeva Reader, edited by Toril Moi. New York: Columbia University Press, 1986.

"The System and the Speaking Subject." In *The Kristeva Reader*, edited by Toril Moi. New York: Columbia University Press, 1986.

*"Semiotics: A Critical Science and/or a Critique of Science." In *The Kristeva Reader*, edited by Toril Moi. New York: Columbia University Press, 1986.

"Reading the Bible." In *New Maladies of the Soul*, translated by Ross Mitchell Guberman. New York: Columbia University Press, 1995.

Julia Kristeva: Interviews, edited by Ross Mitchell Guberman. New York: Columbia University Press, 1996.

Strangers to Ourselves. Translated by Leon S. Roudiez. New York: Columbia University Press, 1998.

*(With Catherine Clément) *The Feminine and the Sacred*. Translated by Jane Marie Todd. New York: Columbia University Press, 2001.

About Kristeva

Beardsworth, Sara. *Julia Kristeva: Psychoanalysis and Modernity*. Albany: State University of New York Press, 2004.

Joy, Morny, Kathleen O' Grady, and Judith L. Poxon (eds). *French Feminists on Religion: A Reader*. London and New York: Routledge, 2002.

Lechte, John and Margaroni, Maria. *Julia Kristeva: Live Theory*. Continuum Books, 2005.

Oliver, Kelly (ed.). *Ethics, Politics, and Difference in Julia Kristeva's Writings*. London and New York: Routledge, 1993.

*O'Neill, K. "Aeschylus, Homer, and the Serpent at the Breast," Phoenix. 52.3–4 (1998), 216–29.

Oliver, Kelly. *Reading Kristeva: Unraveling the Double-Bind*. Bloomington: Indiana University Press, 1993.

Smith, Anne-Marie. *Julia Kristeva: Speaking the Unspeakable*. London: Pluto Press, 1998.

22 Jacques Lacan

Key concepts:

- orders: Symbolic, Imaginary, and Real
- unconscious
- *objet a*
- subject
- mirror stage
- phallus/phallocentrism
- lack
- castrate
- real
- desire
- gaze

Jacques Lacan (1901–81) was born in Paris to a Roman Catholic family. He earned a medical degree at the Sorbonne and then trained as a psychoanalyst. His relationship with mainstream psychoanalysis in Europe was tense, and he resigned from the Société psychanalytique de Paris in 1953— the same year he gave his famous lecture "The Function and the Field of Speech and Language" at the International Psychoanalytic Association in Rome (also referred to as "The Rome Discourse"). In that same year he inaugurated his weekly seminar, which continued almost until his death. Lacan's seminar was the primary venue for sharing his work. Most of his published essays were originally given as papers in his seminar, which was attended by many influential intellectuals, including Julia **Kristeva** and Luce **Irigaray**. In 1963 he founded the École Freudienne de Paris.

Focused on the formation of the subject and the role of the unconscious, Lacan's work constitutes a radical reinterpretation of **Freud** and psychoanalysis in the light of structuralism (especially the structural linguistics of **Saussure** and the structural anthropology of Lévi-Strauss). Dissenting from the common conception, widespread among his contemporaries, of the ego or conscious self as autonomous, sovereign, and biologically determined, Lacan theorized that it was interpolated within a system of meaning that it had no part in creating. Far from autonomous and sovereign, it becomes a self or an ego— an "I"—when it is *subjected* to a preexisting **symbolic order**. These ideas are at odds with those classicists, who cling to the idea of a centered subject-hood, with classical Greece as the locus.

The **unconscious**, according to Lacan, is not a biologically determined realm of libidinal drives; rather, it is formed in tandem with the formation of the ego. It is the remainder (what Lacan calls the *objet (petit) a*) of the ego's subjection to the Symbolic (at times also referred to as *Autre*): i.e., it is created as the excess or surplus self of unadulterated pleasure that does not fit with the conception of the self as formed by the primary repression or the acquisition of language, by its subjection by the *Autre* or Other. Thus the unconscious reveals the presence of the **subject** within the construct of the self and reveals the fact that we as subjects are always more than our social selves allow. For this reason Lacan will state that the subject is on the side of the unconscious; that is where it will be found. Far from being an autonomous, sovereign agent in the world, the ego is an illusion, a symbol-ically constructed identity whose excesses and *aporias* are revealed by the eruptions of the unconscious into conscious life.

Lacan develops this understanding of ego formation and the unconscious *vis-à-vis* the structural linguistics of Saussure. For Lacan, the birth of subjec-tivity is one's entry into language, understood as a synchronic system of signs and social codes that both generate and circumscribe meaning. It is the Symbolic that locates and "subjects" you, thereby enabling the becoming of a self, an "I." Before Lacan, most psychoanalysts believed that the develop-ment of the ego as the seat of consciousness was a biological development. Lacan's radical inflection of this premise is to insist that birth into language is birth into subjectivity. As he famously pronounced in "The Rome Discourse," "Man thus speaks, but it is because the symbol has made him man" (p. 65). And later in the same essay: "Symbols in fact envelop the life of man with a network so total that they join together those who are going to engender him 'by bone and flesh' before he comes into the world" (p. 67).

Besides the **Symbolic**, which we return to below, Lacan's theory of the subject relies upon two other orders: the **Imaginary** and the **Real**. (These three orders are inseparable and co-construct each other in his thought.) The Imaginary is developed in tandem with Lacan's well-known formula-tion of the **mirror stage** (for a clear discussion of both, see "The Mirror Stage as Formative of the Function of the *I* as Revealed in Psychoanalytic Experience," first presented in 1949). It is important to note that while Lacan addresses the mirror stage in his early work, he continues to revisit this concept throughout his career, revising and refining it. He identifies the mirror stage as an important means by which the child is inaugurated into the Imaginary. The Imaginary precedes the child's entry into the Symbolic and continues to operate along with her/him throughout life. The Imaginary is the order in which the child becomes aware of itself as a specular image. It is in this order that the ego is created through an illusory representation, which Lacan terms a "misrecognition" [*méconnaissance*]. In general, the Imaginary is the matrix of *self as other* as well as *self and other* structured by this logic of "misrecognition."

Lacan argues that the mirror stage occurs between the ages of six and eighteen months, when the child first recognizes itself in a mirror as a seemingly coherent and whole entity. In this moment, before the child can speak or even walk, the child recognizes itself as *other*, as an objectification of itself in an image whose point of view and position are external. In other words, the mirror stage "describes the function of the ego via the process of identification; the ego is the result of identifying with its own specular image ... The baby sees its own image as a whole, and the synthesis of this image produces a sense of contrast with the uncoordination of the body, which is experienced as a fragmented body" (Evans, in *An Introductory Dictionary of Lacanian Psychoanalysis* p. 115). In this respect the mirror stage, which inaugurates the Imaginary, may be seen as "one of those crises of alienation around which the Lacanian subject is organized, since to know oneself through an external image is to be defined through self-alienation" (Silverman, in *The Subject of Semiotics*, p. 158). The construction of the ego or the self is accomplished through an act at once narcissistic and aggressive. The aggressiveness is between both the subject and its body image and between the subject and others (e.g. the parent that holds the child before the mirror).

According to Lacan's often criticized narrative of child development, the child's entry into language as a subject coincides with its separation from the mother. The mother, therefore, is the child's first experience of lack absence, which creates the condition of desire. The father intervenes in the mother–child relationship at a moment coinciding with the child's entry into the Symbolic and loss of union with the mother. As the child becomes a self within the Symbolic, the father is identified with this order, which constitutes and governs subjectivity. For this reason Lacan sometimes calls the Symbolic *le Nom-du-Pére* ["the Name of the Father"], which in French is pronounced the same as *le Non-du-Pére* ["the No of the Father"], thus creating a play on words, that also signifies God-like authority and prohibition. Thus the child is subjected in two senses of the word: subjected to the law of the symbolic order (identified with patriarchal law/no of the father) and constituted as an acting subject in the world.

This is also where the notion of the **phallus** comes in, so to speak. One of the first childhood experiences of sexual difference, according to Lacan as well as Freud, is the recognition that the mother does not have a penis. But for Lacan, what is most important is the symbolic significance of the penis, a symbolism he emphasizes by consistently using the terms "phallus." What matters in the symbolic order is not the body part, but what it signifies. First, it signifies sexual difference. Second, insofar as the father (identified with the symbolic order) has a penis and the mother (identified with the pre-linguistic state of bliss before entry into the symbolic order) does not, the phallus signifies **lack**/absence within the symbolic order. For Lacan, the phallus comes to signify *both* women's and men's lack, dependence, and subjective vulnerability within the symbolic order. The child may identify the father with the symbolic order, but he too was once a child, subjected to the same law and always inadequate and incomplete in relation to it, never in full possession of it. Thus, the blocking of desire is a product of the constitution of one's own subjecthood, rather than in parental authority as embodied by **Freud**'s concept of Oedipus. No one possesses the phallus, thus all are "**castrated**." As noted by the feminist biblical scholar Deborah Krause, "castration is an equal opportunity employer."

Lacan's insights on the phallus and castration are useful to scholars in gender, the classics, and all cultural and historical disciplines because he insists that there is nothing essential about the androcentric symbolic order with its foundational patriarchal structures of sexual difference. For Lacan, there is nothing essential or "natural" (remembering that the natural is cultural) about sexual difference itself. Woman, man, femininity, and masculinity are symbolic constructions formed arbitrarily and linguistically by a repressive system of meaning that masquerades as the real.

As mentioned above, the **unconscious** is formed at the same time as the self/ego. It is an after-effect of the repression that takes place during subjection. Ego formation requires repression of whatever does not fit the image of the self-constructed within the Symbolic. The unconscious is the "censored chapter" in the history of psychic life ("The Function and Field of Speech and Language in Psychoanalysis," p. 50). Alterity resides at the heart of the self, manifesting itself in and through language, often as interruption— in mis-speakings, slips, and forgetting names. It also occurs in the curious linguistic constructions to which Lacan pays close attention. Constructions like *ne* in French or *but* in English as in "I couldn't help but overhear" are symptomatic of the presence of the unconscious. The agent of this statement is indeterminate. It is Lacan's position that when statements like this are made they indicate the presence of the Real in the Symbolic, which thereby suggests the troubling and illusory nature of specular and linguistic identity. In other words, the intervention of the unconscious within conscious existence reveals the fact that the self is a tentative construct, by no means entirely stable, permanent, or discrete. In Lacan's words, "the unconscious is that part of the concrete discourse ... that is not at the disposal of the subject in re-establishing the continuity of his conscious discourse" ("The Function of the Field of Speech and Language in Psychoanalysis," p. 49). This interruption or encounter indexes the presence of the Real within language, the immanent plane in which the subject is defined through a structure of desire.

Lacan uses the term **Real** in reference to that which is really "there," "in its place" apart from the symbolic order and outside its ordering of things. It is the present, as opposed to that which is represented through language in the symbolic order. The Real is the order in Lacan's system that underwrites, so to speak, the actions described in the Imaginary and the Symbolic. He posits that the subject emerges from its non-individuated, prelinguistic state of being not into unmediated reality but into a culturally constructed world of symbols. The *objet a* is precisely a remnant of the prior state that remains embedded within the Symbolic and, in fact, it determines the entirety of the subject's position within the field of signification. Moreover, the *objet a* is not the specular image of the Imaginary; rather, it is the object cause of desire that makes us seek pleasure or enjoyment [*jouissance*] in the other. The *objet a* is, therefore, an irreducible alterity within the self, residing between the Real and the Imaginary.

Lacan terms this prior, undifferentiated state the Real because it is "absolutely without fissure" (*Seminar II*, p. 97). The Real is that which resists symbolization. For this reason Lacan will argue that the Symbolic introduces "a cut in the real." The constitutive inability to signify the Real is why Lacan discusses it in relation to anxiety and trauma. Nonetheless, throughout the life of a subject there are moments in which the remnant of the Real is approached. In these encounters there is a potentiality for the self to embody that portion of itself—the *objet a*—that it repudiates.

In *Seminar XI: The Four Fundamental Concepts of Psychoanalysis* Lacan states: "Where do we meet this real? For what we have in the discovery of psychoanalysis is an encounter, an essential encounter—an appointment to which we are always called with a real that eludes us" (p. 53). To denote this cause of anxiety, this chance encounter with the Real, Lacan uses the Aristotelian terms *tuché* and *automaton*. The term *automaton* refers to the behavior of the self within the Symbolic or, in other words, the behavior of the signifying chain within language. This behavior is structural because it is formed in relation to that which resists and yet instigates the signifying chain: the *objet a*, the surplus of the Real. For this reason, Lacan understands the *tuché* to be the encounter: "The real is beyond the *automaton*, the coming-back, the insistence of the signs by which we see ourselves governed by the pleasure principle ... The function of the *tuché*, of the real as encounter—the encounter in so far as it may be missed, in so far as it is essentially the missed encounter [is] that of the trauma" (pp. 53–55). Here we see how Lacan reinscribes Freud's notion of the pleasure principle. Lacan explains that Freud's system demonstrates how human beings are always kept just shy of pleasure; there is no pleasure as such because it is never attained. Lacan, however, argues that what we desire is the very structure of **desire**: the frisson between the *automaton* and the *tuché*, the pleasure derived from the chance encounter that interrupts and undermines the very ground on which we stand.

Lacan's views on art are relevant to the role of material culture in classics. In *Seminar VII: The Ethics of Psychoanalysis* Lacan discusses art as one of the primary means by which we take up a relation to the Real. He aligns art with the Freudian concept of repression [*Verdrängung*] by arguing that art represses the Real through sublimation. By developing his idea of art in relation to Kantian sublimation, Lacan tethers his discourse on art not only to that of Kant, but also to the thought of Plato and Martin **Heidegger**. Sublimation, he argues, is a change in status of the object that "raises an object to the dignity of the Thing" (*Seminar VI*, p. 112). The "Thing" in question here is the Freudian Thing or *das Ding*, that which is completely other or alien and therefore an index of the Real (which is interesting in light of Freud's fondness for antiquities). In his later work, Lacan denotes *das Ding* with the idea of the *objet a* or desire as discussed above. A sublimated object, by being elevated to the status of *das Ding*, exerts a power of fascination that ultimately leads to death and destruction. This is one of the reasons why Lacan also links art, via repression, to hysteria. Art represses the Real and yet, through that very act, simultaneously acknowledges it by attempting to represent it.

In addition, Lacan spends nearly the entirety of his eleventh seminar on the **gaze**. The gaze, for Lacan, indicates a split with the eye/sight. Drawing on the phenomenological work of Jean-Paul Sartre and **Merleau-Ponty**, Lacan argues that sight examines the object, but that the gaze comes from the object; there is an asymmetry between the sight of the self and the gaze of the thing that looks back. In summarizing this point, Lacan states: "When ... I solicit a look, what is profoundly unsatisfying and always missing is that—*You never look at me from the place from which I see you*" (*Seminar XI*, p. 103). This schism between sight and the gaze is another indication of the fundamental "misrecognition" of the self, i.e., the distinction that grounds all of Lacan's work: the subject within the self. The gaze can be analyzed in terms of how the discourse, in this case classics, is structured, the power relations involved, and to elaborate on the relationship between subjects and objects.

Beginning from Lacan's astute explication of the distorted skull in Hans Holbein's sixteenth-century anamorphic painting *The Ambassadors*, which becomes legible only when the subject occupies a particular position in the chain of signifiers, art and film historians have elaborated on the concept of the gaze. In addition, bringing the skull into view eliminates or diminishes the presence of the other subjects of the painting. Lacan's emphasis on the gaze as a lure, as a proleptic gesture of the act of traversing the fantasy that marks the end of analysis in his system, also provides him the opportunity to elaborate on some intriguing comments he makes in *Seminar VII*. The most pressing of these is his contention that "at a given moment one arrives at illusion. Around it one finds a sensitive spot, a lesion, a locus of pain, a point of reversal of the whole history, insofar as it is the history of art and insofar as we are implicated in it ... [therefore] the expression 'history of art' is highly misleading" (*Seminar VII*, pp. 140–1). This comment clearly demarcates the difference between Lacan's and Freud's positions regarding art and the illusory aspects of subjectivity. Freud values art in a classical, liberal, and humanist sense. He champions artistic creation and the imagination of "the great artist." Freud reads sublimation as a process by which sexual libido is redirected into non-sexual, socially acceptable outlets. The implication of viewing the Holbein work is to problematize the notion that there is a particular anamorphic perspective from which the past itself will become legible. Instead, there are multiple subject positions from which to place oneself into a relationship with the past.

Lacan, as we have seen, also takes up the idea of sublimation, but in a much different vein. The key distinction is Lacan's complete rejection of "psychobiography" (his term) when it comes to art history. This is why in *Seminar XI*, when explaining his interest in Edvard Munch, James Ensor, and other painters, he declares: "This is not the occasion to begin a psychoanalysis on the painter ... Nor is it a question of art criticism ... [it] is not to enter into the shifting, historical game of criticism, which tries to grasp what is the function of painting at a particular moment, for a particular author at a particular time. For me, it is at the radical principle of the function of this fine art that I am trying to place myself" (pp. 109, 110). Lacan's interest in art and literature stems from his desire to explain the intimate connections between how we represent ourselves *vis-à-vis* desire. It is the gaze that fractures our relation to the work of art; a gaze that implicates us in a larger, delimited structure of individual and social identity construction. Lacan's work sets us two tasks. The first is not to disavow the desire of the viewer. One's reading of a work (artistic or textual) is determined in large part by one's subject position. Similarly, the identity of classics as a discipline is fractured (Greece, Rome, history, prehistory, art, text, material culture, feminism, architecture, etc.), and there is no anamorphic point from which to view the discipline or its objects as a coherent whole. Secondly, Lacan's explications of painting and literature are meant to serve as allegories for the training of analysts: to show them how to listen, read, and interpret the analysand's discourse.

Lacan is emphatic when he instructs his audience to "please give more attention to text than to the psychology of the author—the entire orientation of my teaching is that" (*Seminar II*, p. 153). What the text or work tells us about society or ourselves is just as important as who created it or where they came from. But he is equally emphatic when he derides what he calls "applied psychoanalysis." Rather than merely applying the insights Lacan's thought provides, the ethic of that very thought demands a radical redefinition of what we traditionally refer to as classics. The goal of Lacan's work is to change discourses, to interrupt the fantasy of "misrecognition." Any application of his work that refuses this ethical call misses the point.

With regard to the classics, James Porter and Mark Buchan have discussed how the history of classical culture is a history of the subject's self-discovery and maturation, whether discussing the development of Homeric heroes or Greek art. They argue that simply by applying Lacan and other theorists to classics we can modify the master narratives and paradigms of this discourse. They observe that Lacan challenges us to rethink the world in terms of what the subject lacks or desires. For example, desire to know more and the lack of knowledge about Homer's identity has fueled our interest in the Homeric poems. In addition, Homer's heroes as well as other characters of Greek literature are linguistically constituted and, thereby, subject to the linguistic constraints of the time. Our knowledge of other aspects of the classical past are also fragmented, whether by accidents of preservation or temporal distance, fueling the desire to learn more.

Further reading

By Lacan

*"The Function and Field of Speech and Language in Psychoanalysis," "Mirror Stage as Formative of the Function of The *I* as Revealed in Psychoanalytic Experience," "The Signification of the Phallus," and "The Freudian Thing, or the Meaning of the Return to Freud in Psychoanalysis." In *Ecrits: A Selection*, translated by Bruce Fink. New York: Norton, 2002.

The Seminar of Jacques Lacan Book XI: The Four Fundamental Concepts of Psychoanalysis. Translated by Alan Sheridan. New York: Norton, 1978.

The Seminar of Jacques Lacan Book II: The Ego in Freud's Theory and in the Technique of Psychoanalysis: 1954–1955. Translated by Sylvana Tomaselli. New York: Norton, 1988.

The Seminar of Jacques Lacan Book VII: The Ethics of Psychoanalysis: 1959–1960. Translated by Dennis Porter. New York: Norton, 1992.

About Lacan

Adams, Parveen (ed.). *Art: Sublimation or Symptom*. New York: Other Press, 2003.

Brennan, Teresa (ed.). *Between Feminism and Psychoanalysis*. London and New York: Routledge, 1989.

Conley, Tom. "The Wit of the Letter: Holbein's Lacan." In *Vision in Context: Historical and Contemporary Perspectives on Sight*, edited by Teresa Brennan and Martin Jay. London and New York: Routledge, 1996.

Copjec, Joan. *Read My Desire: Lacan Against the Historicists*. Cambridge, MA: MIT Press, 1994.

* Evans, Dylan. *An Introductory Dictionary of Lacanian Psychoanalysis*. London and New York: Routledge, 1996.

Feldstein, Richard, Bruce Fink, and Maire Jannus (eds). *Reading Seminar XI: Lacan's Four Fundamental Concepts of Psychoanalysis*. Albany: State University of New York Press, 1995.

Fink, Bruce. *The Lacanian Subject: Between Language and Jouissance*. Princeton: Princeton University Press, 1995.

Goux, Jean-Joseph. *Oedipus, Philosopher*. Stanford: Stanford University Press, 1993.

*Porter, James I. and Buchan, Mark (eds). *Before Subjectivity? Lacan and the Classics*. Helios. 31.1–2.

Regnault, François. "Art After Lacan." *lacanian ink* 19 (Fall 2001).

Riggsby, Andrew. *Caesar in Gaul and Rome: War in Words*. Austin: University of Texas Press, 2006.

Silverman, Kaja. *The Subject of Semiotics*. Oxford: Oxford University Press, 1983.

23 Henri Lefebvre

Key concepts:

- everyday life
- perceived space
- conceived space
- lived space

Henri Lefebvre (1901–91) was a French Marxist, social theorist, philosopher, and historian. Born and raised in the Landes region of southwestern France, he studied philosophy in Paris, where he became involved with a group of young intellectuals promoting Marxist ideas. He joined the French Communist Party (Parti Communiste Français, or PCF) in 1928. He was influenced by Marx's early writings, some of which he translated into French. He fought in the French resistance during World War II. Afterward, he became a broadcaster and devoted his time to writing about Marxism, though he regularly skirmished with the PCF over his "humanist" Marxist views that were based, in part, on the Hegel-influenced early writings of Marx. Lefebvre was expelled from the French Communist Party in 1958 because of his anti-Stalinist views (though he became involved again in the late 1970s).

Later, in the 1950s, Lefebvre was appointed to a research position in sociology. It was during this time that he applied Marxist ideas to the sociology of everyday life. He went on to hold sociology chairs, first at Strasbourg and then at Nanterre, from which he played an active role in the 1968 Paris protests. It was during this period that he explored new intellectual currents, embracing ideas taken from sociology, literary criticism, and philosophy.

Lefebvre was antagonistic toward the linguistic and anthropological structuralisms popular among French intellectuals in the 1960s and wrote articles criticizing the work of Claude Lévi-Strauss and Michel **Foucault**.

He also critiqued the anti-humanist Marxist views of Louis **Althusser**, accusing him of turning structuralism into an ideology.

Lefebvre was the author of more than 60 books, although much of this work has yet to be translated into English. His scholarship has influenced such diverse disciplines as philosophy, sociology, literature, geography, architectural history, and political science and has been championed by postmodern spatial theorists, among others. Lefebvre's major intellectual contributions concern the study of "everyday life" and the configuration of social space in capitalist and urban settings.

In his own lifetime, Lefebvre was witness to the rise of industrialism in France and, along with it, the increasing urbanization and suburbanization of French life. These experiences informed his application of Marxist critical theory to problems of **everyday life**. Lefebvre draws attention to the social forms of alienation that appear in the quotidian affairs of human beings as a result of capitalist modernization. For Lefebvre, this alienation is the product of a three-stage process. In the first stage, everyday human activities are spontaneously ordered and largely independent of the state. This spontaneity is then co-opted in the second stage by capitalist forms of rational structure. Finally, in the third stage, these co-opted forms of everyday activity become systems of oppression. Economically, Lefebvre argues, divisions of labor become means for worker exploitation. Similarly, benign political structures become oppressive state ideologies.

In the three volumes of *The Critique of Everyday Life* (the first volume was published in French 1958), Lefebvre delineates the alienating effects of capitalism and urbanization on everyday life. He argues that within capitalist society, human beings lose control of their own self-actualization (as subjects) and increasingly describe themselves as objects within the economic system (as, for instance, "assets" and "consumers"). They objectify and commodify themselves in economic terms and thus become alienated from their own lives.

In *The Production of Space* (1974), Lefebvre turned his critical attention to an analysis of social space. He is concerned not only with how space is produced within a social context but also with how particular forms of space actually produce the forms of life that take place within them. Space is not simply an external location that human occupants act upon and shape, as we so often assume. Rather, space is a subject that acts upon and shapes us, and our social lives.

Lefebvre reads space primarily from a Marxist perspective. He is interested in transcending or sublating a binary view of space as physical form— **perceived space**—and mental construct—**conceived space**. To this end, Lefebvre proposes a three-tiered analysis of space, one that adds a dimension that he refers to as **lived space**. Lefebvre organizes his trivalent spatial analysis in the following way:

> The fields we are concerned with are, first, the *physical*–nature, the Cosmos; secondly, the *mental*, including logical and formal abstractions;

and, thirdly, the *social*. In other words, we are concerned with logico-epistemelogical space, the space of social practice, the space occupied by sensory phenomena, including products of the imagination such as projects and projections, symbols and utopias.

(*The Production of Space*, pp. 11–12)

This tripartite view of space is understood not as three compartmentalized spaces—space separable into three—but is conceived as a synthesis of all three. All territory is composed of all three aspects of space at once. Lefebvre charts his view of space in terms of the interconnections between the three categories of space. Table 1 summarizes the terms he uses to name these three kinds of space along with the meaning assigned to these terms.

Edward Soja (*Thirdspace*) has taken up Lefebvre's spatial trialectics, developing his three categories in terms of Firstspace, Secondspace, and Thirdspace. For Soja, Thirdspace (Lefebvre's social space) is a combination of Firstspace (physical space) and Secondspace (mental space). Thirdspace, then, cannot be separated from the others and must be examined together with them. Firstspace (physical space) is also always Secondspace (mental space) and Thirdspace (social space). When one looks out over a natural (physical) landscape, one does so through a conceptual spatial lens, and one experiences that landscape as lived space. Likewise, one's experience of space (as lived space) is an experience of a conceptualized physical space. In approaching lived space in this way, Soja seeks to move beyond binary logic of either/or into a trialectical logic of both/and.

A simple example may help clarify Soja's theoretical spatial distinctions *vis-à-vis* Lefebvre. Consider the space you are occupying as you read this text. The physical space—dimensions of a room, furniture, window placement, temperature, etc—is perceived space, the space presented to you through your five senses, Firstspace. This same space as conceived space, Secondspace, would be a photograph or architectural drawing of the space, or your mental picture of what the space will look like after renovation. Thirdspace— a synthesis of these two—addresses how one may experience space. The room you occupy might produce any number of possible responses: a sense of

Table 1

Lefebvre's terms		Meaning
Physical space	*perceived space *spatial practice	*physical, material space
Mental space	*conceived space *representations of space	*concepts/ideas about space
Social space	*lived space *spaces of *representation	*space as experienced (physically, emotionally, intellectually, ideologically, etc.)

tranquillity or oppression; fond memories or unpleasant ones; and a variety of experiences as you move about it. The point here is that space is never neutral or merely a physical location that can be represented conceptually through a photograph, painting, architectural drawing, or map, as if the representation was a one-to-one likeness of the physical space.

Although Lefebvre's treatment of ancient space is brief and sometimes essentializing, the Greek agora is an empty, absolute space for the political and religious gathering of free citizens in contrast to the Roman forum (in *Production of Space*, p. 237), filled by objects and things, his work on the social production of space has significant implications for the study of classical texts as well as classical archaeology. Among the different types of spaces we deal with are sacred, social, public, performative, gendered, private, stratified, urban, connected, rural, space as temporally segmented, and the mentally projected and conceptualized spaces found in literature. The tendency to sometimes associate space with architecture, art, or performance, neglects the key role it plays in the literary. Lefebvre has observed that "any search for space in literary texts will find it everywhere and in every guise: enclosed, described, projected, dreamt of, speculated about" (1991, p. 15). Using Lefebvre's approach, Thomas Dozeman has suggested that Herodotus' use of geography "represents a complex interaction of physical geography and social construction" (in "Geography and History in Herodotus and Ezra-Nehemiah," p. 455). Dozeman argues that Herodotus' work embodies Lefebvre's and Soja's trialectics, whereby perceived space is represented in Herodotus' aim to describe world geography, that conceived space is found in his attempt to represent continents and national structures and that the lived space of immediate experience is found in Herodotus' conception of how environmental factors result in different customs among the Greeks and Persians (in "Geography and History in Herodotus and Ezra-Nehemiah," p. 456). In classical archaeology, for example, Ray Laurence has used Lefebvre to inform his understanding of the role of social values in the construction of urban space at Pompeii and more recently on the role of Roman roads. Lefebvre (*Production of Space*, p. 245) suggested that the Roman road was a dominant feature in Roman civil and military society through linking the city with the countryside. In *The Roads of Roman Italy*, Laurence discusses a number of important issues including how the production of social space played a key role in the Roman conquest of Italy as well as the role of travel in creating distinctions in social status. On a number of levels, the work of Lefebvre and Soja has the ability to inform our understanding of the classical past through attention to spatial constructs.

Further reading

By Lefebvre

The Production of Space. Translated by Donald Nicholson-Smith. Oxford: Blackwell, 1991.

Critique of Everyday Life. Vol. 1. Translated by John Moore. London: Verso Books, 1991.

Critique of Everyday Life. Vol. 2. Translated by John Moore. London: Verso Books, 2002.

Critique of Everyday Life. Vol. 3. *From Modernity to Modernism (Towards a Metaphilosophy of Daily Life).* Translated by Gregory Elliot. London: Verso Books, 2003.

Henri Lefebvre: Key Writings. Edited by Stuart Elden, Elizabeth Lebas, and Eleonore Kofman. New York: Continuum, 2003.

About Lefebvre

*Dozeman, Thomas B. "Geography and History in Herodotus and Ezra-Nehemiah." *Journal of Biblical Literature.* 122.3 (2003) 449–66.

Flanagan, James W. "Ancient Perceptions of Space/Perceptions of Ancient Space." *Semeia* 87 (1999) 15–43.

Laurence, Ray. *Roman Pompeii: Space and Society.* London and New York: Routledge, 1994.

*Laurence, Ray. *The Roads of Roman Italy: Mobility and Cultural Change.* London and New York: Routledge, 1999.

Stuart, Elden. *Understanding Henri Lefebvre: theory and the possible.* London and New York: Continuum, 2004.

Wiles, David. *A Short History of Western Performance Space.* Cambridge: Cambridge University Press, 2003.

24 Emmanuel Levinas

Key concepts:
- ethics as first philosophy
- the Other (alterity, *autrui*)
- face-to-face encounter
- transcendence

Emmanuel Levinas (1906–95) was born in Kovno, Lithuania. His parents were devout Jews and part of a distinguished Jewish community. In 1923 he moved to Strasbourg, where he studied philosophy. In 1928–9 he studied phenomenology with Edmund Husserl in Freiburg. It was there that he met Martin **Heidegger**. Although one of the primary figures in Levinas' thought, he would later criticize Heidegger for his complicity with Nazism. Levinas' doctoral thesis was entitled *The Theory of Intuition in Husserl's Phenomenology* (1930). Before World War II, Levinas moved to Paris and began teaching at the École Normale Israélite Orientale. In 1935 he published "On Escape" (1935) in *Recherches Philosophiques*, an essay that evinces his desire to move beyond a discussion of phenomenological being. During the war, Levinas volunteered for the French military, serving as a translator of German and Russian. He was later captured by the Nazis and spent the remainder of the war in a prisoner of war camp. The Nazis captured and murdered many members of his family, including his parents. Fortunately, however, his wife and daughter survived in France. Levinas has described his life as dominated by the memory of exile, Nazi atrocities, and the Holocaust. After the war, he was reunited with his wife and daughter in Paris, where he participated in Talmudic studies with the famous Monsieur Chouchani (who was then also teaching the young Holocaust survivor Elie Wiesel, another Lithuanian).

Levinas became director of the Alliance Israélite Universelle, but did not begin his university career until the publication of his first major work

Totality and Infinity in 1961. He was appointed professor of philosophy at Poitiers, before moving on to the University of Paris-Nanterre in 1967 and finally to the Sorbonne, from which he retired in 1976.

For most of his career Levinas remained a relatively obscure philosopher, known primarily for his essays on the Talmud and interpretations of Husserl and Heidegger. The latter, especially the work on Husserl, exerts a strong influence on Jean-Paul Sartre and Simone de Beauvoir in their construction of Existentialism. Much attention was drawn to his work in 1963 by Jacques **Derrida**'s famous essay on Totality and Infinity entitled "Violence and Metaphysics." Derrida's essay, although critical of some of Levinas' major points, demonstrates how Levinas' articulation of responsibility and alterity provides further possibilities for ethics. Throughout his life, Derrida remained a primary interlocutor for Levinas' work, calling his thought "an immense event of this century" (Derrida, "Law of Hospitality," p. 153). Since the publication of Derrida's essay, Levinas' influence has grown immensely. His work on Jewish experience, Talmudic readings, and philosophy as well as how he employs the premises of phenomenology to reinscribe its discourse plays a central role in any discussion of social theory. Levinas died on December 25, 1995 during Hanukkah and his legacy has yet to be fully established.

Central to Levinas' philosophy is the claim that ethics and not ontology (first philosophy or nature of being) is the basis of philosophy. Instead, **Ethics as first philosophy**—one's responsibility for and obligation to the Other—is what makes metaphysics (study of the nature of reality) possible. Because philosophy posits ontology as first philosophy, Levinas' contention challenges both the very foundations of Western metaphysics as such and the limitations of locating the origins of philosophy in Hellenism. This leads to his examination of what he terms "pre-philosophical" texts, primarily Russian literature and the Hebrew Bible. The central theme of Levinas' ethics is an inescapable obligation to care for the Other, which differs from the subject–object relation as discussed by Sartre. In Sartre's work the subject–object relation is one fraught with antagonism and alienation; it undermines any notion of authenticity, which for Sartre leaves one responsible for sustaining one's situation. For Levinas, the dictum of the Oracle at Delphi to "know yourself" is impossible without knowledge of the Other. The **Other** (*autrui*, alterity) is the not-me, that which is beyond or exterior to my own self-understanding and sense of the world. This other is not an abstraction, but a radical exterior tied directly to another human being. Levinas grounds his argument that we are always responsible for and to the Other in a rigorous discussion of phenomenology and ethics.

The condition of the 'self' or 'me' [*L'même*, the same] in this relation is one of passivity because in the face-to-face encounter with the absolute Other [*Autrui*] one is required to respond: to recognize the Other without any mediating factors such as religion, law, philosophy, etc. Ethics is first philosophy because there are no mediating factors in the primal need to respond to the Other. The **face-to-face encounter** with the Other is one in which the traditional subject does not exist except in its obligation to this Other face whose presence calls to mind the biblical injunction "Thou shall not kill." This prohibition is both literal and metaphorical for Levinas, who argues that to deny the Other's existence by reducing alterity to sameness constitutes "killing." If the subject "makes sense" of the Other according to a preexisting system of thought, explains the Other away, or regards the Other as a means to an end, then alterity is killed. The face-to-face encounter with alterity is the "ultimate situation" because it is "present in its refusal to be contained" (*Totality and Infinity*, pp. 81, 194). It obliges 'me' to open myself to it, thereby sacrificing my own sense of self-contained identity and any sense of security.

This relation with alterity is the primal encounter from which all language and communication are made possible. In the face of the Other we must acknowledge a responsibility for the Other. In this dialogical I–thou relation that Levinas adapts from Buber's famous text *I and Thou* [*Ich und Du*] (1923) to look into the face of the Other is not only to hear the injunction not to kill, but also to experience responsibility for the Other. This inescapable responsibility is not the result of a sovereign decision on the part of an autonomous subject, but rather it is the condition, which pre-exists and founds any notion of a subject. With a term borrowed from Heidegger, one could discuss Levinas' thesis as one in which we are "thrown" into responsibility: it is an unconditional demand that is made upon me. For this reason the face-to-face encounter is an exposure without moralism or pathos; to recognize the Other exceeds even cognition. And, "the responsibility for the Other is structured as the one-for-the-other, indeed even as the one *hostage* of the other ..."(in *Of God Who Comes to Mind*, (1998) p. 172). Derrida (in *Of Hospitality*) has dealt with the ethical implications of the unconditional hospitality to the stranger, becomes a form of oppression that might result from a reading of Levinas' ethical position. Thus, Levinas' ethics do not represent a simple alternative to the concept of being that grounds Western metaphysics. In this condition of responsibility, one does not know what to do or what is expected of one, or where to "draw the line." This is precisely the in-between of ethics as first philosophy.

Levinas' critique of phenomenology, especially Heidegger's ontology of **Dasein**, is a critique of Western philosophy as a philosophy of "totality." Rather than thinking "totality," the same, or being, Levinas thinks ethics and alterity. The stakes of his critique are high, but the consequences of the idealism of "totality"—the dream/nightmare of Western philosophy—are much worse. In *On Escape* Levinas' words are pointed and direct:

> [T]he value of European civilization consists incontestably in the aspi-
> rations of idealism, if not in its path: in its primary inspiration idealism
> seeks to surpass being. Every civilization that accepts being—with the
> tragic despair it contains and the crimes it justifies—merits the name

"barbarian".... It is a matter of getting out of being by a new path, at the risk of overturning certain notions that to common sense and the wisdom of the nations seemed the most evident.

(p. 73)

One can read the trajectory of Levinas' work *in toto* in this early statement. To find "new paths" in order to "get out of being" is a call for nothing less than an escape from the very confines of Western philosophy as such. This is evident in his concept of **transcendence**. The face-to-face encounter with alterity is a form of religious experience, albeit not the kind of religious experience that affirms the foundations of religious certainty. In one's responsibility for the Other, an awareness arises of the wholly Other. Levinas often discusses the individual face of the Other—that singularity—as the trace of God. Thus, the encounter with the Other is one of responsibility that is simultaneously an encounter with transcendence. Transcendence means to experience the "trace of the Other," which is completely outside of the self, what is beyond exterior, and yet that which remains the most intimate relation. For Levinas, transcendence is not the totality of the same that he sees as the barbaric foundation of Western metaphysics and politics.

Levinas' ethics has been subjected to several critiques, not only by Derrida, but also by Alain Badiou in his polemical text *Ethics: An Essay on the Understanding of Evil* (published in French in 1998). But the intersection of Judeo-Christian thought and modern European philosophy has made Levinas' work central to a variety of disciplines, including literary studies. In terms of classical texts and ancient art, there has been little written on the many implications of Levinas' concept of ethics and responsibility.

With regard to the latter, Levinas' essay "Reality and Its Shadow," which appeared in a 1948 issue of the journal *Les Temps Modernes*, has interesting implications. Levinas argues that our "confrontation" with works of art raises questions about the fundamental face-to-face encounter. He argues that art opens an "interval" or "meanwhile" between representation and reality. In an argument that interpellates Plato as well as Heidegger, Levinas argues that art shadows reality. This "doubling" allows art to be a mode of escape [*l'evasion*] from the responsibility we have to others because by focusing on the play of appearance—the shadow of reality—we forget our obligation to the face-to-face (authentic) encounter that precedes any discussion of being and through which a just world is created. Levinas criticizes the position of art for art's sake, what he calls "artistic idolatry." Instead, Levinas asserts that the "world to be built is replaced by the essential completion of its shadow. This is not the disinterestedness of contemplation but of irresponsibility" (p. 126). Levinas requires classical archaeologists to interpret the artwork in its past context: "The immobile statue has to be put into movement and made to speak" (p. 127). The key here is that this concept of "being made to speak" is not ventriloquism, but an ethical responsibility with regard to alterity. This concept has been at the center of many discussions of art and social theory, especially postcolonial theory. But those calls, while ethical, remain within a dimension of the political. With Levinas, the ethical turn is not what remains to be done, but what will have been done if there is to be any discourse between subjects and objects that is not merely the totality of the same.

With regard to texts, Levinas' work has been used to elaborate on the construction of the subject in relationship to the Other, a relationship between self and Other, identity and alterity, which many, but especially Jean-Pierre Vernant, have noted go hand and hand. This is famously illustrated in Levinas' reading of Odysseus, which regards Odyesseus' adventures in the world as "nothing but a return to his native land, a complacency with the same, a misrecognition of the Other" (in "The Trace of the Other," p. 348). The adventures of Odysseus are contrasted with the pilgrimage of Abraham: Odysseus makes a circular journey, which returns him to his home, but Abraham makes a pilgrimage to a strange land where he remains. Odysseus is in retreat from the Other whereas Abraham confronts the Other. Odysseus comes to represent a subject that returns to himself. In "Oedipus in the Accusative," Miriam Leonard summarizes many of the arguments around Odysseus, observing that the strangeness Odysseus encounters in his return ultimately leads him to reject the complacency of the Same. However, she also notes that for Levinas "only the biblical can offer an alternative to speaking Greek" (p. 237). In "Networks and the Emergence of Greek Identity" (p. 59) Irad Malkin has argued that contact with the other through overseas experiences played a key role in the formation of Hellenic identity. Both Malkin and Leonard question the Hellenic heritage of European civilization. Though not acknowledging a specific debt to Levinas, Meyer Reinhold (in "Classical Past and American Present") emphasizes the alien-ness of Greek and Roman cultures. On a broader level, Levinas' work encourages us to write an ethical past, paying attention to its otherness, rather than writing an ancient history that mirrors the present, what Julian Thomas (in "Same, Other, analogue") has called writing about the past under the sign of the same, thereby placing it under erasure, and in effect, killing it.

Further reading

By Levinas

Totality and Infinity: An Essay on Exteriority. Translated by Alfonso Lingis. Pittsburgh: Dusquesne University Press, 1969.

Ethics and Infinity: Conversations with Philippe Nemo. Translated by Richard A. Cohen. Pittsburgh: Dusquesne University Press, 1985.

Time and the Other. Translated by R. A. Cohen. Pittsburgh: Duquesne University Press, 1987.

"The Trace of the Other," in *Deconstruction in Context*. Translated by A. Lingus, edited by M C. Taylor. Chicago: University of Chicago Press, 1986.

Nine Talmudic Readings by Emmanuel Levinas. Translated by Annette Aronowicz. Bloomington: Indiana University Press, 1990.

The Levinas Reader. Edited by Seán Hand. Oxford: Blackwell, 1990.
Of God Who Comes to Mind. Translated by Bettina Bergo. Stanford: Stanford University Press, 1998.
On Escape. Translated by Bettina Bergo. Stanford: Stanford University Press, 2003.
"Reality and Its Shadow." In *The Continental Aesthetics Reader*, edited by Clive Cazeaux. London and New York: Routledge, 2000.
Is It Righteous to Be?: Interviews with Emmanuel Levinas. Edited by Jill Robbins. Stanford: Stanford University Press, 2001.

About Levinas

Assheuer, Thomas. "'The Law of Hospitality': An Interview with Jacques Derrida." *Suitcase 3* (1998).
Badiou, Alain. *Ethics: An Essay on the Understanding of Evil*. Translated by Peter Hallward. London and New York: Verso, 2001.
Blooechl, Jeffrey (ed.). *The Face of the Other & the Trace of God: Essays on the Philosophy of Emmanuel Levinas*. New York: Fordham University Press, 2000.
Caygill, Howard. *Levinas and the Political*. London and New York: Routledge, 2002.
*Cornell, Drucilla. *The Philosophy of the Limit*. New York and London: Routledge, 1992.
Critchley, Simon, and Robert Bernasioni (eds). *The Cambridge Companion to Emmanuel Levinas*. Cambridge: Cambridge University Press, 2002.
Csordas, Thomas J. "Asymptote of the Ineffable: Embodiment, Alterity, and the Theory of Religion." *Current Anthropology* 45 (2004) 163–86.
Derrida, Jacques. "Violence and Metaphysics: An Essay on the Thought of Emmanuel Levinas." In *Writing and Difference*. Translated by Alan Bass. Chicago: University of Chicago Press, 1978.
Derrida, Jacques. *Adieu to Emmanuel Levinas*. Translated by Pascale-Anne Brault and Michael Nass. Stanford: Stanford University Press, 1999.
Derrida, Jacques. *Of Hospitality*. Translated by Rachel Bowlby. Stanford: Stanford University Press, 2000.
Jay, Martin. "The Ethics of Blindness and the Postmodern Sublime: Levinas and Lyotard." In *Downcast Eyes: The Denigration of Vision in Twentieth-Century French Thought*. Berkeley: University of California Press, 1993.
*Leonard, Miriam. "Oedipus in the Accusative: Derrida and Levinas." *Comparative Literature Studies* 43.3 (2006) 224–51.
Malkin, Irad. "Networks and the Emergence of Greek Identity." *Mediterranean Historical Review*. 18.2 (2003) 56–74.
Reinhold, Meyer. "Classical Past and American Present." *The Classical Journal* 84.3 (1989) 239–45.
Thomas, Julian. (1990) "Same, Other, analogue: writing the past," In *Writing the Past In the Present*, edited by F. Baker and J. Thomas. Lampeter: St. David's University College, St. David's University.
Vernant, Jean-Pierre. "Sous le regard d'autrui." In *Entre mythe et politique*. Paris: Seuil, 1996.
Wall, Thomas Carl. *Radical Passivity: Levinas, Blanchot, and Agamben*. Albany: State University of New York Press, 1999.
Yale French Studies 104 (2004): *Encounters with Levinas*.

25 Jean-François Lyotard

Key concepts:

- metanarrative
- postmodern condition
- *petits récits*
- differend
- hyphen
- event
- figure
- aesthetics of the sublime

Jean-François Lyotard (1924–98) was born in Versailles, France. He studied phenomenology under Maurice **Merleau-Ponty**. His doctoral work was entitled *Discours, figure* (1971) and his first major publication is an excellent critical introduction to phenomenology (1954). Lyotard began his academic career as a secondary school teacher in Algeria. It was there that he witnessed first-hand the brutality and oppression of colonialism. Throughout his life Lyotard was politically active. He played a primary role in several leftist political groups, including from 1953 to 1963 one called "Socialisme ou barbarie," which comprised both intellectuals and workers. This group wrote critical pieces about the French presence in Algeria and served as a kind of political model for many of the groups formed in the aftermath of the May 1968 strikes in Paris. Lyotard taught at the University of Nanterre and the University of Paris, in addition to holding posts at several American universities including Yale, Emory, and the University of California, Irvine. Besides being closely associated with postmodernism and a philosophy of desire, Lyotard's work is wide-ranging, covering topics as diverse as linguistic and political philosophy, aesthetics, and literature. His interest in art and art history led to his role as the curator of an exhibition entitled *Les Immatériaux*, which took place in 1985 at the Centre Georges Pompidou in Paris.

From his earliest work, Lyotard resisted the so-called structuralist "linguistic turn" that emphasized the way language shapes experience and which was so influential among his contemporaries in France in the 1950s and 1960s (e.g., Lévi-Strauss, **Lacan, Barthes**). He insisted, rather, that there is always a gap between experience and language and that one must not rule out extra-linguistic experience. Language does not construct experience completely because there are events that language does not and cannot represent.

Lyotard's two most influential publications are *The Postmodern Condition: A Report on Knowledge* (1979), originally written as a report on the current state of knowledge for the government of Quebec, and *The Differend: Phrases in Dispute* (1983). The two texts are closely related and together provide a valuable introduction to Lyotard's philosophy.

A key concept in *The Postmodern Condition* is "**metanarrative**," or "grand" or "master" narrative. Lyotard uses the term to refer to the overarching mythic narratives that individuals and societies use to structure knowledge and legitimate truth-claims. A metanarrative locates a current situation, whether individual or communal, within a larger narrative structure that plots movement toward some ultimate objective—progress, triumph of reason, victory of the proletariat, redemption, etc. These types of single, unified accounts of events are totalizing structures that claim to resolve difference and may also serve an ideological purpose (e.g. **Marx**).

The "**postmodern condition**"—ascribed to the contemporary West by Lyotard—is one in which there is an increasing "incredulity" and distrust toward metanarratives. Lyotard asserts that metanarratives are being replaced by a proliferation of *petits récits*, "little stories" or testimonies that draw attention to the particular as opposed to the universal, that is, to local events, individual experiences, heterodox ideas, and other practices and narratives that are not included in the predominant metanarratives (Christianity, Marxism, etc.). Within the postmodern condition there is a newly found interest in difference and dissension that challenges the drive toward homogeneity Lyotard describes as "totalitarian." Against this drive, he urges us to "wage war on totality; let us be witnesses to the unpresentable; let us activate the differences and save the honor of the name" (*The Postmodern Condition*, p. 82).

Lyotard continues this line of thought, including its ethical imperative, in *The Differend*. Here he uses the term "**differend**" to explain the silencing of particular differences that do not fit within larger conceptual or social totalities. It signifies that someone or something has been denied voice or visibility by the dominant ideological system, which deems what is and is not acceptable. Such radical differences are suppressed because they cannot be subsumed under overarching universal concepts without undermining them. "Differend" means at once dispute, difference, and otherness (alterity).

The logic of the differend undermines certainty and the myth of the transcendental subject because it is premised on an inhuman, radical alterity.

The singularity of the event makes one attentive to the presence of multiplicity, subversion, and potentiality within language. The sublime is an experience of the limits of language within language itself that sets forth the ethical and political task of the postmodern: to change discourse and to destabilize the narrative structure of discourse and its history in order to present the aesthetics of the sublime.

With regard to metanarratives, Lyotard is particularly interested in how the Jews and their history are marginalized within the largely Christian metanarrative of Western culture. The most extreme instance of this may be found in the "forgetting" of the Holocaust, an event that radically undermines the Western myth of progress and humanism. In *Heidegger and "the jews"* (first published in French in 1988), for example, he explores the irony that Heidegger, the great philosopher of forgotten Being, has more or less willfully forgotten the Holocaust and the Jews. We must always remember that something has been forgotten that must not be forgotten and that our very lives are indebted to that something. This was, for Lyotard, Heidegger's sin.

Along similar lines, one of Lyotard's last works, *Hyphen* (first published in French in 1993) argues that the **hyphen** in "Judeo-Christian" marks the subsumption of Judaism within Christianity. While appearing to embrace and identify with Judaism, the idea of the Judeo-Christian places Judaism's actual difference and dissent within the predominantly Christian West under erasure. Patricia Bikai (In "Black Athena and the Phoenicians") has similarly argued that hyphenated terms such as Graeco-Phoenician, Egypto-Phoenician, and Hebraeo-Phoenician, relegate the Phoenicians to the status of a non-people, who are frequently considered only in terms of what they can tell us about Greek culture (e.g. transmission of the alphabet). Alternatively they are stereotyped as an alien 'other' based on biblical representations of them as evil and pagan. Other hyphenated terms that have found their way into classical studies and merit a similar critique include the terms Cypro-Minoan and Levanto-Helladic.

To counter metanarratives, Lyotard forwards the indeterminacy of language games and linguistic play. The critical play of the *petit récits* is evident in his contention that they reveal the incommensurability between metanarratives and the singularity of the event. Metanarratives are unable to fully account for the event. Lyotard's argument here is explicitly post-structuralist and anti-Hegelian. The **event**, for Lyotard, is a singularity, an occurrence or a happening. (His usage here borrows from Martin **Heidegger**'s concept of *Ereignis*.) Lyotard's position is that an event cannot be completely articulated, translated, or represented by discourse. It is here that his reliance upon the aesthetic arena becomes evident. For him, the aesthetic—the production and the reception of the work of art—offers an alternative to the conceits of any metanarrative while simultaneously transmitting the undisclosed aspect of the event. In other words, what discourse is unable to attend to, the work of art can represent as feeling, sensation, or desire. It is important to note that in Lyotard's thought the concept of truth is premised on the notion that sensibility and understanding occur before cognition (see also **Merleau-Ponty**). The artwork communicates pre-conceptual knowledge; it communicates a radical alterity prior to and independent of cognition. Therefore, an artwork's ability to communicate the incommunicable plays an ethical and political role in Lyotard's philosophy. Works of art disclose the limitations of discourse—the hegemony of reason and metanarratives. Although the focus is on modern and contemporary art, it can be argued that all art is contemporary because it is written about in and into the present.

Influenced by classical archaeology, art history has traditionally deployed metanarratives of style and historical development, alongside other inter-pretative frameworks, to explain its subject matter. Social function and meaning, rupture, and even alterity as an aesthetic, as observed in Minoan art (see Hitchcock, "Naturalizing the Cultural") can focus on the event, which stands in opposition to these metanarratives. Lyotard's aesthetics of the sublime—which at once possess the logic of play and games as well as the experience of the event—is a theorization of the particular that erodes the conceits of the grand narratives. The aesthetics of the sublime is a form of judgment counter to established rules and values, a break with the consensus. He articulates this by distinguishing between discourse and the figure. The **figure** is the basic aesthetic form and it occurs prior to any meaning and/or representation. For Lyotard, there is no possibility of mean-ing without figure, which is never fully locatable in the semiotic. The figure is excessive; it is sublime and, as such, it leaves one at a loss for words. In discussing the figure, he relies on **Freud**'s work on desire and the libidinal economy, in which the communicative (discourse) is associated with the conscious and the libidinal (figure) is associated with the unconscious. Lyotard claims that the relation between discourse and the figure reveals that reality is irreducible to representation. There is no discourse without figures, yet the feelings and intense desire represented by figures delimit any discursive contextualization. The release of desire signaled by the figure does not communicate discursively, but rather it foregrounds precisely what is incommunicable and, thereby, what exceeds the boundaries of discourse as such.

"The Sublime and the Avant-Garde," originally published in *Artforum* in 1984, offers a concise summary of the ethical and political importance Lyotard gives the art of the avant-garde through his use of the concept of the sublime (see also Jacques **Derrida**'s *The Truth in Painting* for a related discussion of the sublime). Lyotard's interest in the sublime reinforces his contention about sensation and pre-existing cognition. The sublime is an event that transcends the limits of knowledge and discourse because it is an experience of pleasure and pain, joy and anxiety: the presence of the unknow-able and the unrepresentable is felt in the experience of the sublime and inas-much it indicates the presence of an insurmountable radical difference.

Lyotard's **aesthetics of the sublime** seeks to theorize an aesthetic event that interrupts any narrative tradition of aesthetic experience as well as any residual claim to canonical representation. The sublime is inexorable alterity, a particular event that undermines the foundations of the classical tradition as a metanarrative and traditional aesthetics as a "science."

Although Immanuel Kant occupies a central place in Lyotard's later work (e.g., *Lessons on the Analytic of the Sublime*), in "The Sublime and the Avant-Garde" he relies more on Edmund Burke's conception of the sublime as given in his *Philosophical Inquiry into the Origin of our Ideas of the Sublime and the Beautiful* (1757). Lyotard begins his essay with a reference to Barnett Newman, specifically to his painting *Vir Heroicus Sublimis* (1950–1) and his essay "The Sublime is Now" (1948). In defining his notion of the sublime event—an instant of exultation and despair—in relation to Newman's work, Lyotard writes: "The event happens as a question mark 'before' happening as a question. *It happens* is rather 'in the first place', *is it happening, is this it, is it possible*" (p. 454). He proceeds to further define this sublime event in terms that recall Samuel Beckett's plays *Waiting for Godot* and *Endgame*:

> The possibility of nothing happening is often associated with a feeling of anxiety, a term with strong connotations in modern philosophies of existence and of the unconscious. It gives to waiting, if we really mean waiting, a predominantly negative value. But suspense can also be accompanied by pleasure, for instance pleasure in welcoming the unknown, and even by joy, to speak like Baruch Spinoza, the joy obtained by the intensification of being that the event brings with it. This is probably a contradictory feeling. It is at the very least a sign, the question mark itself, the way in which *it happens* is withheld and announced: *Is it happening?*
>
> (p. 455)

The sublime event, which occurs before perception and cognition, demands that we bear witness to that which is irredeemably other and unrepresentable. This is the basic premise of Lyotard's ethical argument, which bears the influence of the work of Emmanuel **Levinas**.

Lyotard's studies of alterity, the hyphen, the differend (focusing on what is excluded from the discourse), and especially metanarratives, have important implications for the understanding and reception of classics. As has frequently been the case in biblical studies, it can be argued that the study of classics is at the heart of the quest for a metanarrative of Western history. Theories of culture and history are metanarratives of the development of human culture as it progresses from the primitive and/or prehistoric to that which is modern, free, Western, creative, and progressive.

Martin Bernal (in *Black Athena*) argues that the privileging of classical cultures over Egyptian and Phoenician history has to do with their respective roles in different metanarratives: colonial Britain cast itself in the role of the Phoenicians as colonial, seafaring, and mercantile oriented, while in Renaissance times, Egyptian religion was seen as the source of an earlier and mystical religion that could be turned to, to heal religious schisms in Europe. Different aspects of the classics have been privileged as part of the metanarrative in the development of the Western nation state in recent times. For example, Athenian democracy is upheld as part of the genealogy of American democracy, while the Roman republic was privileged as a model in the birth of French republicanism. The rational, logical, and individualistic elements of ancient Greek society have been emphasized over the mystical and irrational: we are like them, because they are like us. In contrast, Hartog (in *Memories of Odysseus*) has looked at how the Greeks have used Egypt as well as other cultures in the constructions of their own metanarratives. Feminist classicists have regarded male-authored narratives such as Homer as metanarratives, which have "received, transmitted, and influenced the traditional male-centered system of representation" (Gold in "Finding the Female in Roman Poetry" p. 84). Standing in opposition to these various metanarratives is the turning away from great men and big events and contemporary interest in the *petits récits*: the history of farmsteads, villages (such as the final Bronze/Early Iron Age site of Kavousi on Crete), households, rural cults, and role of women, which present a very different and particularized history of the classical world.

Further reading

By Lyotard

The Postmodern Condition: A Report on Knowledge. Translated by Geoff Bennington and Brian Massumi. Minneapolis: University of Minnesota Press, 1984.

The Inhuman: Reflection on Time. Translated by Geoffrey Bennington and Rachel Bowlby. Stanford: Stanford University Press, 1988.

"Philosophy and Painting in the Age of their Experimentation: Contribution to and Idea of Postmodernity." Translated by Mária Minich Breuer and Daniel Breuer. In *The Lyotard Reader*, edited by Andrew Benjamin. Oxford: Blackwell, 1989.

The Differend: Phrases in Dispute. Translated by Georges Van Den Abbeele. Minneapolis: University of Minnesota Press, 1989.

Heidegger and "the Jews." Translated by Andreas Michel and Mark S. Roberts. Minneapolis: University of Minnesota Press, 1990.

Phenomenology. Translated by Brian Beakley. Albany: State University of New York Press, 1991.

Libidinal Economy. Translated by Ian Hamilton Grant. Bloomington: University of Indiana Press, 1993.

Political Writings. Translated by Bill Readings and Kevin Paul Geiman. Minneapolis: University of Minnesota Press, 1993.

Lessons on the Analytic of the Sublime: Kant's Critique of Judgment. Translated by Elizabeth Rottenberg. Stanford: Stanford University Press, 1994.

"Les Immatériaux." In *Thinking about Exhibitions*, edited by Reesa Greenberg, Bruce W. Ferguson, and Sandy Nairne. London and New York: Routledge, 1996.

With Eberhard Gruber. *Hyphen: Between Judaism and Christianity*. Translated by Pascale-Anne Brault and Michael Naas. Atlantic Highlands, NJ: Humanity Books, 1999.

About Lyotard

Benjamin, Andrew (ed.). *Judging Lyotard*. London and New York: Routledge, 1992.

Bennington, Geoffrey. *Lyotard: Writing the Event*. Manchester: Manchester University Press, 1988.

Bernal, Martin. *Black Athena: The Afroasiatic Roots of Classical Civilization. Vol. I: The Fabrication of Ancient Greece 1785–1985*. New Brunswick, NJ: Rutgers University Press, 1987.

*Bikai, Patricia M. "Black Athena and the Phoenicians," *Journal of Mediterranean Archaeology*. 3.1 (1990) 67–75.

Carroll, David. *Paraesthetics: Foucault, Lyotard, Derrida*. London and New York: Routledge, 1987.

Foster, Hal. *The Return of the Real: The Avant-Garde at the End of the Century*. Cambridge, MA: MIT Press, 1996.

Gold, Barbara. "Finding the Female in Roman Poetry." In *Feminist Theory and the Classics*, edited by Nancy Sorkin Rabinowitz and Amy Richlin. New York: Routledge, 1993.

*Hartog, François. *Memories of Odysseus: Frontier Tales from Ancient Greece*. Translated by Janet Lloyd. Chicago: University of Chicago Press, 2001.

Hitchcock, Louise A. "Naturalizing the Cultural: Architectonicized Landscape as Ideology in Minoan Crete." In *Building Communities: House, Settlement and Society in the Aegean and Beyond, Cardiff University, April 17–21, 2001*, edited by Ruth Westgate, Nick Fisher, and James Whitley. (British School at Athens Studies 15) 2007.

Jay, Martin. "The Ethics of Blindness and the Postmodern Sublime: Levinas and Lyotard." In *Downcast Eyes: The Denigration of Vision in Twentieth-Century French Thought*. Berkeley: University of California Press, 1993.

Readings Bill. *Introducing Lyotard: Art and Politics*. London and New York: Routledge, 1991.

26 Maurice Merleau-Ponty

Key concepts:

- phenomenology
- primacy of perception
- lived experience
- lived body
- embodiment

Maurice Merleau–Ponty (1908–61) was a French philosopher particularly interested in the nature of human consciousness as embodied experience. He was born in Rochefort-sur-mer, France. As a student at the École normale supérieure, he became interested in phenomenology through the work of Edmund Husserl and Martin **Heidegger**. After graduating in 1930, Merleau-Ponty taught at different high schools, but with the outbreak of World War II he served as an officer in the French army. While participating in the French Resistance during the German occupation, he taught in Paris and wrote *The Phenomenology of Perception* (1945), widely regarded as his most important work.

Following the war, he co-founded the left-leaning cultural and political journal *Les Temps Moderne* with Jean-Paul Sartre. Although the journal itself was never tied to a particular political organization, after the war Merleau-Ponty was an active member of the French Communist Party. His affiliation with the group and his relationship with the political and institutional interpretation of **Marx**'s work became strained however, ultimately resulting in his 1955 work *Adventures of the Dialectic*. He resigned his position on the editorial board of *Les Temps Modernes* after repeated disagreements with Sartre over the latter's support of North Korea during the Korean War. Merleau-Ponty's postwar academic career included positions at the Sorbonne and, from 1952 until his premature death in 1961, at the Collège de France.

Merleau-Ponty's thought centers on understanding the lived, embodied nature of human consciousness and perception. But what makes his work so compelling for subsequent scholars is his incorporation of **Saussure's** structuralist ideas into a phenomenological context. Among noted theorists influenced by his work in this regard were Claude Lévi-Strauss, Michel **Foucault**, Paul Ricoeur, Louis **Althusser**, and Judith **Butler**. More recently, Merleau-Ponty's work has been pursued by social scientists interested in critiquing traditional assumptions about the relationship between body and mind, and the nature of human experience.

In order to understand Merleau-Ponty's philosophy, we need to briefly consider phenomenology, the perspective that informs much of his thinking. As the name suggests, **phenomenology** explores any phenomena [from *phainein* meaning 'to show'; Greek for 'appearance'], which are perceived directly by the senses. The German founder of phenomenology, Edmund Husserl, argues that although philosophical proofs for the independent existence of objects perceived through the senses are impossibly difficult to establish, human beings nevertheless experience the external world as objects of consciousness. That is, knowledge of the world begins with lived experience [*Erlebnis*]. Husserl's method aims at "bracketing out" [*epoche*] or suspending any and all *a priori* ideas and assumptions about the world. By "bracketing out" the scientific and philosophical conceptualization of the world, Husserl believes that pure or preconceptual perception can be identified. He contends that we can isolate the underlying sensory perceptions that constitute our experiences of ideas, images, emotions, objects, and other things that are perceived in consciousness.

One of the main premises of phenomenology is the contention that human consciousness is intentional; i.e., it is always directed at or toward something; it is always an experience of something. Consciousness, is therefore, nothing without its relation to the world, to the environment [*Umwelt*] that is always already there. The concept of the transcendental consciousness that Husserl aims for with his *epochal* method is conceived of as what remains after this process of "bracketing out" has occurred; transcendental consciousness is immediate knowledge of the world of pure experience. In the work of Husserl's followers, including Merleau-Ponty, there is an extended critique of **Freud** and psychoanalysis, especially his concept of the unconscious. Merleau-Ponty argues that phenomenology can already account for fragmented consciousness and for the types of experience Freud seeks to explain by positing the unconscious.

Merleau-Ponty contributes to the phenomenology of Husserl by extending his premises and works against Husserl's privileging of consciousness. The focus of Merleau-Ponty's work is on the concepts of embodiment and perception. In the Husserlian view, which is indebted to Cartesian philosophy, human beings are conscious entities first and foremost. Against this view, Merleau-Ponty insists that human identity—our subjectivity—is informed first and foremost by our physicality, our bodies. He asserts the centrality of the body and the body's influence on our perception of the world. These issues are explored in *Phenomenology of Perception* where Merleau-Ponty critiques and opposes the Cartesian concept of a body–mind dichotomy. It is essential, he insists, to recognize that people are not disembodied thinking minds, but rather bodies connected to a material world. Bodies are, therefore, not abstract, but are concrete entities in the world through which perception occurs and subjectivity is formed (see also Pierre **Bourdieu**, Luce **Irigaray**, and Judith **Butler**).

For Merleau-Ponty, the world is the ground of experience. His position, colored by Heidegger's concept of being-in-the-world, is that subjectivity is of the world, not separate or disconnected from it, and it is fueled by the "**primacy of perception.**" Our access to the world is through the body and concrete perception, and not through, or not only through, the workings of a disembodied mind or consciousness. Contrary to Descartes' principle, *Cogito ergo sum* ("I think, therefore I am"), existence is not thinking but embodiment. Indeed, all thinking is embodied; it derives from consciousness, which itself develops from the subject's bodily perceptions. These perceptions underlie rationalization and other conscious and logical operations in their meaning. Thus, Merleau-Ponty privileges the body over the mind in our experience of the world. Perception is incarnate: perceptions do not exist as bodiless abstractions, but only within bodies. Perception occurs only in the world of lived experience. Perception does not exist as an abstraction transcending or standing outside the lived body.

Merleau-Ponty asserted that it is through **lived experience** that we gain knowledge of the world. He states that the activities of the body in the world constitute lived experience. Such experience is never fixed but is always in process. We both shape and are shaped by our lived experiences. The mind that perceives things is incarnate in the body. Perception and consciousness are not separate from or transcendent of lived experience in the world.

Perception is directly connected to the **lived body**. By lived body, Merleau-Ponty is referring to both the body that experiences the world and the body that is experienced. The subject (person) doing the perceiving is embodied. This embodiment is thus the link to the external, phenomenal, experienced world. Humans consist of conscious components, but it is our bodily aspects that determine who we are. This concept of **embodiment** is central to Merleau-Ponty's work. According to him, it is not just the mind, which perceives, experiences, and represents the world—a traditional philosophical view of the centrality of mind. Instead, the concept of embodiment means that the body plays a central role in how one understands the world.

Despite the insistence by some influential philosophers that consciousness is foundational to what it means to be a human being, Merleau-Ponty argues that whatever we experience in the world or understand about the world derives fundamentally from our bodies and our embodied minds. Perception underpins categorization or theorization even if it appears that we have thoughts and conceptualizations about the world that we only secondarily experience physically. The world can only be viewed from our physical time and place. As Merleau-Ponty states: "Our own body is in the world as the heart is in the organism: it keeps the visible spectacle constantly alive, it breathes life into it and sustains it inwardly, and with it forms a system" (*Phenomenology of Perception*, p. 235). In Merleau-Ponty's schema the world is not merely an external object to think about, but becomes known and recognized through our perceptions and experiences. Philosophical ideas that consciousness does all the work of perceiving the world are thereby erroneous. From Merleau-Ponty's perspective, you cannot have consciousness without the body—body and mind are inextricably bound. Subjectivity, then, is incarnate. For Merleau-Ponty, embodied knowledge precludes the possibility of a realm of autonomous knowledge gained prior to or without the body. Analysis of the world is always the activity of an embodied mind.

The concept of body subject is used by Merleau-Ponty in *Phenomenology of Perception* to refer to the idea that the body, mind, and world are completely intertwined and not separable as Cartesian thought asserts. Merleau-Ponty's phenomenology seeks to understand this interconnection, not to try to locate some immutable consciousness transcending the world as experienced by bodies. The notion of body subject underscores Merleau-Ponty's insistence that it is a body that connects a person to the world. Cartesian duality breaks down at this juncture. There is no disembodied mind that observes objects out there in the world. We live in the world by way of our bodies. Subject and object are a unity, not a duality. That is, you must not treat them as separate realms, but rather as two sides of the same entity that exists—embodied—in the world.

In *The Visible and the Invisible* (1964) Merleau-Ponty writes:

> What there is then are not things first identical with themselves, which would offer themselves to the seer, nor is there a seer who is first empty and who, afterward, would open himself to them—but something to which we could not be closer than by palpitating it with our look, things we could not dream of seeing 'all naked' because the gaze itself envelops them, clothes them with its own flesh.
>
> (p. 130)

Between consciousness and reality, there is "an inside of an outside"—the human body. (Merleau-Ponty's theory of the gaze is taken up by Jacques **Lacan** in *Seminar XI: The Four Fundamental Concepts of Psychoanalysis*.) What Merleau-Ponty posits in this quotation is that "colours, patterns, and textures of sensory experience, *before they are the qualities of objects*, are the thick interactions which manifest the disclosive, intentional structure of experience" (Cazeaux, "Merleau-Ponty," p. 76).

The work of Merleau-Ponty (as well as Giddens and **Bourdieu**) has influenced a number of classical archaeologists who have shifted their attention from the description of objects to the experience of them as a process of embodiment. While not making specific reference to Merleau-Ponty, Minoan buildings have been interpreted based on recreating the experience of those who used them, while others have looked at the relationship between trance, ritual, and gesture as embodied experiences, and the sensuous aspects of feasting and sacrifice, which include smells, heat, chanting, and intoxication. Thus, "thinking through the body" is quickly becoming a catch-phrase in classical archaeology. Embodiment is also of key significance to the study of texts. The study of oral traditions, the pleasure of hearing texts read aloud, the study of performances (whether plays, the recreation of battles, or ancient music) all derive their justification from Merleau-Ponty's ideas on the primacy of perception.

Further reading

By Merleau-Ponty

The Structure of Behavior. Translated by Alden L. Fisher. Boston: Beacon Press, 1963.
The Primacy of Perception and Other Essays. Translated by James M. Edie. Evanston: Northwestern University Press, 1964.
The Visible and the Invisible. Edited by Claude Lefort and translated by Alphonso Lingis. Evanston: Northwestern University Press, 1968.
The Essential Writings of Merleau-Ponty. Edited by Alden L. Fisher. New York: Harcourt, Brace, and World, 1969.
Adventures of the Dialectic. Translated by Joseph Bien. Evanston: Northwestern University Press, 1973.
*Phenomenology of Perception. Translated by Colin Smith. London and New York: Routledge, 2002.

About Merleau-Ponty

Barral, Mary Rose. *Merleau-Ponty: The Role of the Body-Subject in Interpersonal Relations*. Pittsburgh: Duquesne University Press, 1965.
Carman, Taylor and Hansen, Mark (eds). *The Cambridge Companion to Merleau-Ponty*. Cambridge: Cambridge University Press, 2005.
Cazeaux, Clive. "Merleau-Ponty." In *The Continental Aesthetics Reader*, edited by Clive Cazeaux. London and New York: Routledge, 2000.
Dillon, M. C. *Merleau-Ponty's Ontology*. 2nd edn. Evanston: Northwestern University Press, 1997.
Evans, Fred, and Leonard Lawlor (eds). *Chiasms: Merleau-Ponty's Notion of Flesh*. Albany: State University of New York Press, 2000.
*Hamilakis, Yannis, Pluciennik, Mark, and Tarlow, Sarah (eds). *Thinking Through the Body: Archaeologies of Corporeality*. London: Kluwer Academic/Plenum Press, 2001.
Hitchcock, Louise A. *Minoan Architecture: A Contextual Analysis*. (Studies in Mediterranean Archaeology Pocket Book 155). Jonsered: Paul Åströms Förlag, 2000.
Langer, Monika M. *Merleau-Ponty's Phenomenology of Perception: A Guide and Commentary*. Tallahassee: Florida State University Press, 1989.

McGowan, Erin R. "Experiencing and experimenting with embodied archaeology: Re-embodying the sacred gestures of Neopalatial Minoan Crete," *Archaeological Review from Cambridge*. 21.2 (2006) 32–57.

Pietersma, Henry (ed.). *Merleau-Ponty: Critical Essays*. Lanham, MD: University Press of America, 1989.

*Priest, Stephen. *Merleau-Ponty*. London and New York: Routledge, 1998.

Primozic, Daniel Thomas. On *Merleau-Ponty*. Belmont, CA: Wadsworth, 2001.

Sartre, Jean-Paul. "Merleau-Ponty." In *Situations*, translated by Benita Eisler. New York: George Braziller, 1965.

27 Edward W. Said

Key concepts:

- postcolonialism
- representation
- colonial discourse
- Orientalism
- imperialism
- contrapunctal reading

Edward W. Said (1935–2003) was a literary critic and the Parr Professor of English and Comparative Literature at Columbia University. Born in Jerusalem, Said's Palestinian family became refugees in 1948 and moved to Egypt, where he attended British schools. During his youth he also spent time in Lebanon and Jordan before immigrating to the United States. He earned his B.A. from Princeton University in 1957 and his Ph.D. in literature from Harvard University in 1964. He spent his entire academic career as a professor at Columbia University. He died in 2003 after a long battle with leukemia.

Said's work combined intellectual and political pursuits. On the one hand, he is well known for his engagements with literary criticism (he wrote a study of Joseph Conrad) and postcolonial theory, frequently drawing on the methods developed by Michel **Foucault**. On the other hand, he was politically active as an advocate of Palestinian independence and human rights. (See his 1979 text *The Question of Palestine*.) Critical of U.S. foreign policy, especially in the Middle East, he also spoke out against corruption within Palestine.

These intellectual and political agendas are inseparable for Said, who taught that the intellectual is political and vice versa. In his case, both Said's academic work and his political activism address the ways in which white Europeans and North Americans fail to understand—or even try to understand—the differences between Western culture and non-Western cultures. The example Said sets of an engaged intellectual has been extraordinarily influential throughout the world. In terms of the discipline of classics, Said's work is invaluable in challenging its historically privileged position as the primordial origin of Western civilization set in opposition to numerous non-Western areas of study which, in light of Said's work, appears as one of the more problematic artifacts of post-Enlightenment Europe.

Said's work inaugurated the discourse of **postcolonial theory**. With the publication of his groundbreaking study *Orientalism* in 1978, Said focused attention on the issues of discourse and representation in the history of Western colonialism, with particular attention to the Orient. Orientalism refers to a web of related disciplinary practices, particularly the study of Near Eastern and Asian languages and cultures so as to facilitate ruling over them, especially during the height of the colonialist adventures in Britain (which has been alternately compared to ancient Rome and Phoenicia) and France. Through Orientalist praxis, cultures became objects of study that were represented through the mediating grid of European colonizers. At the same time, there was prejudice against these peoples, particularly Arabs and Islam as the enemy of Christianity. Oriental peoples were represented as unfit to govern themselves. Orientalist discourses are compatible with other disciplinary foci such as Indo-European philology, Enlightenment notions of progress and obtaining knowledge through categorization and description. As an exact science of mental objects philology became a tool for comparing cultures: it became another way of racially distinguishing people. Thus Semitic languages and peoples were creations of Orientalist philological study, which enabled the singling out of groups of people, which could then be placed into a subject-object relationship with the West. Even today, such disciplinary separations have resulted in both a widespread reluctance and a lack of training among most classicists to deal with the non-Indo-European etymologies in ancient Greek.

The critical analysis undertaken in *Orientalism* centers on the nature of colonial discourse and the ways it is used to construct the colonizer-colonized, self-other relationship, and how this binary construction of identity both produces and is produced by a social hierarchy predicated on institutionalized racist and hegemonic power. Said's work here focuses especially on the Middle East as "Orient," but his thesis and methodology can and have been extended to other cultural contexts where colonization has occurred (and is still occurring). Thus, Said's work asks critical questions about how colonized cultures are **represented**, about the power of these representations to shape and control these cultures politically and economically, and about **colonial discourse**, that is, the discourse through which the subject positions of the colonized *and* the colonizer are constructed. Following Foucault, Said understands discourse as a system of linguistic usage and codes that produces knowledge about particular conceptual fields, demarcating what can be known, said, or enacted in relation to this archive of knowledge. It is through discursive formations that knowledge of the world is possible.

For Foucault, there are significant ramifications to the discursive process. In any cultural setting there are dominant groups that establish what can and cannot be said and done. This discursive knowledge is wielded against others. Discursive knowledge is invariably connected to power. Those in control of a particular discourse have control over what can be known and hence they have power over others. In the end, however, both poles are subjected to and by this knowledge; everyone lives within the parameters discursive formations allow. The power of these discourses and disciplinary practices have meant that many scholars in non-Western cultures have had to turn to European scholarship to learn about there own civilizations. What Said works to uncover is precisely how this knowledge attains the status or appearance of an independent reality, and how its origins as a social construct are forgotten.

Discourse, as a form of knowledge-power, is central to Said's concept of **Orientalism**: Western discourse about the East that engenders and reproduces the oppressor-oppressed relationship that arises within colonial discourse. Said focuses on the ways in which discursive formations about the "Orient" exert power and control over those subjected to them. This concept has three dimensions: the discursive, the academic, and the imaginative. All three are interconnected, however, and should be understood as such. The *discursive* concerns the notion that "Orientalism can be discussed and analyzed through corporate institutions for dealing with the Orient by making statements about it, authorizing views of it, describing it, by teaching it, settling it, ruling over it: in short, constructing it as something distinct, other, and inferior. Orientalism thus becomes a Western style of dominating, restructuring, and having authority over the Orient" (*Orientalism*, p. 3). The *academic* refers to "[a]nyone who teaches, writes about, or researches the Orient—and this applies whether the person is an anthropologist, classicist, archaeologist, sociologist, historian, or philologist— either in its specific or its general aspects, is an Orientalist, and what he or she does is Orientalism" (p. 2). Finally, the *imaginative* refers to the idea that "Orientalism is a style of thought based upon an ontological and epistemological distinction made between 'the Orient' and (most of the time) 'the Occident'" (p. 2). Said refers to this culturally constructed space as an "imaginative geography" (p. 54), which is enhanced through the exoticizing of the Orient through various modes of representation: artistic, literary, and contemporary mass media.

Said critiques Eurocentric universalism for devising this binary opposition between the putative superiority of Western cultures and the inferiority of colonized, non-Western cultures. Moreover, he points out that colonial discourse has the pernicious effect of treating the colonized as an undifferentiated mass of people. Thus, "Orientals" are perceived not as freely choosing, autonomous individuals, but rather as homogenous, faceless populations identified only by the commonality of their values. In general, they are reduced to a few stereotypical and usually negative characteristics. The racism that pervades colonial discourse is glaringly evident. In support of this position, Said provides numerous accounts of colonial administrators and travelers who describe and represent Arabs, Jews, and others in dehumanizing ways. In one of many notorious examples, Said cites the British prime minister Disraeli: "Druzes, Christians, Muslims, and Jews hobnob easily because—Arabs are simply Jews on horseback." Said remarks: "In such statements as these, we note immediately that 'the Arab' or 'Arabs' have an aura of apartness, definiteness, and collective self-consistency such as to wipe out any traces of individual Arabs with narratable life histories" (*Orientalism*, p. 229).

Orientalism, Said effectively argues, makes possible "the enormous systematic discipline by which white Eurocentric culture was able to manage—and even produce—the Orient politically, sociologically, militarily, ideologically, scientifically, and imaginatively during the post-Enlightenment period" (*Orientalism*, p. 3). His aim is not to refute the frequently spurious truth-claims of this discourse, but to demonstrate how colonial discourse constructs the epistemological possibility of the West and how it continues to do so. "The Orient," Said insists, "was almost a European invention, and had been since antiquity a place of romance, exotic beings, haunting memories and landscapes, remarkable experiences" (p. 1). For Said, the issue is not whether this European representation is true, but rather how we read its effects in the world.

If colonial discourse oppresses the colonized subject, it also affects the colonizer because the concept of "the Orient has helped to define Europe (or the West) as its contrasting image, idea, personality, experience" (*Orientalism*, pp. 1–2). Thus, European identity is framed in terms of what it is not.

The self-identity of Europe, one could argue, is only the antithetical construction of the "Orient." Such framing is a repeated theme in classical texts, going back at least to the Histories of Herodotus while Said regards Aeschylus' play, *The Persians*, as the earliest piece of Orientalist literature. Said has also noted that many of the taxonomic terms separating Greece and Rome as distinct and superior from other kinds of people came from ancient geographers, historians, and public figures, such as Caesar. However, the West's scientific appropriation of the Orient is associated with Napoleon's (who compared himself to Alexander the Great) short-lived conquest of Egypt in 1798 and subsequent production of the 23 volume Description of Egypt. Negative stereotypes about the Orient were virtually enshrined in Greek art where the Persians became synonymous with the chaotic, the irrational, and the feminine. While such constructions may be more revealing of Greek *aporias* than ancient realities, such stereotypes became reified in Enlightenment Europe.

As the literary critic and cultural theorist Ali Behdad has argued, "Orientalism ... is not divided into accepted discourses of domination and excluded discourses of opposition. Rather, such a discourse of power makes allowance for a *circular* system of exchange between stabilizing strategies and disorienting elements that can produce variant effects" (*Belated Travelers*, p. 17). This is a key statement because Orientalism is a seductive, polyvalent discourse that not only coerces, but also seduces and appropriates even its opposition. Resistance to Orientalism must begin with the idea that "Europe" is as much of a fiction as is the "Orient," but it must not end there.

In a later study entitled *Culture and Imperialism*, Said draws a distinction between **imperialism** and colonialism. For him, "'imperialism' means the practice, the theory, and the attitudes of a dominating metropolitan center ruling a distant territory; 'colonialism', which is almost always a consequence of imperialism, is the implanting of settlements on distant territory" (p. 9). Imperialism is embedded in colonial discourse and serves as an important tool for creating the colonized subject. Said argues that any discourse which comments on a colonized culture cannot remain neutral or stand outside of a consideration of imperialism, because all such discourses are invested in how the view of the other is constructed. For instance, the debased depictions of the other found in the literature, history, and other cultural productions of a colonizing nation serve as alibis for political and psychological acts of violence. This insight informs the concepts of filiation-affiliation that Said discusses in *The World, The Text, and the Critic* (1983). The study of Roman imperialism can contribute much to the analysis of Orientalist discourses, particularly with regard to past events such as the destruction of the temple of Jerusalem and taking of the fortress at Masada, which have reverberations in the modern political landscape.

Said's *Orientalism* initiated the discourse of postcolonialism. Postcolonial theory, which became prominent in the 1990s, is concerned with analyzing the relationship between culture and colonial power, exploring the cultural products of societies that were once under colonial rule. It addresses the lingering affects of colonialism on identity, nationality, and the nature of resistance to colonial power. One goal of postcolonial theory is to question humanist claims about cultural products containing timeless and universal ideas and values, themes all associated with the value of the classics in Western culture. When, for instance, colonizing nations make universal claims, the colonized culture is by default seen as stagnant, unoriginal, simplistic, illogical, and at best, merely mimicking white colonizing culture. For example, Victorian British literature often claims to represent the universal human condition. In doing so, however, Indian culture is represented—whether consciously or unconsciously— as irremediably particular and hopelessly benighted. Postcolonial theory refutes this universalist conceit and, instead, seeks to give voice to local practices, ideas, and values. Eurocentrism, which marginalizes non-European cultures, is understood as a hegemonic power that must be acknowledged and resisted. Part of this resistance is the reclamation of the cultural past of colonized peoples and establishing their value. This also leads to problems within postcolonial theory regarding the inherent indignity of speaking for others who have frequently had to learn about their own cultures in Western academic institutions (see **Spivak**).

One of the primary and most effective means of critiquing colonial discourse that Said bequeaths postcolonial theory is his notion of **contrapunctal reading**. Borrowing the concept of counterpoint from music, Said (a lifelong music-lover) describes a reading strategy that exposes elements of colonial discourse hidden within a text. Contrapunctal reading not only unveils the colonial perspective but, more importantly perhaps, it also tries to read for nuances of resistance (counterpoints) that are also present within the same narrative. Said declares that we need to "read the great canonical texts, and perhaps the entire archive of modern and pre-modern European and American culture, with an effort to draw out, extend, give emphasis and voice to what is silent or marginally present or ideologically represented" (*Culture and Imperialism*, p. 66). In practice, reading contrapunctally "means reading a text with an understanding of what is involved when an author shows, for instance, that a colonial sugar plantation is seen as important to the process of maintaining a particular style of life in England" (*Culture and Imperialism*, p. 66).

Viewed from a postcolonial perspective, the very foundations of classics as a discipline, as well as the scholarship it has produced are implicated in Orientalist and colonialist practices. As a discipline, classics has tended to privilege the Greek culture as the ethnically pure childhood of Europe, which emerged fully developed like Athena from the head of Zeus. The result is that external borrowings or influences from the East, are too often unacknowledged, understudied, marginalized, or excluded from the disciplinary framework of classics, although studies such as Walter Burkert's *Orientalizing Revolution* (1992) and Martin West's *East Face of Helicon: West Asiatic Elements in Greek Poetry and Myth* (1997), are reversing this trend. As Irad Malkin (In "Postcolonial Concepts and Ancient Greek Colonization," p. 343) has written, "Too often, ancient Greeks are treated as though they were both 'white' and 'European,' the people who both put together and kept rocking the cradle of Western civilization." These issues emerge as a particular subtext in the prehistoric period, where there is a frequent reluctance to admit the full impact of the ethnically distinct Minoan civilization of Crete on the Mycenaean Greek cultures on the Mainland.

The role played by the modern museum in colonialist and Orientalist discourse has also been moved into the foreground by Said's work. What was once naively believed to be an innocuous institution for the "disinterested" appreciation of art is now read as an aesthetic space laced with social and political discourses and agendas. Said's work makes possible a critique of the means by which the modern civic museums of Europe were used as instruments to justify and police their imperial gains, from the Great Exhibition of the Arts and Manufactures of All Nations at the Crystal Palace in London in 1851 to the privileged treatment of classical objects as "art" located in art museums while the treatment of objects from the Near East and other colonized regions are often marginalized as "culture" and located in museums of natural history.

While one cannot underestimate the importance and the influence of Said's work on contemporary critical theory, art history, historical studies, and anthropology as well as the Romanist side of classics, those working in the Hellenic sphere have not yet reckoned with the full force of Said's impact in a meaningful way, which may be exacerbating the crisis within the discipline. While classics was at one time synonymous with education, enrollments are down, interest in Greek and Latin languages is in decline, and a discipline predicated on universalist Eurocentric notions of a legacy that belongs to everyone (whether they want it or not!) is increasingly out of touch with a multi-cultural and multi-ethnic world. Challenging this hegemonic discourse by continuing to pursue questions of social class, gender, and ethnicity, while investigating the classical world within a larger multi-cultural and historical context may serve to reinvigorate the classics. In an American Philological Association panel entitled, "Classics and Comparative Literature: Agenda for the 90's," Ralph Hexter proposed reading classical texts by authors seeking to "come to voice" such as the Jewish general, Flavius Josephus, in order to "explode what appears too often as merely a Greco-Roman dyad" (*Classical Philology* (Apr. 1997), p. 165). Similarly, Ian Morris has noted a shift toward Mediterraneanization in the study of the classical world emphasizing a fluidity of movement of things, people, and ideas that may reflect contemporary influences of globalization. Finally, the international milieu in which the Greeks and Romans operated needs to be viewed as a source of cultural and symbolic value in its own right, rather than as something borrowed from, co-opted, and reconstituted or as something exotic and other.

Further reading

By Said

Joseph Conrad and the Fiction of Autobiography. Cambridge, MA: Harvard University Press, 1966.
*Orientalism. New York: Vintage Books, 1978.
Culture and Imperialism. New York: Alfred A. Knopf, 1993.
"Opponents, Audiences, Constituencies and Community." In *The Anti-Aesthetic: Essays on Postmodern Culture*, edited by Hal Foster. Seattle: Bay Press, 1983.
The World, the Text, and the Critic. Cambridge: Harvard University Press, 1983.
The Question of Palestine. New York: Vintage Books, 1992.
Reflections on Exile and Other Essays. Cambridge, MA: Harvard University Press, 2000.

"Invention, Memory, and Place." In *Landscape and Power*, edited by W. J. T. Mitchell. Chicago: University of Chicago Press, 2002.
Freud and the Non-European. New York: Verso, 2003.

About Said

*Ashcroft, Bill, and Pal Ahluwalia. *Edward Said*. London and New York: Routledge, 2001.

Ashcroft, Bill, Gareth Griffiths and Helen Tiffin (eds). *The Post-Colonial Studies Reader*. London and New York: Routledge, 1995.

Assante, Julia. "From Whores to Hierodules: The Historiographic Invention of Mesopotamian Female Sex Professionals." In *Ancient Art and Its Historiography*, edited by Alice A. Donohue and Mark D. Fullerton. Cambridge: Cambridge University Press, 2003.

Barringer, Tim, and Tom Flynn (eds). *Colonialism and the Object: Empire, Material Culture and the Museum*. London and New York: Routledge, 1998.

Behdad, Ali. *Belated Travelers: Orientalism in the Age of Colonial Dissolution*. Durham, NC: Duke University Press, 1994.

*Bernal, Martin. *Black Athena: The Afroasiatic Roots of Classical Civilization, Vol. 1, The Fabrication of Ancient Greece 1785–1985*. New Brunswick, NJ: Rutgers University Press, 1987.

Burkert, Walter. *The Orientalizing Revolution: Near Eastern influence on Greek Culture in the Early Archaic Age*. Translated by Walter Burkert and ME. Pinder. Cambridge: Harvard University Press, 1992.

Goff, Barbara E. (ed). *Classics and Colonialism*. London: Duckworth, 2005.

*Malkin, Irad. "Postcolonial Concepts and Ancient Greek Colonization." *Modern Language Quarterly*. 65.3 (2004) 341–64.

*Morris, Ian. "Mediterraneanization." *Mediterranean Historical Review*. 18.2 (2003) 30–55.

Parry, Benita. "Overlapping Territories and Intertwined Histories: Edward Said's Postcolonial Cosmopolitanism." In *Edward Said: A Critical Reader*, edited by Michael Spinker. Oxford: Blackwell, 1992.

Preziosi, Donald. "The Crystalline Veil and the Phallomorphic Imaginary." In *Brain of the Earth's Body: Art, Museums, and the Phantasms of Modernity*. Minneapolis: University of Minnesota Press, 2003.

Sardar, Ziauddin. *Orientalism*. Buckingham and Philadelphia: Open University Press, 1999.

West, Martin L. *The East Face of Helicon: West Asiatic Elements in Greek Poetry and Myth*. Oxford: Clarendon Press, 1997.

28 Gayatri Chakravorty Spivak

Key concepts:

- subaltern
- othering
- worlding
- strategic essentialism

Gayatri Chakravorty Spivak (b. 1942) is a Bengali cultural and literary critic. Born in Calcutta, India, to a middle-class family during the waning years of British colonial rule, she attended Presidency College of the University of Calcutta, graduating in 1959 with a degree in English literature. She came to the United States in 1962 and attended graduate school at Cornell University, where she received her Ph.D. in comparative literature under the supervision of Paul de Man, who introduced her to the work of Jacques **Derrida**. Her 1977 English translation of Derrida's *Of Grammatology* (1967) made Derrida's work available to a wider audience. She gained substantial recognition from her outstanding introduction to that work, quickly becoming recognized among English-speaking academics as an authority on Derrida's thought. Spivak is currently Avalon Foundation Professor in the Humanities at Columbia University.

Spivak operates at the intersections of postcolonial theory, feminism, deconstruction, and Marxism, combining these different strands of discourse. She rigorously interrogates the binary oppositions that animate both postcolonial and feminist discourse. She further questions concepts found in the imperialist language of colonizers, including concepts of nationhood, fixed identity, and the Third World. The numerous articles and interviews that comprise Spivak's scholarly production have been compiled into several books. *In Other Worlds: Essays in Cultural Politics* (1987) is a collection of essays on a wide range of topics, from Virginia Woolf's *To the Lighthouse* to French feminism, to the concept of "value."

The Post-Colonial Critic: Interviews, Strategies, Dialogues (1990) is a compilation of interviews that present Spivak's often inspiring yet difficult thinking in a more reader-friendly format. Her *Outside in the Teaching Machine* (1993) brings together her writings on higher education and globalization.

Fundamental to Spivak's work is the concept of the **subaltern**. Subaltern means "of inferior rank." Spivak borrows the term from the Italian Marxist philosopher Antonio Gramsci, who used it to refer to social groups under the hegemonic control of the ruling elite. In this sense, the term can refer to any group that is collectively subordinated or disenfranchised, whether on the basis of ethnicity, sex, gender, religion, or any other category of identity. Spivak, however, uses this term specifically to refer to the colonized and peripheral subject, especially with reference to those oppressed by British colonialism, such as segments of the Indian population prior to independence. She emphasizes the fact that the female subaltern subject is even more marginalized than the male. In the essay, "Can the Subaltern Speak?" (1985), Spivak observes: "If in the context of colonial production, the subaltern has no history, and cannot speak, the subaltern as female is even more deeply in shadow" (p. 28).

Spivak's notion of the subaltern is thus also implicated in feminist concerns. She discusses the ways that colonialism—and its patriarchy—silence subaltern voices to the extent that they have no conceptual space from which they can speak and be heard, unless, perhaps, they assume the discourse of oppressing the colonizer. "Can the Subaltern Speak?" has been enormously influential in postcolonial theory. But we should note that Spivak critically revised aspects of her theory of the subaltern in her 1999 book, *A Critique of Postcolonial Reason: Toward a History of the Vanishing Present*. Here she explores further the idea of the "native informant" and reconsiders her discussion of that figure in earlier texts (see especially the chapter on "History").

Another aspect of Western colonialism explored by Spivak is the way that colonial discourse participates in a process she refers to as **othering**. Othering—a term derived from a whole corpus of texts by Hegel, **Lacan**, **Said**, Sartre, and others—is an ideological process that isolates groups who are seen as different from the norm of the colonizers. For Spivak, othering is the way in which imperial discourse creates colonized, subaltern subjects. Like **Said**, she views othering dialectically: The colonizing subject is created in the same moment as the subaltern subject. Othering, therefore, expresses a hierarchical, unequal relationship. In her research into this process, Spivak utilizes British colonial office dispatches to reveal othering in a historical context. Yet she makes clear that othering is embedded in the discourse of various forms of colonial narrative, fiction as well as nonfiction.

Spivak's related concept of **worlding** is closely related to the dynamics of othering in colonial discourse. Her understanding of this concept begins with Martin **Heidegger**'s "The Origin of the Work of Art" (1935–6). Worlding is the process whereby colonized space enters into the "world" as crafted by Eurocentric colonial discourse. She argues: "If ... we concentrated on documenting and theorizing the itinerary of the consolidation of Europe as sovereign subject, indeed sovereign and subject, then we would produce an alternative historical narrative of 'worlding' of what is today called 'the Third World'" ("The Rani of Sirmur," p. 247). A worlding narrative of a colonized space is a process of inscription whereby colonial discourse and hegemony are mapped onto the earth. This is a social construct because it is a "worlding of the world on uninscribed earth" ("The Rani of Sirmur," p. 253). A central way in which the practice of worlding occurs is through mapmaking, but there are ideological aspects as well. For instance, Spivak cites the example of an early nineteenth-century British soldier traveling across India, surveying the land and people: "He is actually engaged in consolidating the self of Europe by obliging the native to cathect the space of the Other on his home ground. He is worlding *their own world*, which is far from mere uninscribed earth, anew, by obliging *them* to domesticate the alien as Master" ("The Rani of Sirmur," p. 253). In effect, the colonized are made to experience their own land as belonging to the colonizer. Worlding and othering, then, are not simply carried out as matters of impersonal national policy but are enacted by colonizers in local ways, such as the soldier traveling through the countryside.

Spivak often makes reference to the highly problematic nature of terms like "Third World," "Orient," and "Indian." For her, as for Said, these terms are essentialist categories whose meanings hinge on binary oppositions that are of dubious usefulness because of their history and arbitrary nature. Essentialist perspectives stress the idea that conceptual categories name eternal, unchangeable characteristics or identities really existing in the external world. Hence, a category like "Orient" is essentialist because it conceits to name a real place inhabited by people with the same characteristics and personality traits that are eternal and unchanging, and, by extension, inescapable because they are "naturally" possessed. Classic essentialist categories include masculine-feminine, active-passive, clear-confused, logicalillogical, and civilized-uncivilized. But essentialist categories are unstable because they are social constructions, not universal names for "real" entities in the world. Furthermore, the categories that Spivak discusses were constructed by a colonial discourse whose usage had significant hegemonic and ideological implications and effects. Labels like "savage Indian," "cunning Arab," or "wiley Jew" literally *other* their subjects. That is, such terms force colonized peoples into a subaltern subject position not of their own choosing. Once located in a particular subject position, the colonizing power can treat them accordingly, and the subjects often assume this role.

In her 1985 essay, "Subaltern Studies: Deconstructing Historiography," Spivak posits that although essentialism is highly problematic for the knowledge it creates about the 'other,' there is sometimes a political and social need for what she calls **strategic essentialism**. By this she means a "*strategic* use of positivist essentialism in a scrupulously visible political interest" (p. 205). She argues that it is necessary to assume an essentialist stand—for instance, speaking as a woman or speaking as an Asian—so that the hegemony of patriarchal colonial discourse can be disrupted and questioned. Spivak acknowledges that the application of essentialist categories can have a salutary effect on struggles against oppression and hegemonic power despite the problems inherent in essentialist discourse: "I think it's absolutely on target to take a stand against the discourses of essentialism ... [b]ut *strategically* we cannot" ("Criticism, Feminism, and the Institution," p. 11). Spivak's position is that strategic essentialism is expedient, if only in the short term, because it can aid in the process of revitalizing the sense of personal and cultural value of the dominated. One example of this is when postcolonial cultures essentialize their precolonial past in order to find a usable, strategic cultural identity.

The intersection of theory and social activism runs throughout Spivak's work. She has been critiqued for her view of strategic essentialism on the grounds that she has acquiesced to the very essentialist and universalist language which she so adamantly opposes. But for Spivak, the strategic use of essentialist categories is not a matter of violating some notion of theoretical "purity" but is rather necessary from the perspective of social and political exigencies that require, among other things, certain kinds of discursive tools in order to counter oppression and other ills. Spivak is also critical of Western feminists for sometimes ignoring the plight of women of color and, contrarily, for sometimes presuming to speak for non-Western women on issues about which Western feminists have no direct knowledge or experience. In this latter instance, speaking for non-Western women is to once again mute the voices of women that Western feminists are trying to assist on the geopolitical stage. Such Western feminist discourse constructs non-Western women as subaltern subjects and subverts their attempts to speak for themselves into an echo of the same, rather than allowing for a voice of difference.

The importance of Spivak's work in postcolonial theory, cultural studies, subaltern studies, and feminism has made it especially insightful for classics. Thus, the idea of the subaltern group is a helpful concept for studying those marginalized in the classical world where they can be discerned in ancient literature and religion, through the analysis of archaeological remains, particularly in households, as well as within the Athenian, Hellenistic, and Roman imperial formations. Studies of ancient imperialism, trade, colonialism, and other forms of cultural domination tend to have been preoccupied with the emulation of or identification with the dominant culture, whereas little work has been devoted to the way in which these relationships may have affected the construction of social, ethnic, or gender identity. Spivak's work poses an ethical demand, that classicists reflect upon the complexity of discourse as that which constructs identities, representations, and epistemology. This means that the imbrication of race, gender, and class should be taken as complex whole, rather than as purportedly theoretical elements that can be portioned out and dealt with individually, if at all. Spivak's work exemplifies the kind of critical practice that is able to address the complexities of cultural production *and* its histories.

Perhaps the most impressive reading of these issues is given in the chapter "Culture" from *A Critique of Postcolonial Reason: Toward a History of the Vanishing Present*. This chapter is a virtuoso reading of cultural discourse and politics. While it covers a lot of distance, Spivak grounds her discussion in a re-reading of Frederic Jameson's *Postmodernism; or The Cultural Logic of Late Capitalism* (1991). During her re-reading of Jameson's influential and controversial argument, Spivak constructs a stereoscopic reading between it and the Minimalist artist Robert Morris' essay "Aligned with Nazca" (1975), which Spivak calls a "definitive text of minimalism." She addresses how art, space, and cultural alterity are discussed in each text, concluding:

> The constitution of a radical elite alibi for political practice can dress cool. The comprehension of cultural signifiers such as 'postmodernism' or 'minimalism' is taken as a given here. This is of course one of the ways to perpetrate a kind of 'wild' cultural pedagogy that establishes these terms as quick diagnostic fixes within whatever functions as a general elite culture (which also produces the unnamed subject of Jameson's postmodern cultural dominant).
>
> (*A Critique of Postcolonial Reason*, pp. 337–8)

In many ways this is Spivak at her best. Not only critical of her own former positions, such as the concept of the subaltern, Spivak's criticality extends to the inaugural texts of postmodernism as a system of thought and its critiques thereby revealing the necessity for classical studies to continually examine its theoretical and ideological premises. Spivak's work on art, literature, politics, and postcolonial studies demonstrates how indispensable self-reflexivity is for any discipline, which must address its own contradictions and *aporias* before it can deign to understand its objects of study.

Further reading

By Spivak

"The Rani of Sirmur: An Essay in Reading the Archives." *History and Theory* 24 (1985) 247–72.

"Three Women's Texts and a Critique of Imperialism." *Critical Inquiry* 12 (1985) 243–61.

"Subaltern Studies: Deconstructing Historiography." In *In Other Worlds: Essays in Cultural Politics*. New York: Methuen, 1987.

In Other Worlds: Essays in Cultural Politics. New York: Methuen, 1987.

"Criticism, Feminism, and the Institution." In *The Post-Colonial Critic: Interviews, Strategies, Dialogues*, edited by Sarah Harasym. London and New York: Routledge, 1990.
Outside in the Teaching Machine. London and New York: Routledge, 1993.
*"Can the Subaltern Speak?" In *The Post-Colonial Studies Reader*, edited by Bill Ashcroft, Gareth Griffiths, and Helen Tiffin. London and New York: Routledge, 1995.
The Spivak Reader: Selected Works of Gayatri Chakravorty Spivak. Edited by Donna Landry and Gerald MacLean. London and New York: Routledge, 1996.
A Critique of Postcolonial Reason: Toward a History of the Vanishing Present. Cambridge, MA: Harvard University Press, 1999.
Death of a Discipline. New York: Columbia University Press, 2003.

About Spivak

Eagleton, Terry. "Gayatri Spivak." In *Figures of Dissent: Critical Essays on Fish, Spivak, Žižek, and Others.* London and New York: Verso, 2003.
*Malkin, Irad. "Postcolonial Concepts and Ancient Greek Colonization." *Modern Language Quarterly.* 65.3 (2004) 341–64.
*Morton, Stephen. *Gayatri Chakravorty Spivak.* London and New York: Routledge, 2003.
*van Dommelen, Peter. "Colonial constructs: colonialism and archaeology in the Mediterranean," *World Archaeology* 28.3 (1997) 305–23.
Varadharajan, Asha. *Exotic Parodies: Subjectivity in Adorno, Said, and Spivak.* Minneapolis: University of Minnesota Press, 1995.
Young, Robert. "Spivak: decolonization, deconstruction." In *White Mythologies: Writing History and the West.* London and New York: Routledge, 1990.

29 Hayden White

Key concepts:

- fact as event under description
- metahistory
- history as interpretation
- tropology
- emplotment

Hayden White (b. 1928–) is an American intellectual and cultural historian associated with a narrativist view of history. He earned his B.A. from Wayne State University and his Ph.D. from the University of Michigan in 1956. He held academic positions at the University of Rochester, University of California at Los Angeles, and Wesleyan University. In 1978 White became a professor in the History of Consciousness Program at the University of California at Santa Cruz. He was Presidential Professor of Historical Studies and is now University Professor Emeritus.

White approaches history from the perspective of language, suggesting that historical truth is always constructed through the narratives crafted by historians. Historical knowledge, therefore, is not simply the apprehension of an external reality, the truth of the past, but a product of the historian's discourse. White's work typically takes aim at binary oppositions that pretend to organize "reality" in a logical, objective way. From White's perspective, for example, the traditional opposition of history's facts to literature's fictions is a false one. Congruent with this view, White's own work is located at the intersection of historiography and literary theory and has had a significant impact on both areas.

White acknowledges that his theoretical positions owe a great deal to both older historians and philosophers, as well as to contemporaries such as Northrop Frye and Kenneth Burke. He is critical of positivist views of history that assert that objective observation of the past can uncover historical truths. Such thinking is predicated on binary oppositions such as objectivity-subjectivity, truth-falsity, and fact-fiction. Instead, White argues that historians do not discover the facts "out there" but rather construct the "truths" of the historical past through narratives and tropes. Facts and truths are, therefore, primarily the domain of language embedded in particular cultures. History, for White, is a discursive and rhetorical enterprise, not one of excavating objective, incontrovertible facts. White's ideas about historical discourse are contrary to traditional "realist" views of narrative that assume the posture of an omniscient narrator who tells a story characterized by uninterrupted flow. Such a narrative voice masks the usually fragmentary nature of historical sources and evidence. It creates the appearance of a complete and unambiguous story where none exists.

White describes a "fact" as "an event under description." By this he means that historians construct historical factuality with language. The fact cannot be separated from its verbal description. For White, historical events belong to the domain of reality, but facts belong to historical discourse. White does not deny the reality of past events, but he argues that any claims made about what "really" happened—the facts—are made in narratives of those events. The historian has no access to past reality but only to discourses that assert facts about the past. In this sense, history is primarily a textual practice. When historians describe past events, they are really talking about how other narratives have told the story of the past.

It is here that White makes one of his most important claims, namely that the past does not exist apart from historical representations of it, and those historical representations—historical texts—are themselves "literary artifacts," that is, they too are part of history (see "Historical Text as Literary Artifact," in *Tropics of Discourse*). This claim is predicated, in part, on the observation that past events cannot be verified or "fact-checked." Differing interpretations of past events can be compared and critiqued to determine the most compelling narrative, but the events themselves are inaccessible. On this basis, White claims that history must attend to language, in particular to historical narratives, traditions of history writing, the genres used to narrate a persuasive historical discourse, and other linguistic and textual aspects of telling history. In other words, history must also be **metahistory**. That is, it must be self-conscious and self-critical about the presumptions and strategies it employs in order to make sense of the past.

One of White's operating assumptions is that any mode of human inquiry, including historical research, has political or ideological implications. In *The Content of the Form*, White notes, that "narrative is not merely a neutral discursive form that may or may not be used to represent real events in their aspect as developmental processes but rather entails ontological and epistemic choices with distinct ideological and even specifically political implications" (*The Content of the Form*, p. ix). Historical narratives and other representations of the past are ideological because they promote a perspective on the past that cannot be legitimated as "truth" or "objectivity" given the textual nature of the historiographic enterprise.

White's long career is punctuated by different phases of intellectual interest. Of this work, arguably the most important to classical studies is White's work on historical narrative as described in volumes such as *Metahistory: The Historical Imagination in Nineteenth-Century Europe* (1973), *Tropics of Discourse: Essays in Cultural Criticism* (1978), and *The Content of the Form: Narrative Discourse and Historical Representations* (1987). The first two volumes articulate White's arguments concerning historical narrative, discourse, and literary tropes. The latter text deals with issues of historical representation and narrative discourse.

In *Metahistory*, White uses structuralist ideas to understand the nature and function of historical discourses. It is in this volume that White makes his most important arguments about the narrative nature of history. White's narrativist philosophy of history sees the genre of literary narrative as central to the historian's craft. Against the Aristotelian distinction of fact from fiction that dominates contemporary historiography, White describes history as interpretation that takes the form of narrative. Here, White draws a distinction between science as explanation and **history as interpretation**. Extending this distinction, White wants to expose history's scientific conceit, that is, history's traditional employment of explanatory models that are claimed to describe facts accurately and external events in a logical and objective manner. Against this conceit, he presents history as historical narrative, a mode of discourse that sets forth interpretations of past events in a rhetorical manner. From this perspective, explanation does not present us with objective historical verities, but is rather best understood as a rhetorical device to persuade readers of the truth of a particular view of past events (see "emplotment" below). White's distinction between science and history can be charted as in table 1.

White's theory of tropes (**tropology**) is central to arguments about historical writing he expresses in *Metahistory*. A trope is usually understood as a figure of speech, such as a metaphor. White, however, uses this term to refer to styles or modes of thought used by historical narratives to craft their discursive arguments. Through extensive research into the history of historiography, he shows how historical texts from particular periods have in common the use of certain tropes. For White, "troping is the soul of discourse" (*Tropics of Discourse*, p. 2), and it is one of the chief tasks of

Table 1

Science	History
Models	Tropes
Explanation	Interpretation
Logic	Rhetoric

the historian to identify what tropes are used and to uncover their ideological ramifications.

Following Giambattista Vico and Kenneth Burke, White sets forth a hier-archical typology based on four master tropes: metaphor, metonymy, synechdoche, and irony. He understands the first three tropes as "naïve" tropes, "since they can only be deployed in the belief in language's capacity to grasp the nature of things in figurative terms" (*Metahistory*, pp. 36–7). Irony, on the other hand, is self-reflexive about the problem of universal truth claims and is cognizant of the provisional nature of language. Thus White asserts, that "Irony … represents a stage of consciousness in which the problematical nature of language itself has become recognized. It points to the potential foolishness of all linguistic characterizations of reality as much as to the absurdity of the beliefs it produces" (*Metahistory*, p. 37).

White also discusses modes of **emplotment** utilized by historical discourse. Just as with literary narratives, historical narratives have a plot structure that is utilized by the historian to tell the story of past events. Using Frye, White identifies four primary modes of emplotment: romance, comedy, tragedy, and satire. These modes of emplotment in turn are connected to modes of explanation and ideological implications based on the work of Stephen Pepper and Karl Mannheim. White understands these levels of interpretation in historical narrative as "structurally homologous with one another" (*Tropics of Discourse*, p. 70). He represents this homological relationship in Table 2.

White makes it clear that his interpretive typologies are not meant as rigid containers into which all texts must clearly find a place: "I do not suggest that these correlations necessarily appear in the work of a given historian; in fact, the tension at the heart of every historical masterpiece is created in part by a conflict between a given modality of emplotment or explanation and the specific ideological commitment of its author" (*Tropics of Discourse*, p. 70).

The narrative a historian creates from choices of plot, explanation, and ideology serves as an interpretation of past events. Historical interpretation has, according to White, at least three aspects: (1) the aesthetic (choice of narrative strategy); (2) the epistemological (choice of explanatory mode); and (3) the ethical (ideological choice). Historical discourse consists of these

Table 2

Mode of emplotment	Mode of explanation	Mode of ideological implication
Romance	Idiographic	Anarchist
Comedy	Organicist	Conservative
Tragedy	Mechanistic	Radical
Satire	Contextualist	Liberal

three interpretive aspects and thus presupposes a particular metahistory. "Every proper history presupposes a metahistory which is nothing but the web of commitments which the historian makes in the course of his interpretation on the aesthetic, cognitive, and ethical levels differentiated above" (*Tropics of Discourse*, p. 71). Thus, the issue for historians, according to White, "is not, What are the facts? but rather, How are the facts to be described in order to sanction one mode of explaining them rather than another?" (*Tropics of Discourse*, p. 134).

White's theories on history as narrative pose intriguing questions for classicists to answer. To what extent are we aware of the assumptions, critical strategies, codes, and tropes that ground our studies? Like White's view of the historian narrating a history, classics and classical archaeology are primarily textual practices, with narratives constructed in the primary texts and assemblages of the past as well as in the secondary texts of contemporary and recent practices. Are there patterns of emplotment and ideology in classical texts, or are such ideas incompatible, detracting from historical research, as Arnaldo Momigliano insists (in "The Rhetoric of History and the History of Rhetoric")? White's project breaks down the distinction between historical fact and literary fiction and ideology, rendering as suspect the notion of clear textual genres. On this basis, what makes a text literary or mythical as opposed to historical and how are these sometimes combined (e.g., reference to a Minoan thalassocracy in *Thucydides* I.4)? Craig Gibson (in "Learning Greek History in the Ancient Classroom," p. 125) has proposed that White's emplotment devices might prove illuminating for analyzing the modes of discourse and microgenres employed by ancient historians as well as for understanding their ancient reception. The archaeologist Ian Hodder (in "The Narrative and Rhetoric of Material Culture Sequences") has also found White's scheme relevant to the understanding of archaeological assemblages, whereby an individual interred in a communally constructed monumental tomb might be seen as metonymically standing for the entire community, while White's tropes might be seen as structuring archaeological narratives. Still, one suspects that those focusing on literary texts may be more generally receptive to White's message than ancient historians. White's theoretical perspective challenges us not only to self-reflexively consider our critical methods, but also to think carefully about what counts as the textual, ritual, historical, and objective.

Further reading

By White

Metahistory: The Historical Imagination in Nineteenth-Century Europe.
    Baltimore: Johns Hopkins University Press, 1973.
Tropics of Discourse: Essays in Cultural Criticism. Baltimore: Johns Hopkins
    University Press, 1978.

The Content of the Form: Narrative Discourse and Historical Representations. Baltimore: Johns Hopkins University Press, 1987.

About White

Bann, Stephen. "Analysing the Discourse of History." *Dalhousie Review* 64 (1984) 376–400.

Fox, Matthew. *Roman Historical Myths: The Regal Period in Augustan Literature.* Oxford: Oxford Classical Monographs and Oxford University Press, 1996.

Gibson, Craig A. "Learning Greek History in the Ancient Classroom: the Evidence of the Treatises on Progymnasmata." *Classical Philology*. 99 (2004) 103–29.

*Hodder, Ian. "The Narrative and Rhetoric of Material Culture Sequences." *World Archaeology* 25.2 (1993) 268–82.

Hutcheon, Linda. *A Poetics of Postmodernism: History, Theory, Fiction.* New York and London: Routledge, 1988.

*Jenkins, Keith. *On "What is History." From Carr and Elton to Rorty and White.* London and New York: Routledge, 1995.

Jenkins, Keith. "A Conversation with Hayden White." *Literature and History* 7 (1998) 68–82.

Konstan, David. "The Function of Narrative in Hayden White's *Metahistory.*" *CLIO* 11.1 (1981) 65–78.

LaCapra, Dominick. *Rethinking Intellectual History: Texts, Contexts, Language.* Ithaca: Cornell University Press, 1983.

Momigliano, Arnaldo. "The Rhetoric of History and the History of Rhetoric: On Hayden White's Tropes." *Comparative Criticism. A Year Book. Vol.* 3 (1981) 259–68.

Murphy, Richard J. "Hayden White on 'Facts, Fictions and Metahistory.' I. Metahistory and Metafiction: Historiography and the Fictive in the Work of Hayden White. An Introductory Essay." *Printemps Sources* (1997) 3–30.

30 Raymond Williams

Key concepts:

- Culture vs. culture
- cultural studies
- ideal, documentary, and social culture
- the structure of feeling
- dominant, residual, and emergent aspects of history

Raymond Williams (1921–88) was a British literary theorist, novelist, leading Marxist, and one of the founders of cultural studies. He was born in Wales and raised in a working-class family (his mother was a housewife, his father a railway signalman). In 1939 he entered Cambridge University on a scholarship. There he studied literature and was a member of the Cambridge University Socialist Club. His studies were interrupted in 1942 when he was called to military duty, serving as a tank commander. After the war, Williams returned to Cambridge to finish his degree.

After graduating from Cambridge, he worked in the Adult Education Department at Oxford University for 15 years, during which time he wrote two major works *Culture and Society, 1780–1950* (1958) and *The Long Revolution* (1961). He joined the faculty at Cambridge University as a lecturer in English and drama in 1961 and remained there for the rest of his career.

Williams approached literature from an interdisciplinary and Marxist perspective. He explored ways in which class hierarchy was expressed in literature, usually to the advantage of the upper classes. He was also interested in ways that modes of communication are connected to the material conditions of a society. His theories, especially those on culture, have impacted other intellectual currents such as New Historicism and are often associated with Hayden **White**'s concept of metahistory as well as his focus on historiography as a form of interpretive narrative, which is never disinterested with regard to matters of social power.

Williams' ideas about culture are foundational for the field now known as cultural studies. In *The Long Revolution*, his second major theoretical writing, he explores conceptual issues connected with the term culture. He distinguishes between Culture (capital C) and culture (lowercase c). Culture (capital C) is a moral and aesthetic term originally conceived by English writers such as the Victorian poet and humanist Matthew Arnold and the modern literary critic F. R. Leavis. In their discourse, Culture means "high culture," that is, the sum total of civilization's greatest moral and aesthetic achievements. The not-so-hidden agenda of this idea of Culture, of course, is to assert and maintain social class—"high culture" and "high class" are synonymous with each other. Against this view, Williams develops a concept of culture (lowercase c) in terms of the social. Here, culture is not composed exclusively of those ideas and achievements deemed to be the high points of civilization. Rather, culture includes all products of human activity, including language, social, political, and religious ideas and institutions, and other expressions both conceptual and material. In this sense, culture comprises all that humans create and enact in order to make sense of their existence.

Williams' concept of culture has served as the focal point for literary-cultural studies. By arguing that the concept of culture was irreducible to the product of an elite class, Williams helped create a new academic field—**cultural studies**—that examines the everyday life of non-elite groups. Classical archaeology is uniquely suited to these endeavors with its unusually rich data set that includes not simply the great texts and monuments of Culture, but also the everyday items of culture, which can be used to flesh out a highly detailed view of ancient society (see comments by Snodgrass, "Response: The Archaeological Aspect," (1994)). Increasing the emphasis on everyday life in the study of material culture in ancient civilization also has implications for decentering the privileged position of Culture in the academic arena.

This conception of culture as social is for Williams one of "three general categories in the definition of culture" (*The Long Revolution*, p. 57): the ideal, the documentary, and the social. **Ideal culture** refers to the concept of culture as a "state or process of human perfection" measured by absolute or universal standards. In this instance, cultural analysis "is essentially the discovery and description, in lives and works, of those values which can be seen to compose a timeless order, or to have permanent reference to the universal human condition" (*The Long Revolution*, p. 57). Classical literary works, art, and monuments fit into this category. **Documentary culture** approaches culture as a documentary record, a repository for the artifacts of cultural achievements, including literature, arts, and philosophy. Here, "culture is the body of intellectual and imaginative work, in which, in a detailed way, human thought and experience are variously recorded" (*The Long Revolution*, p. 57). Much of the work in classical archaeology fits into this category, particularly with large data sets such as pottery and other quotidian items. Finally, **social culture**, as mentioned earlier, focuses on culture not simply in terms of the artifacts and achievements of high, elite culture, but in terms of all the many ways that people conceive of and enact their lives. Thus culture encompasses the political, the religious, and the economic, as well as all modes of thought and practice by which people live in the world. A major challenge to classics is to become more bound up in this third category. One example of how this is occurring is in the translation of the first Harry Potter novel into ancient Greek and Latin, which is drawing fans of the series into the study of classics.

For Williams, thinking of culture in terms of this third definitional category, as social culture, breaks down distinctions between elite culture and the "popular" culture of the masses. Social culture claims that the products of elite culture are not to be valorized over the products of popular culture. All cultural products count as culture. In Williams' view, culture is not static, but rather a process that on the one hand always asserts itself and acts on us, and on the other hand is constantly produced and changed by human beings. Cultural process flows both toward us and away from us. The idea of culture as social is meant to express this dynamism. Despite this dynamism, there remains a certain tension between popular and elite culture. Items and texts that are circulated as part of popular culture sometimes make a transition into the elite culture by virtue of their age. Archaeology has demonstrated time and again, that objects are circulated, manipulated, and modified in the process of creating identity and class distinctions. In his classic study of architecture and house decoration, *Houses and Society in Pompeii and Herculaneum*, Andrew Wallace-Hadrill has shown how the development of new styles was driven by an increasing need of the elite to distance themselves from others as decoration became more accessible to greater numbers of individuals.

These three categories, or definitions, are to be understood, says Williams, as a whole and in terms of the interactions and relationships pertaining between these three aspects of culture: "However difficult it may be in practice, we have to try to see the process as a whole, and to relate our particular studies ... to the actual and complex organization" (*The Long Revolution*, p. 60). One of the byproducts of Williams' egalitarian, non-elitist view of culture was that he laid a foundation for the study of popular culture. Because all human products and practices are considered valuable and available for cultural analysis, forms of what we now refer to as popular culture—such as television, film, pop/rock music, sports, and web-logs (blogs)—are arguably more revealing about the nature of culture because it is in these aspects of culture that lived experiences of the non-elite are expressed. The products of high culture tell us only about elites; popular culture tells so much more because of its inclusiveness. Williams further studied popular culture in later works such as *Television: Technology and Cultural Form* (1974). Archaeology fits comfortably within such a framework, and as classical archaeologists have turned more to the study of non-elite items and settlements, our picture of ancient life at all strata has been enriched in areas such as ancient nutrition (flora and fauna studies), trade (undecorated pottery), and household economy (weaving implements and manuring practices).

In his examination of culture, Williams pays considerable attention to what he calls "**the structure of feeling.**" According to Williams, a structure of feeling is the particular character and quality of a shared cultural sense. In general, Williams' notion of the structure of feeling refers to the lived experience of a people—or a generation of people—within particular cultural contexts. The lived experience includes interaction between "official" culture–laws, religious doctrine, and other formal aspects of a culture—and the way that people live in their cultural context. The structure of feeling is what imbues a people with a specific "sense of life" and experience of community. It comprises the set of particular cultural commonalities shared by a culture despite the individual differences within it. As Williams notes, the sense of commonality is not necessarily shared throughout a culture, but is most likely the feeling of the dominant social group. This cultural feeling is not typically expressed in any verbal, rational mode of discourse, though it can often be located in literary texts that reveal it only indirectly. Cultural analysis of the structure of feeling aims at uncovering how these shared feelings and values operate to help people make sense of their lives and the different situations in which the structure of feeling arises. In "What is 'Classical' About Classical Antiquity?" James Porter argues for a structure of feeling with regard to classics, calling for nothing less than a phenomenology of the discipline. In noting that Hellenized Romans (among others) sought to *become classical*, through acquiring a mastery over their classical past, Porter observes that there is an exhaustive repertoire of social and cultural positions for developing a phenomenology of the discipline (p. 42).

In *Marxism and Literature* (1977), Williams examines historiographical issues, arguing that the cultural analyst must recognize the complex interactions that occur within historical contexts and be careful to avoid privileging those dominant, empowered voices within it. In other words, rather than view history as a progression of nameable cultural periods—in which each period determines the one that follows—Williams wants to look at history through the lens of cultural struggle and resistance. To this end, he posits three terms "which recognize not only 'stages' and 'variations' but internal dynamic relations of any actual process" (*Marxism and Literature*, p. 121). These are the "dominant," "residual," and "emergent" aspects of historical periods.

The **dominant** aspects of a historical period are the systems of thought and practice that dictate, or try to dictate, what can be thought and what can be done—that is, the assertion of dominant values, morality, and meanings. For Williams, the concept of the dominant is related to the concept of hegemony. The dominant is at once hegemonic, rigorously promoting the interests of the empowered and suppressing the interests of others. But the dominant does not stand uncontested. Williams reminds us that within any cultural context, the "effective dominant culture" is always under siege by alternative values, meanings, and practices that are not part of it. These alternatives and oppositions to the dominant culture can be found in "residual" and "emergent" forms.

The **residual** aspects of a historical period are past cultural formations. These old values and meanings may have once been dominant but have now been supplanted by the present dominant power. Aspects of these older cultural forms may still be active in the present, exerting pressure on dominant forms, although they are generally subordinate to the dominant. In short, the residual can be incorporated into the dominant culture, and at the same time can have aspects, which stand in opposition or as an alternative to that culture. Williams cites by way of example the residual nature of organized religion in contemporary English culture.

The **emergent** aspects of a historical period are those newly emerging values, meanings, and practices that adumbrate future cultural directions and put pressure on the existing dominant culture. Cultural forms can never be frozen by the dominant culture. Dominant culture is always undergoing opposition by these new cultural forms that threaten to replace the dominant.

Williams views these three relations of cultural process as the ground where struggles over dominance and resistance to hegemony are waged. Further, this tripartite view of historical process requires us to view culture as dynamic rather than static and to be mindful of the interactions and cross-fertilization of these three aspects of cultural movement and change.

Williams' all-encompassing, non-elitist concept of culture and his development of a methodology for cultural studies have implications for classics. For one thing, it calls into question the relevancy of a discipline seemingly devoted to serving as the bastion of universal cultural values. Additionally, Williams' concepts can be invoked to broaden the scope of the data set used by classicists and implicate classics to a minor degree in the study of popular culture. The intersection between classics and popular culture has occurred particularly in the realm of mass media such as movies, video, and fantasy gaming. It is also found in contemporary pageantry and spectacle from the opening ceremonies of the Olympics in Athens (which can be analyzed as a metanarrative) to the contemporary staging of Greek plays. Classicists are further encouraged to pay more attention to the quotidian and material aspects of ancient life, rather than simply in terms of established canons and great texts. Williams' approach to cultural studies encourages classicists to attend to the everyday and ordinary practices of social life in the past.

Further reading

By Williams

Culture and Society, 1780–1950. New York: Columbia University Press, 1958.
The Long Revolution. Rev. edn. New York: Columbia University Press, 1966.

Marxism and Literature. New York: Oxford University Press, 1977.

Problems in Materialism and Culture: Selected Essays. London and New York: Verso Books, 1980.

Keywords: A Vocabulary of Culture and Society. Rev. edn. New York: Oxford University Press, 1983.

The Raymond Williams Reader. Edited by John Higgins. Oxford: Blackwell Publishers, 2001.

About Williams

Eagleton, Terry (ed.). *Raymond Williams: Critical Perspectives.* Boston: Northeastern University Press, 1989.

Eldridge, JET. *Raymond Williams: Making Connections.* London and New York: Routledge, 1994.

Higgins, John. *Raymond Williams: Literature, Marxism, and Cultural Materialism.* London and New York: Routledge, 1999.

*Inglis, Fred. *Raymond Williams.* New York: Routledge, 1995.

*Porter, James I. "What is 'Classical' About Classical Antiquity? Eight Propositions." *Arion* 13.1 (2005) 27–61.

Prendergast, Christopher (ed). *Cultural Materialism: On Raymond Williams.* Minneapolis: University of Minnesota Press, 1995.

Snodgrass, Anthony. "Response: The Archaeological Aspect." In *Classical Greece: Ancient histories and modern archaeologies,* edited by Ian Morris. Cambridge: Cambridge University Press, 1994.

Wallace-Hadrill, Andrew. *Houses and Society in Pompeii and Herculaneum.* Princeton: Princeton University Press, 1994.